Privatis

Privatising Justice

The Security Industry, War and Crime Control

Wendy Fitzgibbon and John Lea

PLUTO PRESS

First published 2020 by Pluto Press
345 Archway Road, London N6 5AA

www.plutobooks.com

British Library Cataloguing in Publication Data
A catalogue record for this book is available from the British Library

ISBN 978 0 7453 9925 6 Hardback
ISBN 978 0 7453 9923 2 Paperback
ISBN 978 1 7868 0166 1 PDF eBook
ISBN 978 1 7868 0168 5 Kindle eBook
ISBN 978 1 7868 0167 8 EPUB eBook

This book is printed on paper suitable for recycling and made from fully managed and sustained forest sources. Logging, pulping and manufacturing processes are expected to conform to the environmental standards of the country of origin.

Typeset by Stanford DTP Services, Northampton, England

Simultaneously printed in the United Kingdom and United States of America

Contents

Acknowledgements

We have been helped tremendously by conversations with colleagues, and in particular with practitioners in various areas of state activity affected by the modern privatisation process. We would in particular like to thank Anne Beech for comments on early drafts of some chapters and Janet Ransom for going through the manuscript with a fine eye for contradiction and non sequitur and thereby saving us from many examples of incoherence. All remaining faults and weakness are of course entirely of our own making.

WF and JL, London, August 2019

Introduction

For some years a debate has been growing on the 'privatisation' of activities formerly undertaken by the state, or by public bodies directly accountable to the state. In many countries in the global north, but in the UK in particular, privatisation is seen as concerned with the cutting back or elimination of the Keynesian welfare state through the transfer to private profit-seeking corporations of public utilities and welfare services such as water, gas, electricity, railways and public transport, and much of health care and education. What the welfare state provided as a social right, funded or subsidised from public taxation, the private market now provides as a commodity to be purchased by those who can afford to pay, with financial subsidies going less to the user than to the private corporations providing the service.

For the political right, privatisation was about two things: first, 'setting the people free' – as Margaret Thatcher described it – from the burden of that portion of taxation which funded the services; and second, allowing the bracing wind of competition to increase the efficiency of services previously run by sclerotic public monopolies under the control of time-serving bureaucrats and civil servants (see Gamble 1988). For the political left, on the other hand, privatisation was about maintaining capitalist profitability by dismantling the gains of the welfare state and transferring large amounts of tax money into the hands of private capital through subsidies to the private sector providing services hitherto provided by the state. It was also about ending the democratic control of welfare services and public utilities through accountability to parliament and replacing it with the accumulation of private profit and power by large corporations unaccountable to the democratic process, resulting in the creation of a private 'shadow state' (White 2016).

There is now a growing public backlash against this form of privatisation, particularly those aspects that directly affect the middle class. The sight of angry commuters on rail platforms inveighing against the money-grabbing inefficiency of private railway companies ironically re-enacts the similar anger of their parents towards the alleged bureaucratic inefficiency of the state-owned railways. There is also growing anger at the declining standard of service due to the lack of funding and alleged profiteering of private companies who benefit from subcontracting by organisations still run by the state, such as the National Health Service. From time to time the private companies who stand to turn public need into profitable business take a direct hit in terms of reputational damage as, for example, when the giant multinational G4S spectacularly failed to deliver on its contract to provide security personnel to the London Olympics in 2012 (see White 2016).

But this book focuses on the role of the private sector in one particular area of state activity: that associated with the exercise of coercive force. Most of this obviously concerns the military and criminal justice activities of the state. Here the distinction between two types of privatisation is important. Outright privatisation means handing over the activity entirely to private corporations or bodies to be sold as a commodity in the marketplace. If we follow the conventional view of the state as the institution that has a monopoly of legitimate coercion within its territory, then obviously things like military force or criminal justice cannot be privatised in this sense without dismembering the state itself. No state could allow the privatisation of its courts, police and military without, most would argue, ceasing to be a coherent state. Decisions on engaging in war or on criminal sentencing and imprisonment taken by private bodies outside the control of the state would be akin to the rule of warlords and mafias.

The second type of privatisation – outsourcing – by contrast is where the state retains ultimate control but delegates certain tasks to private corporations. For example, a state may retain full control over its military forces and decisions about when to engage in armed conflict and what forces to deploy, but nevertheless outsource certain tasks such as logistics, guarding or even combat to private sources. One thinks immediately of mercenaries but nowadays they have the more respectable-sounding name of 'private military companies'. Whatever tasks they perform, the argument is that they will do so under the orders and control of the government and the official state military. In a similar way the private sector may undertake criminal justice tasks such as the construction and management of prisons. But only the state courts will decide who goes to prison and for how long, and state inspectorates will monitor the adherence of private prison management to the terms of their outsourcing contracts with the state. This might appear to resolve questions regarding the legitimacy of the exercise of coercive force by non-state bodies. The state retains ultimate authority and private sector organisations operate as agents of the state. This at any rate is the theory.

However, in reality this is precisely where problems begin. To take one example, a private prison governor, operating under an outsourcing contract, is not solely a government agent: he or she is also the employee of a private company whose prime purpose is to secure a profit. Furthermore, the role of prison governor involves decisions about such matters as prisoner discipline or early release. So a degree of coercive power is being exercised by individuals who are not simply the agents of the state. As we shall see in greater detail in Chapter 5, there may be serious concerns about the legitimacy of such power.

Prison governors are of course dealing with the 'captive' populations of sentenced prisoners. But other aspects of outsourcing directly affect the general public. Even though they may be subcontracted by police authorities, having employees of private security companies patrolling public space and handing out fines for dropping litter may seem trivial but in fact raises fundamental issues about authority and legitimacy. Here we encounter a further complication. Although the state remains the ultimate custodian of the law there are strong traditions of legal rights, particularly in England and Wales and similar common law jurisdictions, enabling ordinary citizens to use a measure of force in defence of their private property. In many legal jurisdictions ordinary members of the public may enact a 'citizen's arrest' if state police are not present. Ejecting an intruder from your house is one thing, but as we shall see in Chapter 4, where 'private property' expands to embrace large areas of public space and where the private owners of that space are permitted by the state to formulate their own regulations regarding the conduct of anyone who enters their property, and to employ private security companies to enforce such regulations, then the degree of autonomous private coercion becomes considerable and controversial. Such coercion is not outsourcing of state coercion but the privatisation or commodification of traditional rights to the protection of one's private property. Of course, the 'one' in this context may well be a foreign hedge fund or global property corporation.

Another important consideration is that the private security companies employed either by governments or by the owners of private property themselves have significant power and influence. While some are small and local, others are vast transnational corporations. Companies like G4S operate, as we shall see, worldwide and in some parts of the globe can be considered more powerful than national states. Even in the well-organised and strong states of the global north these private companies may be sufficiently powerful to influence the formation and execution of policy. Private military companies may influence the conduct and duration of armed conflict even though governments are theoretically in charge, while the private prisons industry may lobby informally for the increased use by the criminal courts of custodial sentences.

There is a final issue, and one that structures the whole organisation and discussion of our book: that these matters change and evolve over time. An activity which at one historical period may appear to be inevitably part of the state's monopoly of legitimate coercion, or 'inherently governmental', may in another historical period be carried out largely by private bodies. For example, today in England and Wales the detection and prosecution of criminal offenders is generally regarded as the natural monopoly of state police and prosecutors. But in an earlier period, the eighteenth and early nineteenth centuries, much of it was carried out by what today would be called private security companies acting on behalf of wealthy groups of citizens or by purely local government bodies. At the same time much of the prison estate was privately managed, while private militaries – mercenaries – or troops in the employ of private trading companies played a leading role in the process of colonial expansion. To understand how the boundaries between state and private coercion are subject to historical change is one of our main preoccupations.

These boundaries change, moreover, in particular ways. What interests us in particular is that for a long period, most of the nineteenth and the first half of the twentieth centuries, the tendency was one of the decline of private coercion, much of which was absorbed or replaced by the expansion of the state. This expansion was regarded as part of the process of modernisation: the extension of the rule of law, democratic accountability and modern ideas of citizenship. In the international sphere the decline of private military forces was associated with the evolution of the modern community of states and modern forms of warfare.

Yet in the recent period, roughly since the mid-1970s, this process appears to have gone into reverse. The changing nature of war and armed conflict has seen the significant return of private military forces, while domestically the expanding role of private prisons and various forms of private policing seems unstoppable. What are the changes in the international system of states and in the structure of modern industrial capitalist societies that have underpinned these changes? How far can terms like 'neoliberalism' capture the dynamics?

In the following chapters we try to take a broad overview of these developments. Chapter 1 attempts an outline of some of the main contours of what we have called 'old privatisation' as it existed during the eighteenth and early nineteenth centuries, from the armed trading companies to private policing and prisons. Chapter 2 traces the steady decline of old privatisation, as public state authority became consolidated and expanded and private hired police were displaced by public forces. Meanwhile the old locally and privately run prison system and the embryonic private charity-run probation systems were reorganised and absorbed by the state. These developments reached their apex in the period following the Second World War: the period of the welfare state and the cold war.

The next three chapters on the private military, policing and private security, and prisons and probation, document the main features of the resurgence of the private sector in these areas. At the same time we attempt to relate this resurgence to the well-known social changes underway in recent decades but with a particular focus on changing notions of citizenship which, in our opinion, make the exercise of private power possible and seemingly legitimate.

In Chapter 6 we draw the threads together and attempt a general assessment of the increasing dependence of government on the powerful private security companies (or *security-industrial complex*) in key areas and the extent to which this dependence, and in particular the claims to legitimate authority on the part of the private companies, alters the character of the state itself and results in the emergence of a new type of 'security state' with one foot, as it were, in the private sector.

Finally, an apology is perhaps in order. We have based our discussion overwhelmingly on the British – indeed the English – case, with occasional references to developments in other parts of the world. This is partly a result of the constraints of trying to write a book of manageable size on these broad issues and also because a comprehensive global comparative study of all the issues we consider important would take a substantially longer period given the limits of our present knowledge.

1
Old Privatisation

This book deals with the issue of the outsourcing of the coercive aspects of state power to private corporations. By the coercive aspects of state power we refer generally to military force, various aspects of policing and the punishment of criminal offenders. Other aspects such as the guarding of frontiers and the private protection of individual and commercial property are also considered, but issues such as taxation fall outside our focus, although these might possibly also be regarded as a form of state coercion.

Discussion of these issues usually begins with a reference to the sociologist Max Weber, who famously defined the state in terms of its ability to claim 'the monopoly of the legitimate use of physical force within a given territory' (Weber 1946: 78). There has of course been much critical discussion of this definition of the state, but it is one we shall work with here because of its historical and intellectual reach. The issue of legitimate coercion is central to the areas of outsourcing we are going to discuss. Until fairly recently, only states could legitimately declare war on other states; warfare by non-state actors was piracy or banditry. Still today, only the state legislature has the power to make laws and only the state courts have the authority to imprison those who violate them. Coercion by any other individuals or organisations is kidnapping and false imprisonment. Only the state, acting in accordance with properly enacted laws, can demand your taxes. Such a demand from any other individuals or organisations is a criminal protection racket.

But there is one aspect of Weber's view of the state that is worth further discussion here. Does the state derive legitimacy from the fact that it is able to secure its monopoly of force? This view was articulated by the historian Charles Tilly (1985), who saw the consolidation of modern state legitimacy as the outcome of long periods of medieval warfare in which regional barons, warlords and bandits competed over the use of violence in a particular territory. Eventually the most powerful group succeeded in establishing its monopoly and that monopoly came, eventually, to be accepted as legitimate. Tilly was well aware that this process of establishing a monopoly of legitimate force is never complete and is periodically challenged by rival non-state organisations. He wrote a preface to Anton Blok's study of the Sicilian mafia (Blok 1974) in which he (Tilly) posed the question of whether the mafia, although powerful enough to challenge the power and authority of the Italian state and to achieve a degree of respect and legitimacy in the eyes of the local population, could ever itself become a state:

> If one mafia network managed to extend its control over all of Sicily, all concerned would begin to describe its actions as 'public' rather than 'private'. The national government would have to come to terms with it, outsiders and insiders alike would begin to treat its chiefs with legitimate authority. It would be a government, it would resemble a state. (Blok 1974: xxiii)

It did not do so, according to Tilly, because it remained a system of competing and periodically fractious clans and families. While we are concerned with the privatising and outsourcing of state coercive power to legitimate private security companies rather than organised crime, Tilly's observation is important. If, under certain circumstances, a mafia could become a legitimate government, under what circumstances might a private company achieve the same status? We might ask whether a powerful multinational security company like G4S could ever come to 'resemble a state' rather than simply provide certain outsourced services to the existing state and to other private corporations authorised by the state.

But this is something for a later chapter. The issue here is that in the eighteenth and early nineteenth centuries, a great deal of legitimacy adhered to private corporations, groups and individuals engaged in activities that would later come to be seen as the legitimate monopoly of the state. The process of change was certainly not that these private organisations came to assume a state-like legitimacy. Rather, their activities were taken over in various ways by means of the expansion of the existing state machinery during the end of the nineteenth and the first half of the twentieth centuries. The most important issue, and our main discussion in later chapters, is why in recent decades their activity and importance has increased.

Part of laying the ground for an answer to this question requires that, as we turn to a broad outline of old privatisation in England during the eighteenth and early nineteenth centuries, we acknowledge an important distinction between types of private power. As industrialisation, urbanisation and the expansion of imperialism and overseas trade gathered pace it became clear that there were some forms of private power which, inherited from previous historical periods, were clearly obstacles to these developments. Aristocratic landowners fencing off their private estates in the middle of growing cities obstructed the increasing flow of people and goods. Progress, as we shall see, demanded their dismantlement. But to regard all forms of old privatisation in this way is problematic. A conventional view of the history of English policing, for example, tends to see the old local and private systems as archaic and inefficient, and their replacement by state-sponsored forces as inevitable. Yet closer inspection reveals that much innovation and modernisation of policing was sponsored by private interests. The consequence is that the eventual demise of private policing has to be explained in terms other than simply those pertaining to efficiency. The important consequence is that, when we come to investigate the resurgence of the private sector in recent decades, an explanation which also goes beyond reference to efficiency or value for money will certainly be required.

We are aware, finally, that the greater extent of private and local institutional power, with regard to the English criminal justice system, at the beginning of our period contrasted with much of continental Europe. On whether or not this reflected some special defect or 'peculiarity' of English capitalist development, as famously debated by Marxist historians such as Tom Nairn, Perry Anderson, Edward Thompson and others during the 1960s and 1970s (see Meiksins Wood 1992), we take no position. What we can, however, take as the starting point of our discussion is the fact that 'by the late seventeenth century the English State lacked the coercive capacity to exact a uniform compliance throughout its social structure' (McMullan 1995: 123).

PRIVATE WARFARE AND COLONIAL SOVEREIGNTY

From an early stage the inefficiencies of the English state were evident in its overseas activity – colonial conquest – which was as crucial a part of capitalist expansion as the growth of the domestic economy and social structure. The demands of warfare both between European states and as an aspect of early colonial expansion in the seventeenth and eighteenth centuries necessitated expansions of military force supplemented from private sources. In 1701, 54 per cent of British military forces were foreign mercenaries (Thomson 1996: 29). The hiring of foreign professional soldiers, as individuals or corporations, as a supplement to domestic militaries goes back to the ancient world and long predates the modern nation state (see Holmila 2012).

But the important innovation from the seventeenth century onwards was the growing demands of colonial expansion, which far outstripped the capacities of the English state (the British state after union with Scotland in 1706). The seventeenth and eighteenth centuries were the age of the armed trading companies of which the most well known are the British and Dutch East India Companies, which began to assume state-like powers in colonial conquest. 'Because of the limited capacity of the early modern state, the extension of imperial sovereignty to overseas territories necessarily relied ... on the delegation of legal powers to these non-state entities or persons' (den Blanken 2012: 7–8).

The (British) East India Company was described by Edmund Burke as 'a delegation of the whole power and sovereignty of this kingdom sent into the East' (quoted in Thomson 1996: 32). Philip Stern rejects the notion of the company as 'state-*like*' in favour of the notion of a 'company-state' (Stern 2012: 6; see also Wilson 2009). That is to say, the company's charter from the British Crown – in that sense, of course, it remained an *outsourced* power of the English state – which began in 1600 as a trading monopoly, was progressively extended until it became

> a claim to jurisdiction over all English subjects in Asia and the Eurasian populations resident in its growing network of settlements. Grant after Grant from English monarchs progressively expanded this purview, giving the Company leave to establish fortifications, make law, erect courts, issue punishment, coin money, conduct diplomacy, wage war, arrest English subjects, and plant colonies. (Stern 2012: 12; see also Thomson 1996: 35)

By the late 1700s, the East India Company's own army of around 100,000, including foreign mercenaries, was larger than the British army. The activities of the company in India can only of course euphemistically be described as 'trade'. The realities of its rule included outright looting and pillage, impoverishment through ruinous levels of taxation imposed on Indian communities and massive levels of bribery and deception. These were the realities of the foundation of the British Raj

(Dalrymple 2015). Much of this wealth flowed directly to the coffers of the company rather than the British state, such that what may have begun as 'outsourcing' ended up as more or less complete privatisation – until the British Crown reasserted control well into the second half of the nineteenth century. But until then the virtual monopoly and indeed independence from British state control certainly enabled the company to 'resemble a state' in the sense elaborated by Tilly. This independence included the initiation of military conflict independently of the orders of the British government. This was established early on. In 1622, in collusion with Persian forces, company troops attacked Portuguese garrisons in India despite government orders to the contrary (Singer 2007: 33–4). Company-initiated wars of conquest continued well into the nineteenth century (Kinsey 2006: 39).

Furthermore, during the seventeenth and eighteenth centuries the monopoly of the right of the sovereign government of a country to wage war was less clear than it became later in the nineteenth century. David Kennedy, in his discussion of the legal and moral dimensions of warfare, notes that earlier discussions 'did not distinguish between legal and moral authority, or between national and international law, or between the public and private capacities of sovereign authorities' (Kennedy 2006: 48). Thus, 'all sorts of entities had rights – rulers of many different kinds, individuals, citizens, pirates, merchants. Later would come the East India Tea Company' (Kennedy 2006: 61). In other words, the right of the East India Company to wage war was not simply a matter of outsourcing by the British state, but rather derived from a world in which the capacity and right to use military force was not yet clearly limited to the sovereign governments of states. In England in particular – where at the same time, as we shall see, substantial areas of the domestic criminal justice machinery remained in private hands – this would hardly have seemed strange.

Nevertheless, the autonomy of the company was a necessary part of early colonial expansion rather than some anachronistic survival. It reduced the military and administrative burden on the British state as well as providing the latter with a strategy of plausible deniability in cases of failure or morally dubious action (Thomson 1996: 44; Whyte 2015: 41). The autonomy of the 'company-state' resolved the difficulty of stretched lines of communication in the early period of rapid colonial expansion where 'requiring companies to wait for the sovereign's instructions would probably not have been a viable option' (Holmila 2012: 60). This was the case particularly with respect to the important role of the company in combatting rival aspiring colonial powers such as the Netherlands, which promoted the powerful Dutch East India Company.

The East India Company was not simply a trading company but also operated textile factories in the areas of India under its control and

> the transformation of the company into an increasingly powerful territorial organisation enabled it to deploy its coercive apparatus in support of its intervention in the labor process, as it did through the assignment of military personnel to protect and support the *gumashtas* (supervisors) and their staff, or through the later enactment of legislation requiring weavers to work exclusively for the company. (Arrighi and Silver 1999: 111)

It was precisely those coercive measures designed to produce a docile labour force habituated to factory discipline and wage work which also played a major role in the reforms of the English police system, reforms led, as we shall see presently, by the London merchant and magistrate Patrick Colquhoun in the form of his own private system of police. The private sector (as it would now be called) laid down the foundations for a modern police force and, indeed, the formation of the modern working class.

POLICING AND CRIME CONTROL

There were certainly aspects of private power in the area of policing and crime control which were anachronistic obstructions to capitalist modernisation. The resistance, during the early years of the nineteenth century, of the rural gentry and landowners to police reform is well known. Douglas Hay wrote of the eighteenth-century landowners: 'A regular police force did not exist, and the gentry would not tolerate even the idea of one ... In place of police, however, propertied Englishmen had a fat and swelling sheaf of laws which threatened thieves with death' (Hay 1975: 17). For the enforcement of that 'sheaf of laws' the landowners had their own armies of retainers, gamekeepers and supporters. As late as the 1830s, during the Captain Swing riots in Hampshire, the Duke of Wellington 'induced the magistrates to put themselves on horseback, each at the head of his own servants, retainers, grooms, hunters, gamekeepers armed with horse whips, pistols, fowling pieces, and what they could get, and to attack in concert ... those mobs, disperse them and take and put in confinement those who could not escape' (Kent and Townsend 2002: 126, quoted in Clement 2016: 124–5).

The recourse to private arrangements for the defence of private property was not simply a rural phenomenon. Even in rapidly growing cities private land, guarded by what would now be called private security and initially resistant to the incursions of public authority, was a major factor. During the eighteenth and early nineteenth centuries,

> large sections of urban centres such as London, were owned by a small group of wealthy landlords who controlled vast swathes of the capital ... Reflecting both the social divisions of the time and the management practices of the private landlords, the capital in this period was characterised by numerous gated squares and private streets, where public access was restricted or blocked by hundreds of gates, bars and posts. (Minton 2006: 9)

This enclosure of public space by private landowners dates back to the seventeenth century. The Dukes of Bedford were major private landowners in London and 'Upper Woburn Place, originally a private road for the Dukes, had gates in the eighteenth century. By 1798 this road was closed off to traffic, and from the early 19th Century, parts of the Bedford Estate had gates at all entrances' (Mudlark 2016). By the 1820s the Duke of Bedford had over 200 gates on his properties and employed his own private security to guard them. Private control of urban space was increasing well into the nineteenth century:

> the West End was a gilded cage of privilege, the limits of which were constituted not only in the informal and subtle manipulation of the 'quality' of its residential neighbourhoods and communities, but also more crudely through the blockading of streets to keep out undesirables and to restrict or ban access to traffic ... The Bedford Estate, one of the most stringent in the protection of its territory, employed uniformed ex-prison officers to vet traffic, and these men acquired a reputation for unflinching defence of their domain, occasional surliness and even violence. At an 1874 court hearing of the reasons for a fracas at the Gordon Street gate, the keeper declared that 'he would suffer death rather than let the cab through'. (Atkins 1993: 266)

Alongside this private system of what would now be called 'gated communities' there existed, as far as the detection of crime and the general policing of public space was concerned, a traditional localised system of parish constables and night watchmen together with a privately paid system of crime detection. The principle of payment for service was a powerful driver of the 'old' police and prosecution system (McMullan 1996; Rock 1983; Zedner 2006). Constables were unpaid: any victim of crime who wanted a constable to apprehend a perpetrator was expected to pay the expenses (Friedman 1995: 475–6). It is true that the system had its contradictions, in particular that private thief-takers hired by victims and paid 'by results' for property recovered and/or perpetrators apprehended for prosecution had an incentive to collude with criminals; there were some celebrated cases of this (Zedner 2006; McMullan 1996).

At least some of the criticism of the old system might be special pleading to frame Robert Peel's new police, which took to the streets of London in 1829, as a great step forward in state-led reform. Indeed, to anticipate our later argument, the alleged inefficiencies of the private system were not the main reason for the eventual predominance of Peel's police. Where policing was less associated with the general disciplining of the working class and the symbolic control of public space, and more focused on the protection of the propertied classes from robbers and burglars – in other words when security was still to a considerable extent seen as a *private good* available to those who could pay – then a system of fee payment for thief-taking made sense. Payment by results (in modern parlance) for the detection and apprehending of offenders appeared natural to the urban middle classes in eighteenth-century London, as it is beginning to appear once again (as we shall see in Chapter 4) to their twenty-first-century descendants, who are increasingly hiring private security companies to defend their property.

Furthermore, the system reflected an older pre-industrial tradition which considered it a duty for men of property to participate in the governance of their communities as magistrates and constables (Dodsworth 2004). The origins of private payment for policing functions lie in the desire to delegate these functions to others. This, particularly in the duties of constables and watchmen, was not private enterprise in quite the modern sense but a commutation of traditional civic duties. The legitimacy of payment for service being established, it could then seem obvious, in the face of rising theft and street robbery, to pay private thief-takers and informers. Thus it is not surprising that reformers –

such as the London magistrates in the mid-eighteenth century onwards led by the Fielding brothers – should seek to extend and reform this private paid police system.

The focus on payment by results as the appropriate organisation of policing was also favoured by another characteristic of the decentralised English system of the eighteenth century, namely the responsibility of the victim – or their relatives – to initiate prosecution. This lasted well into the nineteenth century before being gradually assumed by the new police, there being no office of local public prosecutor in the English system. The duty of the victim to prosecute – like the duty of personal service as a constable – are residues of a world in which much crime took place between victims and offenders who either knew each other personally or who could easily be put in contact. The notion of crime as above all a violation of the law had yet to fully inscribe itself. Writing about the second half of the seventeenth century up to 1750, Beattie explains what was considered the normal relationship between traditional constables and the victims of crime: 'constables could be hired, just as any other private citizen could be hired, to help find offenders … They could also use their office to engage in free-enterprise thief-taking, an activity much encouraged by the establishment of statutory rewards in this period' (Beattie 2001: 131).

So as urban life became more complex, and criminal offenders increasingly unknown personally to their victims, the employment of a thief-taker to recover the property or track down the offender flowed naturally from this system. It is therefore unsurprising that the private system of 'monied police' should be the focus of intense reform activity during the second half of the eighteenth century. Victims collaborated in private subscription Associations for the Prosecution of Felons (APFs). These associations, which estimates suggest numbered as many as 4,000 between 1750 and 1850 (King 1989; see also Shubert 1981), acted to share the costs of hiring thief-takers and of funding prosecution. Meanwhile, on the policing side the reformers – notably the London magistrates led by the brothers John and Henry Fielding – acted to extend the role of private thief-takers paid from fees and rewards from victims (Harris 2004).

Henry Fielding became a magistrate at Bow Street in 1748 and his court became something of a national coordinating centre for information. His private thief-takers, or 'runners', increasingly served as a de facto London police force. Like Patrick Colquhoun (of whom more presently), he understood the importance of significant eyes and ears in the community such as turnpike (private road) keepers, market traders and inn-keepers. He adopted the practice of information dissemination through handbills and posters (McMullan 1996; Johnstone 2015). John Fielding, meanwhile, was active in the more general policing of urban space, organising armed horse and foot patrols which extended to the highways into and out of the metropolis (Emsley 2010: 22). By the time of Peel's 1829 Act creating the new state-organised Metropolitan Police in London there were already substantial round-the-clock street patrols (Johnstone 2015: 44), so much so that it was not immediately obvious to some that Peel's 'New Police' added greatly to efficiency. As Clive Emsley pointed out:

> Long before the creation of the Metropolitan Police, good night watchmen had got to know their beats and the people who lived on them; they were observant and, on occasions, it was their watchfulness which led to the arrest of offenders. The new police extended this system ... and they introduced a measure of uniformity, but whether they thus deterred burglars and street robbers it is impossible to say. There were those who expressed doubts. (Emsley 1996: 59)

Nevertheless, the days of the old system were numbered. It was not just that with urban growth and complexity, security had become a *public good* necessarily provided for the general population of an area rather than to individuals who paid for it. It was a matter of the general stabilisation of class relations and urban life in the new industrial capitalism. This meant the control of public space and the general disciplining of the urban poor and, more precisely, subordinating the new working class to the rhythms of wage labour and factory discipline. At the end of the eighteenth and the beginning of the nineteenth centuries these problems were magnified by the shadow of the French revolution and the rise of working-class radicalism. The Gordon Riots in London in 1780, the numerous food riots up and down the country, the disastrous use of the military in public order situations, notably at the demonstration at St Peter's Fields in Manchester in 1819 (Peterloo), concentrated the minds of reformers on problems and solutions which could not possibly be solved by piecemeal private initiatives. Such was the backdrop to the organised public police founded by Peel.

In this respect the other great police reformer at the end of the eighteenth century, the London merchant Patrick Colquhoun, is a complex character. He is celebrated for his private initiative in founding one of the first modern police forces, the Thames police. But his general project, nothing less than the struggle against the 'indigence' of the new urban working class, was a blueprint for the general development of social policy well into the nineteenth century, something that, despite Colquhoun's suspicions of the state, certainly could not have been sustained by private initiative alone.

A major concern of merchants at the time was the tendency of workers, derived from older pre-industrial traditions, not only to imprecise time-keeping but also to walking off with a small portion of the cargoes stored in their employers' warehouses. In London, the West India Merchants' Committee employed, from the mid-1760s, informal security guards to prohibit 'all perquisites from Sweepings of Sugar' (Linebaugh 2003: 426). In 1798 they were persuaded by Colquhoun, who was also a magistrate, to fund his new Thames Marine Police based at Wapping. The organisation included a resident magistrate and 60 armed employees (Johnston 1992: 16). Colquhoun's force is often heralded as the precursor to Peel's police into which it was later absorbed. But in many respects it seems to resemble a private security company engaged, with the convenience of an attached magistrate, in the guarding of commercial property. Colquhoun's police searched workers as they left his warehouses and he even put them in charge of the payment of wages (Linebaugh 2003: 428). Other merchants in Liverpool and Bristol followed rapidly with their own 'docks police'.

But for Colquhoun and his associates, the delinquency of the warehouse labour force was but a microcosm of the general problem facing the further development of capitalism: the indigence of the poor, their unwillingness to work. The term referred of course to the broader issues, not of unwillingness to labour as such, but of resistance to the discipline of wage labour as the sole source of income and subordination to the organisation of work determined by the employer rather than by custom and tradition (see Thompson 1967). This was the significance of Colquhoun's police at Wapping and their war on pilferage and perquisites. In his writings (e.g. Colquhoun 1806) and discussions with his friend, the philosopher Jeremy Bentham, Colquhoun inveighed against the working class as a 'general army of delinquents' in need of 'humane improvement by police' (Linebaugh 2003: 428).

The war on indigence led Colquhoun in a number of directions. The prevention of pilferage from his warehouses led him to distinctly modern notions of crime prevention. As David Garland noted, Colquhoun

> presents a meticulous analysis of crime events, which identifies many of the 'ten thousand different ways' in which mobile property is 'exposed to depredation', and offers a detailed account of precisely how particular crimes are facilitated by the situation in which they occur. Following on from this, he proposes methods of regulation, inspection, guardianship and design which would substantially reduce the opportunities for crime and increase the risks of an offender being caught. Moreover, this 'correct system of police', as he calls it, is to be put in place not by the state (which barely had the capacity for such extensive action) but by men of influence, philanthropists, patriots, ale-house keepers, merchants, ship-owners, those in charge of parishes, the clergy, and magistrates in charge of business, commerce and the city – in other words, by the institutions of civil society. (The new 'superintending agency' suggested by Colquhoun is often identified as the origin of the public police force which emerged 30 years later, but it is clear that this was only one of a long list of agencies which were to be involved in his scheme of city regulation.) (Garland 1996: 465)

This 'long list of agencies' included embryonic forms of what today would be considered private security. Banks, places of entertainment, race courses, taverns, hotels, all expanding areas of commerce in the early years of the nineteenth century, employed their own guards and bouncers as well as, particularly in the case of banking houses, private detectives to track thieves, forgers and counterfeiters (see George and Kimber 2014). These worked alongside and as part of the various systems of private prosecution and thief-taking already mentioned. For Colquhoun such developments were part of a more general strategy of social control in which Colquhoun distinguished, as Mark Neocleous (2000) noted, between 'municipal' and 'criminal' aspects of police. The former included what later became the notorious New Poor Law which, from the 1840s, was infused with the principle of 'less eligibility', that is the enforced habituation to work by making sure that living conditions obtainable on 'relief' (social security) were below those obtainable on the lowest wages. Criminal police (police in the modern sense) dealt with those who rejected the discipline of municipal police and turned to crime as a strategy of survival.

Colquhoun's antipathy to the state and his reliance on informal agencies and private initiative arose mainly from his perceptions of the inefficiency of the English state. He was in fact a great admirer of the French system of a militarised *gendarmerie* and advocated the suitability of such a model for England. Robert Peel was also an admirer of the French system. Before becoming Tory home secretary in 1822 he had been chief secretary in Dublin and was able to create just such a *gendarmerie* in the form of the Royal Irish Constabulary (RIC) (Johnstone 2015: 45–6). The RIC (the Irish Constabulary until 1867, when it acquired the 'Royal' prefix) became the general model for British colonial policing. The inefficiency of the English criminal police system at the time lay in the reliance on a 'sheaf of laws' and severe penalties, but with little chance – especially in the growing urban context – of detection. But in this as in other areas, as the nineteenth century progressed it was the private sector that for a time drove innovations. Eventually these came to be seen as parochial and inefficient in the face of the modernising state-led and state-organised police.

THE PRIVATE SECTOR AS ANACHRONISM: THE PENAL SYSTEM

As with policing, the old penal system was a mixture of private and local government-administered workhouses, bridewells and local and county gaols. The appalling conditions existing in most of these establishments were famously documented by the reformer John Howard, who travelled and documented *The State of the Prisons in England and Wales* published in 1777. As is of course well known, the main form of punishment at that time was public hanging and lesser forms of physical punishment, including transportation. Prisons were mainly either holding places for those awaiting trial or for the detention of debtors. In his survey Howard found that only 16 per cent of prisoners were incarcerated as a result of sentence. The rest were either on remand or indeed the greater proportion (69 per cent) were in prison for debt. As, during the nineteenth century, the prison became the main form of punishment, so it was that state control of the system was consolidated and the widespread local and private ownership and management of prisons disappeared.

While his main concern was that of the welfare of inmates, Howard remarked throughout his report on the particular conditions pertaining in privately run gaols. In characterisations that have a significantly modern ring, he reported for example that:

> some gaols are private property: in these the keepers, protected by the proprietors, and not so subject as other gaolers to the control of magistrates, are more apt to abuse their prisoners when a temptation offers. One of these gaols some years ago was quite out of repair, and unsafe; and the proprietor not choosing to repair it, the gaoler to confine his prisoners took a method, that to all who saw it was really shocking. Some years before that, a prisoner in another of these gaols was tormented with thumb-screws. The grand jury took up the case and remonstrated to the proprietor; but in vain. I had the account from a worthy friend of mine who was upon that very jury. (Howard 1777: 34)

As he journeyed around the country he noted the ownership of local gaols. He discussed Halifax private debtors' prison which was located on the manor of Wakefield and 'is the property of the Duke of *Leeds*' (Howard 1777: 415). He then proceeded north to Durham where 'the High Gaol is the property of the Bishop' and where 'by Patent from his Lordship, Sir *Hedworth Williamson* Bart is perpetual Sheriff' (Howard 1777: 417).

These forms of ownership of course were nothing like the private sector prison estate of modern times. They were remnants of pre-capitalist feudal and ecclesiastical forms of ownership mixed in with the traditional rights of towns and boroughs. Nevertheless, the most important aspect is that they were not directly administered by the state. One area in which private enterprise in the modern sense flourished was in the form of the freedom of the wardens and gaolers to charge fees for board and lodging, and also (less common) to pay prisoners themselves for various tasks – Howard mentions sweeping out the prison yard. He also observed that fees for board and lodging tended to be higher in private gaols: 'I wish my reader be not tired of so many Tables of Fees even for the Counties. Yet I must not omit the Fees which I saw in this private prison at *Rothwell:* because some of them are high and at *Halifax* they are the same' (Howard 1777: 414). Howard's negative view of the role of the private sector in the old prison system was, many years later, reiterated by Sidney and Beatrice Webb in their historical study of *English Prisons Under Local Government*:

> the long drawn-out tragedy of prison life is to be ascribed less to any culpable neglect of the Sheriffs and the Justices, in the discharge of duties which had never been precisely defined or even explicitly imposed on them, than to the amazing administrative device, at that time almost universally adopted, of converting the keeping of a prison into a profit-making private business. We can now realise that so long as the keeper of the gaol was permitted to make a profit out of the prisoners committed to his charge, it was quite impracticable to secure conditions of health or decency, or even of common humanity – let alone uniformity or reformative treatment. (Webb and Webb 1922: 18)

Indeed, the Webbs emphasised the widespread penetration of the private profit systems throughout local government and state machinery in the eighteenth century – the obviously still prevalent traditions of royal sale of offices and tax farming being not so distant at that time. An indication of the widespread prevalence of the private profit system is that in a footnote the Webbs drew attention to the fact that in his famous design for the 'panopticon', a revolution in prison design which Foucault famously used as a general metaphor for the new systems of discipline and surveillance developing in early industrial capitalism, Jeremy Bentham thought it quite acceptable to see outsourcing to private entrepreneurs as the best way of funding the new prisons: 'It is to be noted that, even at the beginning of the nineteenth century, so wise a man as Jeremy Bentham was seriously proposing, as the basis of his "panopticon" letting the management by contract to the highest bidder' (Webb and Webb 1922: 18 note 1).

Bentham's scheme was in fact highly ambitious. Both his proposed panopticon prison and a parallel scheme for managing workhouses for the non-criminal poor envisaged private ownership and management and profits from the labour of inmates. He proposed a National Charity Company modelled directly on the East India Company. The latter impressed Bentham not just as a form of joint stock ownership but also as a company-state. If the company could rule large parts of India then placing the management of criminal offenders and the poor in England in the hands of a single private monopoly surely presented few problems. Gertrude Himmelfarb quotes Bentham's original opinion that 'the government of such a concern as that of the proposed National Charity Company would be but child's play to a Director of the East India Company' (Himmelfarb 1970: 83–4). It would be well over 200 years later that Bentham's ideas on private management would see the light of day, by which time the East India Company would have been replaced by G4S and Serco.

Meanwhile, overlapping with the old prison system was penal transportation. Some commentators have suggested that the transition of punishment from the public spectacle of capital punishment to incarceration behind closed walls celebrated in Foucault's (1977) account needs to be modified to include transportation. Anderson et al. (2015) argue that the period from 1750 to the early nineteenth century might be more appropriately characterised 'as a period of complementary and competing regimes of punishment, and in certain contexts as an age of triumphant convict relocation' (Anderson et al. 2015: 1). What was clear, however, was that penal transportation was by no means simply an archaic form of punishment by banishment, but in many respects assimilated into the early versions of strategies of discipline and moral rehabilitation through combinations of regulated labour and solitary confinement, which for Foucault characterises modern institutional discipline. Transportees 'progressed through a regime of separate confinement by night and associated labour by day in official hope of moral reformation. Their character was observed in the isolated confines of the transportation ship' (Anderson et al. 2015: 5) where regimes of 'moral reclamation' could be imposed.

Regimes of penal transportation were especially amenable to a flourishing sector of private entrepreneurs – merchant ship-owners in particular and private subcontractors for penal labour in the destinations. In a period in which mercenaries and privateers, and importantly the slave trade, were common at the colonial periphery, this is only to be expected. As Beattie explained:

> From the beginning the actual machinery of transportation was in the hands of private merchants … who looked upon the trade in convicts as they would any other commodity: their willingness to engage in it depended on the supply of convicts available, on the demand on the other side, and on the profit to be made … The merchant made his profit by selling the convicts as indentured servants in the colonies. (Beattie 1986: 479; see also Feeley 2018)

Indeed, the combination of private trading in convicts and the prison ship as a form of solitary confinement made the system of penal transportation, much more than the system of public penitentiaries which rapidly replaced it, a grim parody of the modern private prison.

As we have already noted, and will discuss further in Chapter 2, the process of penal reform during the nineteenth century is virtually coterminous with the rapid absorption of the prison estate into a centrally state-administered system. Unlike the development of policing there was no significant initial period of the expansion of private initiative or reform to cater for the new need for punishment in urban capitalist society.

This might be explained by the fact that the expansion of the state sector and the radical change in the function of the prison itself were simultaneous. The first was the vehicle of the second. The transition to incarceration as the main form of punishment was a profound change and has been well documented (e.g. Foucault 1977; Ignatieff 1989; Spierenburg 1991). Prisoners of course continued to be held on remand awaiting trial but this was done increasingly within the state system. The changes in penal regime and conditions required by the shift to discipline and rehabilitation (see particularly Foucault 1977) were beyond the capacities of a fragmented local and partially privatised sector. Indeed, it is a misnomer to talk of a private *sector* in the modern sense of the private security industry. The main forms of private ownership were archaic arrangements of landownership dating back to feudal and ecclesiastical landholding, and the main private activity within prisons was the profiteering by individual gaolers and wardens.

Nevertheless, the shift to the modern system of incarceration as the predominant form of punishment did provide a context for some late eighteenth-century reforms – leaving aside Bentham's imaginative thinking – in a fairly localised and fragmented way. DeLacy (1986) and Hardman (2007) emphasised the reforming practices of the county magistrates in raising money to improve prison buildings and imposing tighter control over the profiteering activities of gaolers and wardens. This sort of activity was the nearest equivalent to Fielding's development of a privately funded system of thief-takers. A belief in the private sector as *capable* of such tasks of major reform was perhaps illustrated by Bentham's proposal for outsourcing his panopticon, noted by the Webbs. But the shift to large prisons with a rehabilitative agenda rapidly shifted emphasis away from such localised initiatives and placed the state at an advantage. If the tradition of local county goals and bridewells had continued then it is likely that private property would have played a larger role. But 'the transformation of the gaoler or master from an independent profit-maker into a salaried servant of public authority' (Webb and Webb 1922: 33) was already beginning to become associated with issues of *legitimacy* which only the state, as we shall see, could provide.

THE VOLUNTARY SECTOR AS INNOVATOR: PROBATION AND WELFARE

During the second half of the nineteenth century the state gradually came to regulate and absorb many of the private forms of crime control we have discussed so far. The prison was certainly, as we shall see, the leading sector in this regard. But this did not prevent new initiatives developing in the non-state sector. At the same time as the prison system was being consolidated as a state-run system, private charity organisations were developing resettlement schemes for former prisoners. These would eventually in their turn also be absorbed by the state in the form of the professional probation service.

The latter decades of the nineteenth century saw decisive changes in penal and social policy. In the early decades, as we have seen, the preoccupation of the bourgeois reformers was the 'dangerous classes' as a whole, the problem of indigence and that of the need to subordinate the masses to disciplined labour. The criminal offender was seen very much as a rational calculator who needed to be deterred by heavy penalties. The period roughly after 1860 saw the development of a much more sophisticated approach to governance of the working class. As the industrial working-class communities became more stable and integrated and the franchise was extended, and as trade unions and political aspirations developed, in particular among the 'labour aristocracy', the strategy of the ruling class moved away from pure repression to a more sophisticated strategy of incorporation. Colquhoun's concept of 'correct system of police' had helped to initiate this shift.

The ruling class, at least the bourgeoisie, began to understand better the need to develop a more sophisticated relationship with the increasingly powerful and organised working-class movement, and indeed to pay attention to the urban environment in general. David Harvey succinctly summarised the attitude of the bourgeois reformers in the second half of the century:

> The nineteenth century faced the difficulties of the urban in a very positive and powerful way. It blended socialist sentiments, anarchist ideas, notions of bourgeois reformism and social responsibility into a programmatic attempt to clean up the cities. The 'gas and water socialism' of the late nineteenth and early twentieth centuries did a great deal to improve the conditions of urban life for the mass of the population ... Some of that concern would be helpful to have back in our cities right now. (Harvey 1997: 20)

This reforming spirit was diffused through a number of channels, which included central state action but also the 'gas and water socialism' of Joseph Chamberlain's local government-led reforms in the 1870s. It also involved private charity and philanthropy directed at the poor, which became increasingly coordinated as the century wore on. In 1869 the Charity Organisation Society (COS) aimed to improve charity work by organising and regulating it and deploying expertise in the task of classifying those to whom charity could be usefully applied: the separating out of the 'deserving' from the 'undeserving' poor.

The recognition of the problem of poverty of course in no way implied a critique of capitalism as such. Indeed, by 1881 COS was in 'no doubt that the poverty of the working classes of England is due, not to their circumstances … but to their improvident habits and thriftlessness' (Charity Organisation Review 10 (1881): 50, quoted in Jones and Novak 1999: 80). Colquhoun's view of the indigence of the poor still persisted, but now it was applied not to the working class as a whole but to the very poor and marginalised sections. These were the targets for the developing profession of social work. A major development was the foundation of the National Society for the Prevention of Cruelty to Children (NSPCC) in 1884. In the context of the political turbulence that gripped Europe after the First World War, the role of social work in the political pacification of the working classes was of fundamental importance. Thus, 'In one of his wilder flights of fancy, J. C. Pringle, the General Secretary of the COS for most of the inter-war period, declared social casework to be the answer to Bolshevism' (Lewis 1995: 18).

Developments in the criminal justice and penal system reflected these broader developments. The working class and the new police (as we shall see in Chapter 2) came to an accommodation, while in the penal field the criminal offender came to be seen increasingly as a pathologically weak individual (Wiener 1990) in a similar way to those who had fallen into poverty. Just as the 'deserving poor' who accepted responsibility for their plight should be helped to return to a productive existence, so those petty criminal offenders who showed sufficient remorse – in particular by abstaining from alcohol – could be rehabilitated by a spectrum of non-penal measures both within and outside the prison rather than penal servitude and deterrence. These were the beginnings of *penal welfare* (Garland 1985; Gard 2014).

This was the starting point for probation as an alternative to prison: the major provider of probation was the religious charity sector. As with developments in policing prior to Peel's new police, it was the magistrates who were the innovating force, and the focal point of this innovation was (as with the Fieldings almost a century earlier) the central London court at Bow Street. The freedom of the magistrates to innovate regarding non-penal sentences was made possible by the expansion of summary jurisdiction. A raft of legislation from the Juvenile Offenders Act 1847, the Summary Jurisdiction Act 1879 and the Probation of First Offenders Act 1887 increased the range of offences which could be tried summarily and enabled magistrates to differentiate more precisely between different categories of offenders with different levels of culpability, such as juveniles, women and women with infants (see McWilliams 1983: 130). The religious charity workers became known as the London Police Court Missionaries, and were drawn mainly from members of the Church of England Temperance Society. They began work at Bow Street in 1876 and,

> working throughout the metropolis ... became instrumental in the daily functioning of local courts and an indispensable counterpoint to the work of the magistrates. Although the task of the first missionaries was confined to temperance work in and around the police courts, the role of these early agents very rapidly expanded into almost every aspect of the courts' operations. Within a few years of their introduction, the missionaries were collecting pretrial information on the accused, mediating interpersonal and marital conflicts, advising the magistrates, monitoring the post-trial behaviour of the courts' clientele, and even providing employment, funds, and tools for those in the community deemed worthy. (Auerbach 2015: 628)

The role of missionaries and the particular emphasis on temperance was sustained by the widespread focus during the period on alcohol as the cause both of poverty in general and petty criminality in particular (Wiener 1990: 79). This view was given official status by the Gladstone Committee of 1895: 'Habitual criminals, habitual drunkards, mentally disordered offenders, first offenders, young prisoners, women, women with infants, remand prisoners and debtors were all believed to require distinct methods of treatment in special institutions' (Rawlings 1999: 120).

The focus of the missionaries on getting those placed in their charge by magistrates to sign the abstinence pledge eventually became, as McWilliams (1983) observed, their Achilles' heel and enabled their later replacement by state-employed secular psychiatrically trained social workers. Nevertheless, an important element would remain, namely the fact that the status and work of these early probation officers remained 'at a distance' from official state control. Though the support of the magistrates was crucial, this element of independence remained an important factor in their status and ability to operate in working-class communities (see Auerbach 2015: 636). The role of the missionaries as court probation officers was formalised by the Probation of Offenders Act of 1907. This was the beginning of the process of absorption into the state. Nevertheless, the essentially non-state character of the probation officer remained for some time to come: 'The probation officer appointed after 1st January 1908 could also be the agent of a voluntary society: Church Army, Church of England Temperance Society, Police Court Mission, Discharged Prisoner's Aid Societies, Catholic Societies, Salvation Army and NSPCC' (Whitehead and Statham 2005: 24).

CONCLUSION

The brief but wide-ranging survey that we have undertaken in this chapter might seem to stretch the bounds of eclecticism. What could the early history of the East India Company have in common with private thief-taking, let alone the origins of the English probation service? The common thread is that as British capitalism began its long period of expansion, both in overseas colonialism and into the reorganisation of the domestic urban social structure, private power, in particular private coercive power, existed alongside the state. It was something to which the state had to respond. Some of these forms of power were anachronistic – as with private gated and guarded estates and turnpikes in the middle of expanding cities, or the corrupt and inefficient system of local and private prisons. Understanding that these were swept away in the process of state-led reform is both well documented and discussed by historians and presents few analytical problems. The developing state represented modern efficiency and the embodiment of humane values as the basis for reform.

That is, however, a one-sided view. In many other areas – the development of colonial administration, domestic police reform, the modernisation of the penal system through the development of probation – private organisations were there first: reorganising power structures and innovating in many areas that were later to be absorbed as characteristic attributes of the state. It may be that, during the late nineteenth century and first half of the twentieth century, it seemed that Tilly's problem – the coexistence of the state with other organisations capable of exercising various forms of coercive power – was being resolved by absorption into or regulation by the state; the story that in the areas of military organisation, policing and penal systems the state was not simply more efficient but more legitimate is familiar. But if so, why has it been so easily put into partial reverse? Why has the popular discourse that private military companies, private prisons and private police are more efficient in various ways and, while in no way capable of replacing the state, certainly capable of taking over large sections of state activity, gained political purchase? Why is the private sector to be regarded as more efficient and legitimate today if in earlier periods it was the greater efficiency and legitimacy of the state which seemed beyond doubt? What has changed in the interim? An attempt to answer this conundrum, we argue, has to begin by understanding the real reasons why the state displaced private activity in the first place.

2
The Consolidation of State Power and Legitimacy

In Chapter 1 we noted how during the late eighteenth and early nineteenth centuries there was still a good deal of space for private coercive power to coexist with that of the state. Mercenary troops were widely deployed in the British army while the East India company-state, with its own private army, furthered the interests of British colonialism. Domestically, alongside the survival of anachronistic forms of private control – urban space, some prisons – new private initiatives in prosecution and policing responded to the demands of expanding urban capitalism. Private (charity) initiatives in the development of social work and probation continued until almost the end of the nineteenth century.

Nevertheless, from the first decades of the nineteenth century onwards right through to the middle of the twentieth century, the state consolidated its monopoly of legitimate coercive power in both the international and domestic spheres. Mercenaries and private military forces became regarded as not so much inefficient as illegitimate in modern warfare. A similar development occurred with private forms of policing. Urban modernisation required the removal of private gated estates and spaces, while the reform and changing role of the prison system was at the same time undergoing a process of incorporation by the state. Finally, and much later, the probation system was absorbed by the state as part of a process of modernisation and professionalisation. The broad outlines of the developments we discuss in this chapter are familiar enough. But it is necessary to be clear about why private forms declined in order to understand their later revival.

THE DECLINE OF PRIVATE MILITARY FORCE

The East India Company and similar forms of the colonial company-state or 'corporate sovereignty' could not survive for long in the epoch of competitive capitalism and free trade. If one company has a monopoly of political control and trading rights in a particular geographical area then it can possibly afford the expenses of a private military and state apparatus. However, the opening up of colonial trade to many companies meant that the company providing the state apparatus was at a competitive disadvantage. Other companies entering the area would be 'free-riders' because they did not bear such costs, and it was implausible that each company could have its own private army. The solution was that all companies paid taxes to a general provider of military and state functions. The general provider could not be itself one of the trading companies taking taxes from the others because it would have had an incentive to maximise its own advantages in terms of colonial trade – not to say plunder. In short, the most appropriate general provider is the state. This is the simple economic argument for the non-viability of a company-state in the epoch of competitive capitalism and explains why the state tended to take over such functions. The problem would eventually be solved, as in the recent period, by a new type of specialist private security company providing security services to all trading companies for a fee. But such a company could not itself function as a state, only as the outsourced agent of a state.

Meanwhile the opening up of the colonial (Indian and Chinese) markets to competing modern joint stock companies and the ending of the East India Company monopolies in India in 1813 and in China in 1833 sounded the death knell of the company-state. The final end in India was when, following the Great Rebellion of 1857 against the company in particular and British rule in general, the company was forced to give up all its administrative functions to the British Crown. India became part of the British Empire. The company was an unviable relic of the mercantilist epoch, depending on its trading monopoly to finance its military and state functions and using the latter to defend its monopoly (Robins 2006). The company had overseen a highly successful phase in British imperialism in India. It had 'penetrated the subcontinent by making use of its buoyant markets in produce and land revenue', but at the same time 'had tended to snuff out that buoyant entrepreneurship of revenue farmers, merchants and soldiers which kept the indigenous system functioning' (Bayly 1990: 135, cited in Arrighi and Silver 1999: 112). There was of course plenty for a coercive British colonial state in India to do, in particular to carry on what the East India Company had begun: the suppression of local Indian commercial enterprise to facilitate the market expansion of British companies and to guarantee low raw material prices (Arrighi 1994: 262).

As British colonialism expanded during the nineteenth century, particularly into Africa, some of the conditions which had favoured the monopoly of a single company were reproduced. The British South Africa Company (BSAC) was granted its Royal Charter in 1889. The charter was modelled on that of the old East India Company. The BSAC was formed by Cecil Rhodes mainly to pillage mineral resources in what is now Zimbabwe. The subsequently established colonial settler states, Northern and Southern Rhodesia, were administered by the company until the early 1920s when 'democratic' (that is to say, white settler-controlled) regimes assumed control, under the watchful eye of the British state (see Blake 1978; Loney 1975).

As part of its machinery of company rule, the BSAC established its own paramilitary police force, the British South Africa Company Police (BSACP). The history of this private company police force illustrates an important characteristic of the private administration of coercion that we shall see illustrated repeatedly. It is rarely a question of 'either the state or the private sector' in a mutually exclusive sense. Rather the two interact and combine in various ways. The BSACP was closely modelled on Robert Peel's Royal Irish Constabulary which, as we noted in Chapter 1, became the model for British colonial policing. Early BSACP officers were trained in Dublin (see Cramer 1964). The training and organisation was sufficiently military-oriented for the BSACP to see service during the First World War. Indeed, the police force rapidly became independent of the BSAC itself and came to serve as the state police force in the new white colonial settler states.

Meanwhile, during the nineteenth century there were more general pressures for the decline of private military force. In the sphere of international relations, the problem posed by Tilly (outlined in Chapter 1) was solved: war between states comes to be regarded as exclusively the right of the sovereign, that is of the national state. Thus, 'private armies, mercenaries, privateers – all these were outmoded, not only because they were part of an aristocratic past, but because they did not fit with the new, exclusively public nature of sovereign war' (Kennedy 2006: 64; see also Thomson 1996: 143). As we shall see, the state simultaneously consolidates its monopoly of domestic coercion and international coercion. Only the state can wage war against other states. War and peace become state matters exclusively. States required exclusive control of which conflicts they were to be involved in. This ruled out initiatives by private companies like the East India Company but also created problems for mercenaries. The last mercenary recruitment by Britain was during the Crimean War in 1854, though the troops never saw combat (Thomson 1996: 88). Even if citizens of one state were fighting under the flag and command of another, the state of which the mercenaries were citizens found it difficult to argue that it was not involved in the conflict precisely because warfare was now firmly between states. Thus, 'in the 1814 treaty between Britain and Spain, this principle was explicitly articulated for the first time as there was a provision whereby Britain agreed to prevent its subjects from serving Latin Americans seeking independence' (Leander 2006: 37–8).

There were also technical reasons for the decline of mercenaries. Advances in military technology and organisation requiring high investment in skills, discipline and command structures meant that there were no longer private military entities in existence with anything like the resource and skill mix to make subcontracting viable. The state had to provide these (Smith 2002; Muenkler 2005). This, together with the increasingly uneconomic nature of rehiring military assets for specific engagements (Singer 2007), made the demise of the mercenary as a serious component of the military machine inevitable.

However, arguably the most important function of the pre-eminence of state military was associated with nation building. If war was between states and all soldiers were citizens of those states, then military service was a potent force in building a sense of nationhood and identity. Indeed, well before the end of the period in which the British military ceased to employ mercenaries, 'service in the armed forces brought together the English, Welsh, Scots and Irish in a common endeavour, and presented to the wider public an image of Britishness at work. Military and naval triumphs were the focus for much British pride' (Conway 2001: 893).

Linda Colley (2009) stressed the combination of warfare and the Protestant religion, shared by the Scots, Welsh and English, as crucial in the forging of a common British identity against a variety of non-British, non-Protestant 'others', notably France. Meanwhile in continental Europe, from Napoleon's *levée en masse* onwards, large standing armies became 'central to the construction of and cementing of national identities … [and] played a central part of the shaping of the modern state not only militarily but also socially and politically' (Leander 2006: 41). The role of military service as part of a unifying 'national' endeavour would have been undermined by a primary loyalty not to sovereign and country but to the wage from a private employer who, at least in principle, could offer the military services it purchased elsewhere.

The end of the nineteenth century and the early twentieth century consolidated these tendencies further. The First and Second World Wars brought the mobilisation not just of mass military service but most sectors of the economy and civil society as part of the war machine (van Creveld 1991; Hobsbawm 1994). The requirements of industrialised total war required national consensus and sacrifice. Public support for the military as 'the nation in uniform' precluded any notion of mercenary employment. Debate about the relative merits of the private sector as opposed to the state was entirely suppressed in the general national mobilisation in which all sectors, public and private, were mobilised for the war effort.

THE DECLINE OF PRIVATE SECURITY

Within the territory of the British state the nineteenth century was a period of continuous decline of privately managed coercive force, and much of this was also associated with the development of national identity.

Gated private urban space was frequently a direct obstruction to the free flow of goods and people required by capitalist urban development. The Victorian public 'became increasingly intolerant of perceived hindrances to the efficiency of daily life, their political spokesmen stressing the utilitarian gains of public access through private streets which were key links in the network' (Atkins 1993: 269). The key innovators were local public bodies authorised by the central state. The London County Council and the Metropolitan Board of Works in London and similar bodies in other major cities played a key role.

The liberation from gated streets – and their associated private policing – was just one aspect of a massive expansion of state competence and acquisition of regulatory and inspection powers which characterised the late Victorian period in British urban history. From street lighting, sewerage, the hygiene of slaughterhouses to elementary education, social security and public health, the state became the leading innovator and absorbed many of the private or voluntary initiatives of earlier periods (see Daunton 2000). In particular, the opening of public space was a crucial tool for the social integration of the more prosperous sections of the working class. The other side of the coin was the destruction, through railway building and street widening, of the old criminal ghettos – the *rookeries* – inhabited by the poorest and most socially marginalised sections of the population.

There was also a movement of people off the streets and into organised sites of education, leisure and entertainment – pubs and music halls, parks and public spaces (Daunton 1983). There was developing what Phil Cohen (1979) called 'a new moral economy of place and space' whereby 'a system of informal, tacitly negotiated and particularistic definitions of public order were evolved which accommodated certain working-class usages of social space and time, and outlawed others' (Cohen 1979: 131). As Cohen notes, public space was highly gendered as well as dominated by class. Indeed, the notorious Ripper murders of 1888 were used by the media to control women through 'a cautionary tale for women, a warning that the city was a dangerous place when they transgressed the narrow boundary of home and hearth to enter public space' (Walkowitz 1992: 3; see also Daunton 2000: 10). These emergent conceptions of space had profound implications for the nature of policing not simply as crime control but in the enforcement of public order and urban governance in accordance with the new norms of shared public space.

If policing is regarded as simply thief-taking then it is perhaps harder to understand why the earlier, expanding private systems of policing discussed in Chapter 1 were in decline. Some neoliberal commentators argue that institutions such as the APFs could well have continued had they not been crushed by the advancing juggernaut of the state (see Friedman 1995; Koyama 2012). Various forms of legislation in the early nineteenth century propped up the old tradition of the victim as prosecutor by providing for financial aid to prosecutors (Hay and Synder 1989). The same principle, it might be argued, could have been applied to APFs, in particular those that provided patrolling services and therefore a measure of general deterrence against crime and disorder in public space. In the same way the local street patrols organised by the magistrate John Fielding could have received greater central government subsidy. The result of course would have resembled precisely the growth of private security of the type we have witnessed in recent years. So what happened in the intervening period, and in particular how did policing relate to the emergence of the type of public space we have just described? Could an adequate policing of public space have been undertaken by a private force akin to an APF? If not, as historically seems to have been the case, what has happened to public space in recent years to make a partial return of private policing possible? This final question will be taken up in Chapter 4.

First, it is necessary to understand the nature of the 'new police' begun by Robert Peel with the foundation of the Metropolitan Police in London in 1829. This was a state force in the sense that it was answerable to the home secretary and neither to any private agent nor to the decentralised local authorities which had hitherto provided policing in London. It did not build upon the existing system and had a different orientation:

> While the new police emphasised crime prevention, this was not in terms of deterring potential criminals by the certainty of detection, which had been at the core of John Fielding's work, rather they looked to the moralisation of the poor and the continual harassment of those identified as the least moral sections of the poor – the 'trained and hardened profligates' … the vagrants and the drunks. (Rawlings 1999: 77; see also Storch 1976)

Though the force did undertake thief-taking, this was not its main task. Detectives only appeared in 1842 and then only a very small number. The modern Criminal Investigation Department did not materialise until 1877. The continuity of Peel's police was much more with Colquhoun's vision of a generalised struggle against indigence and the general habits of the working class. The police were a 'bureaucratic instrument for the ordering of the promiscuity of the urban mob by cleansing the disorderly, the disreputable, and street hawkers from the main streets and central thoroughfares of the capital' (Pile et al. 1999: 116, quoted in Brogden and Ellison 2012: 134). It was less crime as such than autonomous working-class street life and leisure that were the focus of police attention, upon which they descended like 'a plague of blue locusts' (Storch 1976).

What Colquhoun and, later, Peel shared was an admiration for the French *gendarmerie*, a militarised state police oriented towards public order and control of the streets. Peel had been able to create just such a force in Ireland in the form of the Royal Irish Constabulary. In London, the middle classes would not have stood for this, so much so that Peel initially had to put his officers in top hats and blue tunics to underline their thoroughly 'civilian' nature, though by the end of the nineteenth century the standard police Noddy helmet was not dissimilar to the headgear of many British army infantry regiments.

However, as the new system of police spread outside London under legislation such as the Municipal Corporations Act of 1835, the decentralised nature of the English state drew the new forces back towards the existing traditional structures of power and authority. Even in the capital Peel had been obliged to respect the powerful commercial interests governing the financial district of the City of London and so exclude the square mile from the jurisdiction of his new police. The City of London formed its own police in 1839. Outside London the new police fell under local government jurisdiction, there being no equivalent to the French office of *préfet* (prefect) who represents the authority of the national state at the local level. Thus local arrangements for the new police were in fact very close to the old system of local watchmen and constables which, in London, with the direct accountability of the new police to the home secretary, had been side-stepped.

In provincial England the powerful commercial interests represented on local government watch committees were not afraid to give direct instructions to 'their' chief constables (see Brogden 1982). In northern English cities there were also numerous examples of the 'employment of public police by private individuals or organisations for the performance of policing duties, largely on private property' (Williams 2008: 191). Police attendance at theatres, football matches and other sporting events, paid for by event organisers, shows a continuity with the old system of private and local policing. This private use of public police, which continued well into the present period, is a mirror image of recent developments in which private security companies are emerging from their role in security and guarding of private property to acquire a foothold in the policing of public space (see Chapter 4). Other areas of English criminal justice responded only slowly to the advance of the state: 'the police directed most theft prosecutions only by the 1880s, and ... charges of common assault were still routinely handled by private individuals by this point. In other words, police prosecution developed piecemeal, and there remained a significant role for victims of crime in bringing cases before magistrates' (Churchill 2014: 141).

Nevertheless, the direction of travel is clear and there were various devices for the increase of central government control of local police forces. As early as the 1840s, ruling-class fear of a popular uprising led by the Chartist movement provoked the Home Office to take direct control of some large city police forces such as those in Birmingham and Manchester (Williams 1998). The County and Borough Police Act of 1856 initiated the gradual, and by no means conflict-free, process of centralisation and monitoring by the Home Office Inspectorate of Constabulary aimed at ensuring consistent standards of training, promotion, operational methods and, most crucially, control of a substantial part of police funding (Brogden 1982; Hale et al. 2004). But the independence of chief constables from direct control by local government watch committees was only established gradually (see Williams 2003). Prior to 1914 the chief constable was still seen as servant of the local watch committee, and not until a court case in 1934 (*Fisher vs. Oldham*) was it established that police officers, including the chief constable, were accountable 'to the law' rather than to the watch committee itself (see Emsley 1996: 164). Despite the continued existence of 43 separate regional forces, various mechanisms of centralisation have continued to develop right up to the present period, while the London-based Metropolitan Police, as the largest force and directly answerable to the home secretary, has acted in some respects as a national force in major incidents.

However much it was decentralised, the police as an institution nevertheless developed a symbolic significance that certainly could not have been achieved by any private organisation. As the better-paid sections of the working class developed stable urban communities, the directly repressive activities of the police – the last rounds of the struggle against indigence – shifted their focus away from the working class as a whole to the very poor and permanently unemployed. The police were aided by such well-established legislation as the 1824 Vagrancy Act which enabled the arrest of a person on suspicion of likelihood of committing an offence. Relations between police and the stable, and increasingly politically organised, working-class community gradually took more the form of a 'grudging acceptance' on both sides (Brogden 1982: 184; see also Cohen 1979). This fragile truce was periodically disrupted by massive police action against trade union organisations during industrial disputes.

Nevertheless, as part of normal urban life, of the 'moral economy of place and space' mentioned above, the police role became increasingly that of the symbolic demonstration of public power. The appearance of accountability to the law rather than to a particular social group – local employers for example – and acting as the 'state on the street' (Brogden 1991) enabled the police to carry the symbols of national cohesion and order into the working-class community even while exercising coercive force (Loader 1997; Emsley 1999; White 2014a). This sense of the paternal – and patriarchal – authority of the police reinforced their status at the pinnacle of a number of traditional informal authority figures in working-class communities (Minton and Aked 2013) such as park-keepers, bus conductors and caretakers – respected adults, all of whom regulated public space and especially its use by young people. Their status as the formal pinnacle on top of this system of informal authority enabled police constables to draw from a reservoir of intervention strategies, ranging from arrest to a good talking to. Policing had, in other words, become more than simply a public good in the economic sense of a service that had to be supplied universally rather than on the basis of individual payment. It had become an important form of authority.

Police domination of the streets played a similar role to that of military service in the building of a sense of national identity increasingly shared by working and middle classes in the new urban context. There was no way that such symbolic integrative functions could have been performed by a group of private security companies any more than a regiment of mercenaries could have symbolised loyalty to monarch and nation. It goes without saying that this legitimacy ebbed and flowed historically with the general state of class relations. Major industrial conflicts and the role of the police against strikers left resentment and contempt for police in working-class communities from the transport strikes of 1911 to the coalfields in 1985. But these were episodic disruptions of the everyday relations between police and community. The symbolism of legitimacy of course changed over time. During the nineteenth and early twentieth centuries much of it linked directly to the monarchy and the colonial empire. Following the two world wars it necessarily took on a more democratic hue.

TRANSFORMATION OF THE PRISON SYSTEM

As we have seen, at the beginning of the nineteenth century much of the prison estate was in local and private hands. The idea of private ownership of prisons was certainly not strange. Indeed, in the imagination of Jeremy Bentham, as we noted in Chapter 1, it amounted to a programme of private-led reform which would have rivalled that of the Fieldings in policing had it borne fruit. But as with policing, the reform of the prison system during the nineteenth century was firmly under the direction of the state. And like policing, the absorption by the state involved changes in orientation: in policing, the shift to public order and control of space and in prisons, the replacement of pre-trial detention in favour of punishment and rehabilitation as the main purpose of the prison system.

The period of the modern prison system in England began with the construction in 1816 of Millbank Prison under the direct responsibility of the Home Office as the first national prison housing offenders from all over the country. Subsequent development involved the construction and modernisation of more large prisons such as Pentonville in 1842 and the progressive closure – in the interests of imposing a consistent disciplinary regime in all penal institutions – of local authority prisons during the 1870s. Of equal importance was the development of a bureaucracy capable of administering the prison estate as a state responsibility. The Prisons Act of 1835 appointed the prison inspectorate, a surveyor general of prisons was appointed in 1844 and prison directors (governors) were appointed by the Home Office in 1855. The theme of development was the increasing centrality of the state as regulator and controller. This process was completed by the Prison Act of 1877 whereby the prison system became a state-run service under its first commissioner, Edward Du Cane, who oversaw the building of Wormwood Scrubs prison in London.

It might be asked why Bentham's plan for a domestic version of the East India Company to run prisons and workhouses failed to attract support. As we know, the East India Company, in the areas where it operated, functioned as the (colonial) state. In England the state already existed and a large private monopoly would have challenged, or at least obstructed, its authority. In fact it is likely that such a corporation would in any case itself have had to be put together by the state, leading to pointless duplication. Modern outsourcing to private companies of the management of prisons presupposes, as we shall see later, the state as the overall enforcer and maker of policy. During the nineteenth century the state was engaged in equipping itself to perform precisely this role. Investment in a large private corporation to give effect to the imaginings of Jeremy Bentham would have been entirely diversionary. The state was engaged in the reconstruction of a prison system some parts of which were already in local and private hands. It is not surprising that governments did not see the creation of a large private monopoly as a suitable vehicle for delivering change.

One of the aims of state-led centralisation was the achievement of a more consistent application of punishment in accordance with the new reforming ideas of the period. The rule of law – the idea that the law will be applied uniformly throughout the national territory and irrespective of social class – is a core component of the legitimacy of the modern state and essential to the building of a sense of national community of citizens, a sense which was increasingly seen to involve the working class. As the Webbs pointed out in their classic study:

> From the standpoint of criminal jurisprudence it seemed intolerable that persons convicted of similar crimes and sentenced to identical punishments should be in one place subjected to physical privation and torturing labour in another, contaminated by dirt, disease, idleness and licentious intercourse whilst in others they were supplied with plentiful food, profitable employment, comfortable lodging and technical and religious instruction. (Webb and Webb 1922: 110; see also McConville 2015)

The continuation of a system of decentralised private prisons, particularly in the absence of a strong centralised controlling state, would undoubtedly have perpetuated this state of affairs. The elimination of 'physical privation and torturing labour' implied a strong state directorate to supervise rebuilding and modernisation and – in the form of the prisons inspectorate – to monitor the standardisation of conditions. Further, the desire to do so implied the steady advance of the principle of rehabilitation as the focus of penal policy. The centrality of incarceration and the decline of transportation and capital punishment reflected the shift of punishment from the body to the soul of the offender (Foucault 1977) and the gradual development of rehabilitation as a key ingredient of punishment.

Early nineteenth-century notions of rehabilitation were harsh and based largely on religious moralising about repentance – a philosophy that also characterised the early days of the probation system. Gradually the notion of the criminal was unpacked into different categories of offenders such as young offenders and the mentally ill, all in need of different regimes of punishment and rehabilitation. By the middle of the twentieth century these had evolved into what Garland (1985; 2001) characterised as a system of *penal welfare* which linked rehabilitation to preparation for the reassumption of *social citizenship* on release from prison. Social citizenship implied 'regularity, political stability and industrious performance' (Garland 1985: 249) in return for guaranteed welfare rights and a political voice. Incarceration gradually emerged from pure 'civic death' to include preparation for reintegration through a system of education, training, therapy etc. 'One of the great animating impulses behind modern punishment, [is] the desire to convert people into proper citizens rather than excluding them, as with transportation, or making a spectacle of them, as with capital punishment' (Vaughan 2000: 26).

In this way the *legitimacy* of penal policy is linked to the state as the superintendent of citizenship. The legitimation of constraint over the prisoner becomes heavily linked, not just to prior deviance, but to the process of rehabilitation into full citizenship. The legitimacy of constraint takes on a developmental element: the reconstruction of the criminal into the citizen. Obviously the provision of particular rehabilitative services and expertise may often only be found outside the prison – in voluntary and professional organisations and, as we shall see in a moment, in the probation service. These rehabilitative services can be brought into the prison under the direction of the state authorities without interfering with the running of the prison as an embodiment of state authority. As the state consolidated its control over the administration of the prison, the legitimacy of incarceration came to rest with the state both with regard to the determination of the sentence by the court and with regard to its enactment and supervision by the prison authorities. The prison governor and staff were in effect an extension of the court from which they derived their legitimacy. The idea of a separation of the determination of punishment by the court from the allocation, or carrying out, of punishment, and the idea that the latter could be carried out by a private company according to its own decisions made in accordance with the requirements of profit making, belonged to the past, the era of transportation, and to the future. In both cases the separation makes sense only when, once the sentence has been passed, it is not so important how it is carried into effect. In neither case is the prisoner a conditional citizen.

These profound changes in penal orientation were predicated on an equally profound enlargement and increasing competence of the state itself. Colquhoun at the beginning of the nineteenth century was, as we noted, critical of the inefficiency of the English state apparatus, and Bentham's plan for a domestic version of the East India Company reflected similar sentiments. It was this inefficiency and chaotic decentralisation which guaranteed that initial moves to cope with the problems of industrialisation and urbanisation would take a private and commercial form. The Webbs, in their study of English penal administration, pointed to the situation in the early nineteenth century as one of 'almost complete lack of responsibility of the Cabinet for what was being perpetrated in the prisons of the King ... Right down to ... 1822 we find the very scantest attention paid in Whitehall to what was going on in the local gaols and bridewells' (Webb and Webb 1922: 106–7). The Webbs went on to point out that this lack of central state competence entrenched the magistrates as the locus of power in the management and control of criminal justice. Magistrates had remained central in all the innovations we have discussed up to this point in policing, prisons and probation.

The advance of central state control required the centralisation of knowledge about existing prison conditions, and so 'Government inspectors, appointed to monitor and inform on the workings of the local institutions, were an important instrument in gradually undermining the credibility of local authorities to administer their prisons' (Brown 2003: 62–3; see also Forsythe 1991). By the end of the nineteenth century the development of penal policy in the direction of 'scientific' rehabilitation was crucially linked to leadership from the centre and in particular the new career civil servants sympathetic to ideas of 'scientific administration' who became influential in the Home Office and prison administration in the 1890s (Bailey 1997: 292).

This growth of a cadre of professional civil servants at the Home Office was, of course, part of a much wider growth of state competence, far beyond the criminal justice and penal systems and related to the whole project of administering the great metamorphosis of urban social and political life occasioned by industrialisation and imperialist expansion. As Karl Polanyi put it: 'The state was never absent from the process of industrial development and the liberal principles of the free market, the regime of "laisser-faire" itself was enforced by ... an enormous increase in the administrative functions of the state' (1957: 139).

The modernisation of British state administration developed rapidly during the early nineteenth century under the impetus of reformers like Jeremy Bentham and Edwin Chadwick and enabled substantial increases in efficiency at tax-gathering. The most significant reforms of the civil service were those introduced by Sir Charles Trevelyan during the 1840s, which resulted in the modern civil service recruited by entrance examination and a system of promotion based on talent. However, Trevelyan's reforms 'were modelled upon the system first organised by the East India

Company – the private organization to which the government had delegated control over the [Indian] subcontinent – where Trevelyan had spent fourteen years of his career' (van Creveld 1999: 141). An earlier age of private corporate sovereignty thus provided the model for the competence and legitimacy of the modern state. Bentham's image of a domestic East India Company as the vehicle of reform of the penal and workhouse system in fact came about in a perverse form: the modelling of central state reform itself on the original private corporation.

In the criminal justice agencies in particular, an important aspect of the strengthening power of the central state was the role of Home Office inspectorates. The inspectorate principle is quite compatible with a degree of decentralisation – the government does not incorporate the local and regional elements as government departments and part of a bureaucratic chain of command, but sends inspectors to monitor adherence to standards to be maintained and policy to be carried out by still formally independent local and regional bodies. The key mechanism of control is the control of funding. We saw this clearly in the case of the regional police forces, and prisons became more centralised as central government took over their building and management.

But at the end of the nineteenth century and the early years of the twentieth century such developments were a long way into the future. They were certainly not applied in the case of the last sector of the penal system to be absorbed by the state, the probation service. Here was a private, religious charity-based organisation which, although independently run, was seemingly fully committed to the type of humane rehabilitation which inspired penal reform. Why was it not allowed to continue as such, subject to the periodic surveillance of Home Office inspectors?

THE PROBATION SYSTEM AND THE STATE

Taking up the story from Chapter 1, it seems that it was simply the religious association of the London Police Court Missions which explains their absorption by the state after the First World War. The Probation of Offenders Act 1907 formalised the powers of the courts regarding placing offenders on probation, and placed the relationship of the missionaries to the courts on a statutory footing. But this served to increase concern regarding the motivations and orientations of the missionaries themselves, in particular that an important task such as monitoring offenders of probation could not be left to 'religiously motivated amateurs'. The result was that the court missionaries became probation officers recruited and trained by the Home Office. 'By the mid-1930s, the men and women fulfilling this purpose in London courtrooms were formal representatives of the metropolitan legal bureaucracy' (Auerbach 2015: 662–3).

The Home Office had two main conflicts with the independent court missionaries which led inevitably to their demise. First, the Home Office, as part of the orientation to rehabilitation, was sponsoring new ideas of 'scientific' social work based on casework and therapy. This clashed with the religious orientation towards 'saving souls' through repentance on the part of the offender. In his classic discussion of this period in the history of English probation, Bill McWilliams (1983; 1985) argued that the religious motivation of the missionaries made it impossible for them to resist the incursion of 'scientific' social work. This was because, from a religious perspective, the offender (the 'sinner') had to repent of their own free will, and if this failed to happen then the religious perspective was powerless before the new 'scientific' orientation of therapy and casework. The incorporation of the diagnostic skills of this new orientation required a centralised initiative to change the character and qualifications of probation officers.

The second aspect of this was the institutional issue of the dual loyalty of the missionaries on the one hand to the magistrates, whose agents they had become, and on the other hand to their religious societies, who still expected them to 'save souls' and also to engage in extrajudicial activities such as fundraising. This was seen as a conflict which could only be resolved by state control, and by 1936 the Departmental Committee on the Social Services in the Courts of Summary Jurisdiction (Home Office 1936) concluded that it was 'essential for the efficient development of the service that in future it should be organised on a wholly public basis' (quoted by McWilliams 1983: 129).

As professional social work training became a requirement for probation officers, so the involvement of the Home Office committees in defining the parameters of such training increased around the then fashionable deterministic psychological theories (e.g. those of Cyril Burt). Thus,

> by the time the Second World War broke out the Home Office had created a state run, largely state financed, secular and social work trained system of Probation Officers. That social work was based

> on a broad liberal education and influenced strongly by a branch of psychology typified by the work of Burt. Ideas like calling, character, religious zeal and good influences were ousted from the service. In roughly 12 years the whole probation system, its finances, organisation and methods, had been radically reformed by central government. (Gard 2012: 335; see also Gard 2014)

However the probation system never became completely absorbed into the state. Most probation officers, as McWilliams (1985) noted, welcomed the shift to professional training while at the same time retaining a measure of relative autonomy derived from the traditions of the old court missionary organisations (Canton 2011; Mair and Burke 2011; Whitehead 2010). Well into the early twenty-first century, probation was able to retain 'a textured and semi-autonomous cultural history – semi-autonomous because it has developed over 100 years according to its own internal dynamics, professional routines, primary tasks and ethical-cultural configurations, within the material and ideological parameters of the state' (Whitehead and Crawshaw 2013: 10).

This relative autonomy initially enabled a different type of legitimacy for the probation service which was not based solely on the legitimate authority of state coercion but also on the relationship between the probation officer and the offender under supervision, expressed in the motto 'advise, assist and befriend'. It is true that the actions of a probation officer, in reporting a breach of probation conditions, could result in a client being returned to prison. But this was the decision of the court, informed of details by probation officers, rather than a decision of the probation officers themselves. It is therefore an interesting historical irony that by the 1930s the religious orientation of probation practitioners was seen as an obstacle to efficient rehabilitation work while many years later, by the 2010s, the commercial profit-taking orientation of the 'community rehabilitation companies' run by large private security companies was seen as an aid, rather than an obstacle, to rehabilitation. What had changed, as we shall see later, was the entire concept of rehabilitation and the required skills of the probation officer.

THE WELFARE STATE, WAR AND CRIMINAL JUSTICE

These tendencies, both gradual and uneven, towards the absorption of private arrangements by the state reached their highest point during the

Second World War and the decades immediately following. The war, as industrialised total war, involved the mobilisation of all sectors of society around the war effort. Social and economic life was subject to detailed state intervention and planning, but not along the lines of either the Soviet Union or the fascist states. British wartime state planning stood as a democratic contrast to the Nazi totalitarian state. In the latter, nearly all of civil society was incorporated as an aspect of the state, subject to elaborate surveillance, and the private sphere was virtually abolished (Neuman 2009). The British war effort was considered a democratic alternative.

True, there were special government emergency powers enabling a degree of coercive surveillance by police and security services. But the consensus which lay behind these – limited to the duration of hostilities – was achieved in the main by recognising the working class as a political actor with a legitimate set of interests which should be the basis of political compromise. Labour Party ministers acquired key responsibilities in the wartime coalition government and trade unions retained their workplace bargaining rights and also engaged in various wartime activities such as ensuring food supplies. The war effort was a process of democratic exhortation and voluntary coordination backed up by minimalist (compared with the fascist states) wartime emergency powers (Addison 1994; Calder 1992). It is no surprise that Beveridge's famous plan for the postwar welfare state appeared, together with other plans for the extension of the public sector, in 1942 during what turned out to be the middle of the war. This type of mobilisation gave complete priority to the state and the war effort. It was privatisation in reverse. Rather than the war effort being outsourced to private companies, it was the latter that were incorporated and directed by the state as part of the war economy. Private profiteering outside central state planning was heavily regulated and in many cases criminalised.

Meanwhile the military – its numbers augmented by mass conscription – was literally the nation in uniform, and this was the basis of its popular support. In 1940 a large force of British troops, together with French and Belgian forces, were stranded at Dunkirk on the French coast having failed to halt the German advance. Operation Dynamo was launched to evacuate them to England despite heavy aerial bombardment. In addition to naval vessels and commandeered civilian craft, an army of civilian volunteers set sale in small boats from ports in southern England to help in the rescue effort. One can only imagine how few of these civilians would have bothered to risk their lives if the British contingent had been made up of hired mercenaries or, as they are now called, private military companies. Volunteers from non-combatant states (Ireland, the US before 1941), and soldiers and aircrew from states invaded by Germany, fought with the allies. But they did so wearing the uniform of, and under the command of, allied officers, and in no way as mercenaries. Similarly, partisan and resistance fighters within the occupied states were entirely volunteers.

The Labour government, elected by a landslide at the end of the war in 1945, sought to continue the wartime social cohesion as a basis for postwar reconstruction. The result was the welfare state, which guaranteed basic minimums in health care, housing, education and social security benefits. Some of the services, such as health care and state pensions, were available on a universal basis irrespective of income, the aim being that all social classes would have a vested interest in the welfare state and this would enhance social cohesion. The welfare state was combined with proactive state economic intervention inspired by the economist John Maynard Keynes and aimed at maintaining economic growth and full employment. This would both minimise the dependence of the population on some aspects of the welfare system such as unemployment benefit, and at the same time provide the resources to fund it.

The principle of social solidarity and collective provision obviously marginalised the private consumer and profit-making sectors in these areas of provision, although private provision, such as in health care, was not entirely eliminated. The organising principle, at least in theory, in most areas of social and urban planning was that the collective good should take precedence over private interest. Thus the 1947 Town and Country Planning Act governing planning and land development aimed to ensure 'subordination to the public good of the personal wishes and interests of landowners' (Minton 2013: 7). Urban renewal to relocate slum dwellers, and create public space open to all, public libraries, public swimming pools and other public recreational facilities were key themes of the welfare state.

Such a development naturally emphasised the state as a benevolent and democratically accountable provider. The police were therefore symbols not just of the state but of a state that guaranteed these public rights. Policing blended with notions of egalitarian social citizenship associated with the welfare state. The police officer in public space symbolised, at least for a time, the democratic access of all social classes to that space in a world of stable employment and rising working-class incomes (see Lea 2002: 85 *et seq.*). Robert Reiner described the immediate postwar years as the 'high point of police legitimation'. The social survey conducted for the Royal Commission on the Police of 1961–2 found that over 80 per cent of respondents 'professed great respect for the police' and only 1 per cent had 'little or no respect'. Reiner concluded:

> By the 1950s 'policing by consent' was achieved in Britain to the maximal degree it is ever attainable. The police enjoyed the whole-hearted approval of the majority of the population who did not experience the coercive exercise of police powers ... and the de facto acceptance of the legitimacy of the institution by those who did. Police power, that is, the capacity to inflict legal sanctions including force, had been transmuted into authority, power which is accepted as at least minimally legitimate. (Reiner 2010: 70)

Such conditions certainly left little or no opportunity for the incursion of private policing into public space. Meanwhile, in the penal system, the centrality of the prison was confirmed even as reformers talked of 'alternatives to prison' and the necessity of diversion away from incarceration for various categories of less serious and young offenders. As rehabilitation strategies became more sophisticated so the role of non-penal agencies increased in importance. 'In the post war decades criminal justice became the territory of probation officers, social workers, psychologists, psychiatrists, child-guidance experts, educationalists and social reformers of all kinds' (Garland 2001: 36). This meant much outsourcing, not to private prison managers or guards from private security companies, but to experts from other welfare state agencies such as health and education and from the voluntary sector, to work within prisons or with probation officers in new varieties of rehabilitation 'in the community'. While many radicals criticised the new therapeutic rehabilitation as 'soft coercion', the management of the actual prison remained firmly in the hands of the state. It was taken for granted that a penal sentence by the courts should be carried out in an institution in seamless continuity with that juridical structure and run by officials similarly employed by, and accountable to, the state: prison governors and their staff every bit as much as judges and magistrates.

Wartime social solidarity and the postwar economic expansion of the 1960s underpinned these orientations. The recognition of the working class as a legitimate political actor strengthened the idea of a legitimate, non-criminogenic working-class life and community into which the 'conditional citizen' could be reintegrated. It cleared away the last remnants of nineteenth-century notions of the indigence of the working class. The success of rehabilitation and helping offenders to leave criminogenic environments presupposed the ready availability of good jobs, social welfare benefits and social relations which would help the offender leave crime. The success of the probation officer and social worker as anything other than religious moraliser depended on this.

Meanwhile the immediate aftermath of the war included some modification to the relations between sovereign states. The consequences of the Nuremberg Trials of Nazi war leaders (1945–6) were to modify the international order by identifying new international crimes such as crimes against humanity and genocide. But most important, the United Nations Charter (1945) inaugurated new rules of international conduct which outlawed war between states – except in self-defence and with the authority of the UN. The hope that this would lead to peaceful relations and mutual recognition between states was based on the assumption that postwar economic expansion would produce a gradual equalisation of levels of economic development between the West (the US and western Europe) and the rest of the world (Rostow 1962). States would become equal citizens of the international community with mutual respect for one another's sovereignty and favourable to increases in trade and cultural interchange. The innovation of the formerly belligerent states of western Europe in laying the foundations of the European Union could be seen as the embodiment of this trend.

The system of international relations between sovereign states would be, in other words, reinforced. Peaceful relations would be aided by internal developments within the advanced states. Economic expansion, rising wages and the growth of the consumer society would, by fostering a decline in militarism as a component of national culture, reinforce the stability of the international order. The military had indeed functioned as a major instrument of national cohesion during the war, but this role would decline in the face of an expanding 'post-military society' (Shaw 1991). War would be seen as increasingly tangential to the pursuit of national interests through diplomacy, and trade and military forces would become smaller and staffed by professionals rather than mass conscription. Military service would be seen pragmatically as a useful way of acquiring technical skills for civilian life as much as service to monarch and country.

It could be plausibly assumed in the immediate postwar period that these internal and international developments would reinforce each other. Recognition, within states, of the legitimacy of different social classes and their interests as matters for political compromise rather than class war would reinforce the recognition of the legitimacy of other states and the methods of diplomacy and trade rather than armed conflict.

Of course, the period from 1947 was also that of the cold war and the nuclear stand-off between the Western NATO alliance led by the United States and the Warsaw Pact alliance led by the Soviet Union. This balance of terror in which both sides frequently saw themselves a hair's breadth from total nuclear annihilation rather disrupted this peaceful scenario, as did the outbreak of numerous local conflicts in the global south. But, although the cold war lasted right up to 1991 (the year of the dissolution of the Soviet Union), the Western powers did not seek to deny the Soviet Union the status of legitimate sovereign state with interests that had to be recognised, even if cautiously and grudgingly. Kees van der Pijl characterised the period of the welfare state and the cold war as one of *corporate liberalism*,

> in which the West recognised the reality and by implication, legitimacy, of the organisation of blocs against it, just as the capitalist class recognised the existence of organised labour. All negotiation through the era of what I call corporate liberalism (roughly from the 1930s and 40s to the 1980s) was premised on the sovereign equality of the other side. *It was this recognition that was abandoned in neoliberalism.* (van der Pijl 2013)

The consequences of this abandonment will be in effect the background to the following chapters.

CONCLUSION: THE PRIVATE SECTOR UNDER THE RADAR

For a few decades after the war this system of mutual recognition and accommodation between states and between social classes seemed to be working. But it was not long before the contradictions and underlying conflicts began to appear. These will be the starting points of subsequent chapters. However, it should not be thought that the private sector, although marginalised by the dynamics of the welfare state and cold war, couldn't find a foothold for survival and indeed growth. This was true both in the domestic situation and as regards international conflict.

In the domestic context the period of economic expansion which sustained the welfare state also tended to expand the opportunities for the fledgling private security industry. It is important here to underline the distinction between private *security* and private *policing* (see South 1988). Rather than the extension of private policing into public space – and the de facto privatisation of large areas of public space – which characterises the present period, the expanding consumer economy of the 1960s increased areas where property owners took steps to protect their property and which did not normally impinge on the people using public space. The growth in cash transit (wages still being paid predominantly in cash) to banks and companies, and the guarding of warehouses, offices, factories, nightclubs and leisure locations – which expanded during the postwar boom – could all be expected to increase the opportunities for a form of security which used no more than the powers of the property owner to deploy agents (see Sarre 1994) and initially had little to do with public policing. It is during this period that 'employment in security and related occupations outstripped that of public police officers in Britain' (Jones and Newburn 1999: 227). But whether 'security and related occupations' can really be compared with 'public police officers' is questionable. As the authors note, both sectors were expanding at that time.

Similarly, the diminished role of the armed forces in a post-military society (compulsory military service in the UK ended in 1960) and the consolidation of the military into a small, technologically sophisticated professional force would in the long run open up new opportunities for private military subcontractors or new mercenaries, particularly when, as we shall see, the whole character of war and international armed conflict was undergoing profound change. Some of these changes would bring the mercenary out of the shadows and into the mainstream of international armed conflict, as the assumptions of a new age of harmonious interaction between sovereign states proved to be a mirage.

3

The Re-emergence of Private War

In Chapters 1 and 2 we took a broad survey of the decline in the role of private organisations in warfare, in policing and in the penal system. In this and the following chapters we document and attempt to explain why this tendency has, in recent decades, gone into reverse gear, with the role of the private sector expanding across all three areas. In particular we are interested in whether there is some common development which has affected all three areas. In this chapter we deal with the resurgence of the private sector in international armed conflict. The growing contribution by private organisations ranges from shadowy mercenaries of dubious reputation to the more or less legitimate 'private military' or 'private military and security' companies/contractors (PMCs or PMSCs) working for the armed forces of major states. Additionally, civilian contractors engaged in non-combatant support roles such as operating surveillance technology and logistics seem to have acquired significant decision-making power in the conduct of military operations.

As we described at the end of Chapter 2, the institutional innovations following the Second World War – the United Nations Charter of 1946 and the Declaration of Human Rights of 1948 – promised the consolidation of an international society of sovereign nation states each respecting the legitimacy of the others. This built upon the idea that gathered pace during the nineteenth century that armed force was only legitimate between the militaries of sovereign states. Member states had now conceded this entitlement to the UN which reserved the right to intervene, through the resources of its member states, to punish violators of this new global peace. Military force was therefore only legitimate for states acting explicitly as the agents of the UN to punish unauthorised aggression and in short-term self-defence (under Article 51 of the Charter) against such aggression until the UN was able to intervene.

In such a scenario there seemed to be little role for private armed force. The activities of private mercenaries would threaten UN attempts to enforce relations between sovereign states as matters of peaceful negotiation. The cold war nuclear stand-off between the US and Soviet-led alliances of states (1946–89) was of course a threat to this system of peace. Indeed, there were occasions when matters came perilously close to actual nuclear exchange (see Lewis et al. 2014). Nevertheless, the West did not seriously attempt to deny the Soviet Union the status of a legitimate sovereign state with its own interests. Moreover, the attempt by both sides to contain the threat of accidental nuclear war left no room for any weakening of the chain of command by a combat role for private mercenaries. However integrated into the military command structure they are, mercenaries have their own interests and may make their own decisions.

This optimistic scenario gradually unravelled in the face of slowing global economic expansion. By the mid-1970s the postwar economic boom was succeeded by a period of recessions and stagnation culminating in the financial meltdown of 2008, the effects of which are still being felt. In domestic politics, the welfare state and the political compromise between social classes began to be replaced by a neoliberalism that stressed the importance of the free market and the pursuit of self-interest and individualised responsibility. The trade union movement – as a legitimate working-class representation built into the welfare state structures of democratic political compromise – gave way, under the Thatcher governments in the UK and Reagan in the US, to a frontal assault on labour organisation as illegitimate interference with the free market.

The consequences for international armed conflict were twofold. First, slowing economic growth undermined the equalisation of economic and social development between states upon which the assumption of peaceful international relations was based. The international community remained highly differentiated in terms of economic and political power. While the ruling classes of some poorer states – in particular those having substantial oil fields – have been integrated into the global elite, much of the global south has remained in the grip of poverty, state fragility and armed conflict. Second, neoliberalism, in particular for the US, replaced the doctrine of harmonious interstate collaboration with one of self-interest and the aggressive pursuit of the free market as the only feasible global economic system. After the collapse of the Soviet Union in 1991 the US became the most powerful state, the global hegemon, and US governments and their allies felt free to marginalise the UN and attempt to mould the rest of the world in the image of neoliberalism through economic domination and armed force. Both ends of the spectrum –

the armed conflicts in weak global south states and the militarism of the US and its allies – have seen a resurgence of mercenary and private military activity.

MERCENARIES AND 'NEW WARS'

The idea that decolonisation following the Second World War would be a smooth process proved fanciful. The former colonial territories took their place in the new community of sovereign states under the auspices of the UN, but not without violent attempts at repression by the former colonial powers. In British colonial territories, popular movements for liberation during the 1950s were met with direct police and military repression, as in Kenya and Malaysia. French troops fought to retain control of Indo-China (Vietnam) and Algeria. Private mercenaries made their re-entry in this context. The new political atmosphere made the repression of colonial independence unpopular. Former colonial states could deny involvement as mercenary organisations recruited 'newly discharged soldiers from the metropolitan states to crush, sabotage, frustrate or delay the aspirations for self-determination' (Musah and Fayemi 1999: 20). This role of mercenaries in colonial repression came to a head in the mid-1970s in the anti-colonial struggle and civil war in Angola. Beginning in the early 1960s the armed struggle against Portuguese colonial rule, aided by the 1974 revolt in Portugal itself, resulted in Angolan independence in 1975. However, this was followed by a civil war between different Angolan resistance groups, with interventions from Cuba, South Africa and mercenaries recruited in Britain. The mercenary intervention was a disaster. The majority of the mercenaries were captured, tried and received substantial prison sentences. Some were executed (Wrigley 1999).

The Angolan civil war continued until the early 2000s, but this particular chaotic episode led to resolutions and declarations by both the UN and the Organisation of African Unity directed specifically at the use of mercenaries against anti-colonial liberation struggles. In 1995, UN Resolution 1995/5 reiterated that the recruitment, use, financing and training of mercenaries ought to be considered offences by all states. In 1989, the UN General Assembly passed resolution 44/34, the International Convention against the Recruitment, Use, Financing and Training of Mercenaries (which only came into force in 2001 due to the slow accumulation of state signatories), which declared that all states should refrain from using mercenaries.

The use of mercenaries, mainly recruited from former military forces, as part of a last-ditch resistance to anti-colonial liberation movements might have been seen as a painful hiccup in the assimilation of former colonies to the community of sovereign states. However, the episodes illustrated by the Angolan war were just the initial phases of a long-term return of private military force. A small part of this was the continuation of mercenary involvement in coup attempts against governments of independent African states. In 2004 an attempted coup d'état in Equatorial Guinea, a small but oil-rich West African state, involved mercenaries allegedly organised by British financiers. The plotters were arrested in Zimbabwe before they could go into action, but the incident attracted media attention because of the alleged financial involvement of Sir Mark Thatcher, son of the former UK prime minister (Sengupta 2008). Fourteen years later, in January 2018, an alleged mercenary group including operatives from Chad, Cameroon and the Central African Republic attempted another coup which was repelled by government forces (BBC 2018). But mercenaries also started to get involved in the action in support of governments: this was their route to legitimacy.

Impoverishment of much of the global south by the powerful northern capitalist states in no way ended with decolonisation. Rather, the end of colonial rule signalled a shift in the driving force of exploitation to international institutions such as the World Bank, the International Monetary Fund and transnational corporations. This fragility is continually reinforced under conditions of slowing global economic growth, climate change and growing socio-economic marginalisation of the majority of the populations of the global south (Rogers 2017). A result is armed conflict in the form of internal wars associated with the redrawing of ethnic and ideological boundaries and the capture of vital natural and mineral resources. Such wars rapidly weaken notions of state legitimacy both because the seizure of the resources of the state machinery is a major goal of conflict, and because of the increasing involvement of non-state groups such as Islamic State and other jihadi terrorist groups who themselves deny the legitimacy of secular states. Both rebels and the occupants of the existing state structures have little hesitation in availing themselves of outside assistance whether from other states, ideologically motivated volunteers or private mercenaries. The private sector is simply another resource, and one that is often better armed and trained than the contending parties to the conflict.

Thus, rather than the mercenaries retreating into the shadows as the anti-colonial struggles were completed, their activity expanded and became more durable and visible to the world's media. As they became associated with the support of governments rather than their overthrow, mercenaries began to acquire an aura of legitimacy. This is not to suggest that the governments being supported were necessarily progressive. Nevertheless, in this context the terminology of private military company (or contractor) (PMC) and private military and security company (PMSC) came into common usage. The key case of this transition to legitimacy was the Sierra Leone civil war.

The war began in 1990 with an uprising against the government by the Revolutionary United Front (RUF) against which government forces were weak, despite support from other regional states (Ghana, Nigeria and Guinea). Numerous economic and human rights issues characterised the conflict (illegal diamonds, brutality, use of child soldiers by the RUF). A decisive role in the conflict was played by the mercenary/PMC, Executive Outcomes. This organisation had been founded in 1993 by Simon Mann, a former officer in the British Special Air Service (SAS). Mann himself went on to be allegedly involved in the 2004 Equatorial Guinea coup. Executive Outcomes had been regarded as a dubious organisation with strong white South African ex-military mercenary connections. Indeed it was subject to criminal investigation and closure by the South African government in 1998 (Barlow 2008). But sometime around 1996 its resources had been transferred to another company, Sandline, which from 1995 to 1997 was decisive in repelling the RUF from the mineral-rich areas of Sierra Leone and bringing about the eventual cessation of hostilities in 2002.

Sandline started off being seen by the UN as a malign influence in that it was clearly supporting the Sierra Leone government against the rebels in violation of a UN arms embargo aimed at stopping the conflict. Nevertheless, Sandline played a key role in the conflict and at one stage was more or less running the Sierra Leone army. It was supplying briefings for Royal Navy helicopter pilots officially aiding the Sierra Leone government and was eventually acknowledged by the UN as a crucial contributor to the defeat of the RUF and the cessation of hostilities in 2002 (see Kinsey 2006; Petersohn 2014).

This led the UK government to revise its attitude towards the organisation. The company was cleared by UK investigators of wrongdoing and a UK government Green Paper was published arguing for the need for a licensing regime to distinguish reputable from disreputable operators in the fast-changing market for private military force. In the introduction to the document, the UK foreign secretary at the time, Jack Straw, noted that 'Today's world is a far cry from the 1960s when private military activity usually meant mercenaries of the rather unsavoury kind involved in postcolonial or neocolonial conflicts' (Foreign and Commonwealth Office 2002: 5). The UK government was therefore, in response to Sandline's role in the Sierra Leone conflict, moving in a different direction from the 1989 UN Convention against mercenaries. Christopher Kinsey (2006), in a detailed account of the whole episode, remarks that: 'during the time it took [the UK government] ... to investigate the affair, and the publication of a Green Paper in February 2002, there occurred a significant, though subtle, shift in the perceived legality of the activities of PMCs and thus how the government came to understand PMCs as legal entities' (2006: 91). Mercenaries were coming in out of the cold even though critics saw the difference between mercenaries and PMCs as simply a matter of whitewashing by name changing (Murray 2009).

The activity of Sandline in Sierra Leone was a situation in which a private military force is recruited by a weak state government which more or less subcontracts the conduct of a conflict to a better-armed, better-trained and more logistically organised private force. In such situations the balance of power between the state and the private military is decisively in favour of the latter. Sandline had considerable leeway to make its own major decisions as to the conduct and duration of the conflict. The company was said to have its own agenda relating to agreements with various diamond and oil corporations operating in the region and was able to guarantee the protection of its clients' interests (see O'Brien 1999; Joireman 2011; Keen 2012).

More recent examples also illustrate that, notwithstanding the adoption of a more respectable-sounding nomenclature, the older mercenary organisation and ethos continues. The spread of jihadi terrorist groups to sub-Saharan Africa over the last decade has caused mounting problems even for the militaries of relatively powerful states in the region. Nigeria, for example, during 2015 and 2016 was employing South African mercenaries to assist in the struggle against the Boko Haram jihadi group. The mercenaries were able to deploy heavier firepower than the Nigerian military – in particular the use of armoured helicopters. The American former mercenary turned academic Sean McFate commented in an interview that:

> this was a more full-blooded mercenary operation than the sort that we are used to of late. These were real, hardcore mercenaries. This was very different from the ways PMCs were used by the coalition in Iraq, say, where they did convoy protection, defence of buildings or people. This was pure offense, and they did a great job. Well ... an effective job, at least. (Quoted in Bayley 2016)

These 'real, hardcore mercenaries' were allegedly employed by a PMC called Specialised Tasks, Training, Equipment and Protection International (see Pfotenhauer 2016). As McFate implied, organising and engaging in front-line armed combat is, at least formally, distinct from the support and guarding roles in which PMCs have been employed by the US-led forces operating in Afghanistan and Iraq (see below).

The types of situations we have been describing correspond in some respects to the concept of new wars popularised by a number of writers (Kaldor 1999, 2003; Duffield 2001; Muenkler 2005). The concept refers to conflicts resembling civil wars but associated with state breakup, and in particular the frequently genocidal targeting of civilian populations as a primary war aim. Kaldor developed the concept in the early 1990s in response to the conflicts involved in the breakup of Yugoslavia. Nevertheless, the aspect applicable to some of the African examples we have mentioned is where the fighting is conducted by a 'disparate range of different types of groups such as paramilitary units, local warlords, criminal gangs, police forces, mercenary groups and also regular armies including breakaway units of regular armies' (Kaldor 1999: 8; see also Holsti 1996; van Creveld 1991).

This list must of course be updated to include the jihadi groups mentioned above such as Islamic State and Boko Haram. Such groups sometimes recruit globally as well as locally and carry a strong ideological rejection of the whole concept of the secular sovereign state and its territorial boundaries. They thereby further undermine the distinction between state and non-state actors participating in the conflict. In such conflicts the weakness or absence of state law and protection combines with extreme poverty to strip away any notion of citizenship or human rights, to produce what the Italian philosopher Giogio Agamben

(1998) aptly termed 'bare life'. The territorial dimension of this might well be termed 'mere terrain' where – devoid of any trappings of state-like existence; or with a cacophony of different groups claiming state legitimacy – there is no special status for private mercenaries or any other groups as somehow legitimate or illegitimate as state actors. The discourse of legitimacy transfers to the moral and legal dimension of the behaviour of such actors, in terms of war crimes, genocide or other forms of criminality.

THE UN AND PMCS

It is mainly in the context of these conflicts in weak and fragmented states that the UN has been able to make some attempt to stabilise conflict, both indirectly, through arms embargoes aiming to 'starve' the participants of supplies, and by direct intervention through peacekeeping missions, usually following a negotiated ceasefire between the belligerents.

In 2017 there are 14 UN peacekeeping operations in existence, the majority in sub-Saharan Africa and the Middle East (UN 2017). The limited resources at the disposal of the UN, together with the interests of the more powerful states represented on the UN Security Council, has resulted in such humanitarian intervention being inevitably selective (see Binder 2017). The same resource limitations have also provided new opportunities for the private sector. The UN has come to accept the role of PMCs by tolerating them as stabilising elements in some conflicts, as with Sandline in Sierra Leone, but also by directly employing them, albeit, as the UN General Assembly resolved in 2013, as a last resort (see Boutellis 2019).

A key reason for this is partly pressure on UN resources and also the fact that humanitarian interventions usually involve, in addition to armed peacekeeping by UN blue helmet troops and police, contributions by various non-governmental organisations (NGOs) and aid agencies helping to deal with the social consequences of armed conflict: food aid, disease control, care of refugees and displaced persons. From the early 2000s these NGOs, working for UN interventions, have become themselves increasingly security-conscious and engaged in elaborate risk assessments regarding such matters as the location of refugee camps, the route of aid convoys and the security of agency personnel. There has been a tendency to retreat to the safe zones of fortified camps and 'green zones' (van Brabant 2010; Duffield 2012), with private security being hired to guard aid-storage facilities, refugee camps and aid convoys.

In UN peacekeeping anything resembling independent mercenary activities could have disastrous consequences for delicate peace negotiations and the maintenance of ceasefires. It is difficult to imagine private military and security companies having the requisite skillset to deal effectively with complex situations requiring negotiation and restraint. The legitimacy of UN involvement in such fragile situations is dependent on the visible neutrality of UN armed contingents. Private security hired by UN missions is therefore focused on the guarding duties noted above. Of course, in unstable conflict situations the distinction between guarding and armed intervention can become blurred. If an aid convoy or UN infrastructure is attacked then a PMC may find itself involved in armed combat. In the Democratic Republic of the Congo in 2004, private security companies employed in the maintenance of UN airfields played a key role in managing the orderly retreat of UN forces under attack (Østensen 2013: 17).

For these reasons the distinction between mercenaries and legitimate PMCs is of the utmost importance for the legitimacy of peacekeeping operations. The UN rather finds itself facing in two directions: on the one hand rightly condemning the type of mercenary activity seen in Angola or the coup attempts in Equatorial Guinea, while on the other hand employing PMCs itself. The key issue is therefore distinguishing between the two. In 2010 a UN working group concluded that 'PMSCs have remained largely unregulated, insufficiently monitored and rarely held accountable for the international crimes and human rights abuses they have committed' (Shameem 2010). A more recent UN working group report 'showed that States regulate PMSCs in an incoherent and inconsistent manner, resulting in accountability gaps and serious risks to human rights' (UN 2018: para. 21). The group had 'witnessed first-hand how non-State armed actors can destabilize entire countries using violence and committing human rights atrocities, often with impunity ... some PMCs have been involved in human trafficking and child soldiers' (UN 2018: para. 25).

Indeed, according to critical commentators, the UN has not taken sufficient steps to monitor the quality of the PMCs to which it outsources private security work, and 'in the absence of guidelines and clear responsibility for security outsourcing, the UN hired companies well known for their misconduct, violence, and financial irregularities – and hired them repeatedly' (Pingeot 2014: 4). One recent attempt to find a solution to the problem has been for the UN to establish its own 'guard units' – an element of deprivatisation – to take over some of the work formerly outsourced to PMCs (Boutellis 2019). An example of the problems of unreliable PMCs comes from 2011 in Somalia, where a company called Saracen International, which apparently had UN accreditation, was also allegedly training local militia in violation of the UN arms embargo in the region. Accused by the UN of 'representing a threat to peace and security in Somalia', the company undertook to suspend operations (Powell 2012). Saracen is an interesting company in that it was believed both to be a descendant of Executive Outcomes and also linked to the American PMC Blackwater which, as we shall see, achieved notoriety in Iraq. Of course, a focus on the corruption of private contractors should not remove the spotlight from the UN itself. Peacekeeping missions have attracted numerous corruption allegations relating to the behaviour of constituent military forces (Pyman 2013). At the time of the Sierra Leone war, UN officers were alleged to be involved in illegal diamond trading (MacAskill 2000).

Obviously, the UN is anxious to separate dubious mercenaries from reliable and law-abiding PMCs by means of a system of effective vetting. As we have seen, the British government voiced support for a vetting system in its Green Paper of 2002. This call for the regulation of the private military industry exactly parallels the evolution of the domestic private security sector. When the latter emerged from the shadows of guarding building sites, warehouses and nightclubs and entered the market for outsourced government contracts (reaching as far as the criminal justice system itself), a system of regulation separating the 'cowboys' – small security companies employing unskilled operatives, many with criminal records – from the 'respectable citizens' of the larger global private security companies became necessary. We shall return to the issue of regulating PMCs after a brief look at their role in the service of the US and its allies in the occupation of Iraq.

PMCS IN THE SERVICE OF POWERFUL STATE MILITARIES

As noted above, the postwar settlement also collapsed at the level of the most powerful states. In particular, the US and its allies were able to pursue interests through armed force, effectively marginalising the UN. US military action in Korea, Vietnam, Cambodia, Panama and elsewhere, as well as the Soviet invasions of Hungary and Czechoslovakia, all demonstrated the weakness of the UN system from the outset of the postwar period (Jacoby 2007; Parmar 2018). US belligerence has provided opportunities for the return of private military force integrated into US military campaigns. There are a number of reasons for this. Some relate to the general changes in the post-Second World War period already mentioned. Others relate to specific factors arising from the so-called 'war on terror' following the terrorist outrages of 2001 and subsequent developments.

We have already briefly mentioned the way in which the development of post-military society following the Second World War disconnected military action from national culture and political mobilisation (Mann 1987; Shaw 1991). This in itself helped to neutralise resistance to the outsourcing of some military activities to PMCs. The economic slowdown and consequent pressure on profit rates from the 1980s onwards encouraged commercial corporations to cut costs by focusing on their 'core competences' and outsource to other companies those aspects of their work which were necessary but not their central focus. This model was adopted by military planners: 'several armed forces have followed this business model by outsourcing roles not regarded as part of their core competences to PMSCs' (Pattison 2014: 15). This process both reinforces and is made possible by post-military society. On the one hand, the outsourcing to civilian contractors of military activities designated as support services not directly related to combat may further reinforce the isolation of the military from the rest of society, because soldiers 'are less likely to be serving in occupations that have civilian equivalents' (Ricks 1997: 5). On the other hand, the power of the government to declare activities traditionally performed by the military itself as suitable for 'civilianisation' presupposes the weakening of the status of the military as a core national icon.

It is worth pausing to emphasise that the identification of non-core activities is a key basis for outsourcing to the private sector across all the state institutions with which this book is concerned. The police attempt to separate 'front line' – note the military analogy – from 'back office' functions, so that the latter can be outsourced, is an obvious example. Meanwhile the penal system distinguishes the core 'determination' of punishment by the courts from its 'allocation', which can then be handled by the private sector without, it is argued, compromising the state monopoly over legitimate coercive force. However, in all cases, including the military, the separation of core competences from support or ancillary services becomes increasingly problematic.

It is important to see outsourcing as a two-way process. In the case under discussion it is not simply the military deciding to offload non-core tasks, but also a powerful private lobby which pressures for outsourcing. This private lobby – in this case the 'military-industrial complex' – includes not just PMCs but the wider sphere of arms manufacturers and information technology and data analysis companies. This type of outsourcing has been going on since the end of the cold war. In domestic private security, as we shall see, the larger companies, many of whom are involved in both the military and domestic security fields, constitute powerful lobbies. Commentators talk, for example, of the 'prison-industrial complex' or the 'security-industrial complex'.

There is also the unevenness of demand for military services. The period immediately following the end of the cold war and the collapse of the Soviet Union led to a notion of a 'peace dividend'. In the UK, the new peace led to an 18 per cent reduction in military manpower. There were similar measures in the US. In such circumstances the failure of military planners to anticipate the outbreak of new wars in various parts of the globe, let alone the invasions of Afghanistan and Iraq, all of which required increased troop deployment, created a significant pressure for new resources. These could be found by outsourcing to PMCs. The result has been, in the US case, that despite the large number of theatres in which military forces are now deployed, the actual number of US military personnel on active duty overseas is the lowest for decades (Bialik 2017). Similarly, although UK and US military deployments in Afghanistan and Iraq have lasted far longer than the Second World War, they have remained relatively marginal, and indeed politically contested, operations. So resource shortages combined with the dynamics of post-military society made outsourcing legitimate and created openings for the private sector.

A second general change derives from the determination of the powerful states to pursue interests through armed force, irrespective of the requirements of the UN Charter. The end of the cold war and the collapse of the Soviet Union left the US as the global hegemon – the most powerful state without any challengers. Even today, the resurgence of Russia, China and other states to counterbalance US power is still in its early stages. During its period of global hegemony the US arguably attempted to act in some respects as a world government, displacing any such pretensions on the part of the UN. An aspect of this was the effective US denial of the legitimate sovereignty of states which incurred its displeasure. Kees van der Pijl refers to the 1992 US Supreme Court ruling 'that the US government is allowed to abduct people from foreign countries and bring them to trial in the US ... the citizenship of another state ... can be suspended by the United States' (van der Pijl 2006: 402). This process, known as 'rendition', is the mechanism whereby many individuals whom the US government suspected of terrorist activities have been captured in many locations around the world and then incarcerated in Guantánamo Bay detention camp.

This denial of legitimacy often takes the form of characterising those states that incur US displeasure – such as (currently) Russia, China, Iran and Syria – less as sovereign states with their own legitimate interests, than as 'regimes' characterised by reference to their present leadership, implying that this is temporary or abnormal. Thus Syria is currently the 'Assad regime' and Russia the 'Putin regime'. Such characterisations aim at the delegitimisation of the government, rendering it a suitable target for 'regime change' and the replacement of the current leadership by one more amenable to US influence (see for example Lennon and Eiss 2004). Recently the US government labelled a major military arm of the state of Iran – the Republican Guard – as a 'terrorist organisation' (Gambino 2019). Until recently, the characterisation of a major component of the military of another sovereign state as 'terrorist' would have been a quite unthinkable attempt at undermining the legitimate sovereignty of that state. The denial of the legitimacy of other states with whom one has a conflict of interest not only makes war more likely but obliterates completely what Kennedy termed the 'exclusively public nature of sovereign war' (see Chapter 2). This negation of the legitimacy of other states, in combination with increasingly belligerent US defence of its national interests (or what the ruling elite perceives as its national interests) in maintaining global domination – particularly of the oil-rich Middle East – has massively increased the role of PMCs.

AFGHANISTAN, IRAQ AND THE PRIVATE SECTOR

More specific factors in the growth of PMCs derive from the character of major US-led military commitments, in particular the invasions and subsequent occupations of Afghanistan (2001) and Iraq (2003). Both these engagements resulted in an initial US 'victory' quickly followed by a prolonged and chaotic insurgency. For the sake of brevity we shall focus mainly on the US-led invasion of Iraq in 2003 and the subsequent occupation, which lasted until 2011.

The US-led invasion of 2003 was a straightforward invasion of another sovereign state. Initially the US and its allies claimed that Iraq had developed 'weapons of mass destruction' (WMDs) which threatened world security and therefore (it was argued by US President George Bush and UK Prime Minister Tony Blair) that invasion was an act of legitimate self-defence under Article 51 of the UN Charter. In the face of well-founded scepticism concerning the existence of WMDs the justification for invasion switched towards human rights enforcement. The invasion was now seen as 'humanitarian intervention' in response to the brutal treatment of its own citizens by the Iraqi government of Saddam Hussein. This effectively dispensed with the notion of Iraq as a sovereign state. Others have seen the invasion of Iraq as simply 'performative war' to demonstrate the power of the US as global hegemon (Butt 2019).

Following the invasion, the US-led coalition then found itself fighting a new war of its own creation. Traditional international humanitarian law (IHL) governing armed conflict (e.g. Article 43 of Hague Convention of 1907) requires the victorious invading state to 'take all the measures in his power to restore, and ensure, as far as possible, public order and safety, while respecting, unless absolutely prevented, the laws in force in the country' (see Bowers 2003: 20). The UN, giving retrospective legitimacy to the invasion through Security Council Resolution 1483 of 2003, also called on the US and the UK as the 'occupying authorities' to 'promote the welfare of the Iraqi people through the effective administration of the territory' (Bowers 2003: 25).

Any notion of humanitarian intervention to rescue the Iraqis from human rights abuses might have been expected to lead the Coalition Provisional Authority (CPA), set up by the US and UK to administer post-invasion Iraq, to comply with this body of legislation. Whether it did so is debatable. Paul Bremer, the US-appointed head of the CPA, simply abolished by decree most of the major institutions of the Iraqi state including the military, local law enforcement and major government ministries. Meanwhile, members of the CPA organised the privatisation of Iraqi oil fields with major concessions to the large US and UK oil companies. The US, as Kaldor put it, 'behaved as though they had won World War II ... And the impact of fighting a reconstructed "Old War" was not victory over an enemy state but state disintegration and "New

War'" (Kaldor 2005: 495). This might be characterised as a demolition of the last remnants of Iraqi citizenship. Iraqis were not going to be treated as conditional citizens deserving of rehabilitation, but reduced to bare life existing on mere terrain, to be placed at the disposal of the major oil companies. This was in effect the restoration of a colonial relationship.

In any case the result was a breakdown in law and order involving widespread looting and arson and the growth of armed sectarian violence. A failure effectively to fulfil the traditional duties of the occupying power created the conditions for both the growth of armed sectarian militias engaged in new war and the widespread deployment of PMCs. A distinction between legitimate and illegitimate force meant little as Iraq fractured into sectarian identities and militias on the one hand and coalition military forces with their associated PMCs on the other. In such circumstances any type of force was free to function if it provided security for those who sponsored it or could afford to pay for it (see Paul and Nahory 2007). The growth of the private military sector was rapid.

In his comment cited above, the former mercenary Sean McFate contrasted the role of mercenaries in Nigeria with the role of PMCs in Iraq and Afghanistan, where they were relegated mainly to a support role. This is to be expected. The well-organised militaries of the US and its allies didn't need PMCs to take over major combat roles (as with the Sierra Leone and Nigerian examples). The expansion of PMCs in Iraq was initially in a support role. General statistics on the growth of PMCs are relatively easy to come by as far as the US is concerned. During the Second World War private contractors constituted around 10 per cent of the US military 'workforce' and were not deployed in any combat roles. In the first Gulf War (1990–1) following the Iraqi invasion of Kuwait the ratio of private contractors to military personnel was roughly 1:100. In the second Gulf War (from 2003 onwards, following the invasion of Iraq by the US-led coalition) the ratio was 1:1. By 2010, in all war zones in which the US military was involved, the number of private contractors came to considerably exceed the (US) military (207,000 contractors to 175,000 military (figures from McFate 2014 and Pattison 2014). By April 2017 there were estimated to be 26,000 private military contractors in Afghanistan compared with 9,800 US troops (Peters et al. 2017).

Figures for the employment of private military forces by the UK are, however, not readily available (House of Commons Foreign Affairs Committee 2002). Some commentators (e.g. Cusumano 2014) suggest that a lower UK use of PMCs derives from the greater historical experience of the British military in dealing with popular insurgencies during the colonial period. The US, by contrast, has a greater focus on conventional war fighting, and so when encountering insurgencies and new wars – as in Iraq and Afghanistan – is more likely to turn to the private sector to assist in operations where policing civilian populations, guarding and security are major components. Be that as it may, UK-based companies were among the leading suppliers of private military services in both Iraq and Afghanistan. According to a report by the NGO War on Want: 'the leading British PMCs are sprawling corporate entities, with complex structures and a global footprint. Companies like G4S (which acquired ArmorGroup in 2008), Aegis Defence Services (now part of Garda-World), Control Risks and Olive Group make hundreds of millions of pounds in profit' (War on Want 2016: 2).

At the height of the occupation of Iraq (which lasted from the invasion up until 2010), around 60 British companies operated in the territory (the total was around 180). Large US corporations such as DynCorp, and in particular Blackwater (by 2018 trading under the innocuous name of Constellis Holdings), are well known. But there was a much larger number of smaller companies, including many UK-based enterprises providing particular services. The interconnections between them were reinforced by mutual subcontracting. David Isenberg (2009), surveying the situation during the US and UK occupation of Iraq during the mid-2000s, identified key UK-based PMCs such as Aegis Defence Services, which in 2004, competing against Blackwater and DynCorp, won a $293 million three-year contract to provide anti-terrorism support and analysis, and to serve as a clearing house for information sharing between coalition forces and private security contractors. Other significant UK companies operating in Iraq at that time have included Control Risks Group, Kroll Security Group, Edinburgh Risk Security Management and ArmorGroup. In 2008 the final company on this list became part of G4S – a name with which, by the end of this book, the reader will have acquired a certain familiarity.

But in the chaos of post-invasion Iraq, the distinction between military combat and support services rapidly became blurred. The outsourcing model establishes, at first sight, a clear distinction between the military core competences of armed engagement with the enemy and the various support services, which include, guarding, training, transportation, logistics, intelligence analysis and technical support (see Singer 2007; Avant 2005; McFate 2015). The Red Cross-inspired Montreux

Document, one of a number of attempts to regulate the private military industry (discussed below), defines legitimate PMCs, as opposed to mercenaries, as:

> private business entities that provide military and/or security services, irrespective of how they define themselves. Military and security services include, in particular, armed guarding and protection of persons and objects, such as convoys, buildings and other places; maintenance and operations of weapons systems; prisoner detention; and advice to or training of local forces and security personnel. (ICRC 2015: 9)

The problem is that the distinction between core competences and support activities has blurred in the context of new wars and new technologies of war, with the result that PMCs in Afghanistan and Iraq moved rapidly towards quite central combat roles. Dunigan (2014), among numerous commentators, pointed out that the distinction between front-line combat and support services was becoming progressively blurred. She noted that many PMCs, for example the well-known US company Blackwater, started out as military training providers but, in the type of conflict prevalent in Afghanistan and Iraq, rapidly became active combat units. According to some estimates, between 10 and 15 per cent of private contractors working for the US military in Iraq and Afghanistan were involved in actual combat (Akulov 2016). In the battle spaces characteristic of new wars and insurgencies the distinction between rear areas and front lines easily blurs. Fighting may break out anywhere. Additionally, most of the enemy forces in such situations are by definition non-state actors – Islamic State, the Taliban, local militias, etc. – using improvised weapons such as car bombs, suicide bombs and improvised explosive devices (IEDs) as well as small arms. Such forces focus on ethnic defence as much as fighting the invader, and therefore – as the use of car and suicide bombs in crowded markets illustrates – blur the distinction between civilians and combatants. Finally, such forces frequently eschew recognisable uniforms or insignia and use the non-combatant civilian population as a shield. This means that a squad of regular military seeking out an armed militia to engage in combat, and PMC employees guarding a supply convoy, may face identical situations regarding the difficulties of anticipating danger.

CRIMINALITY AND THE PROBLEM OF REGULATION

Such unpredictability is highly criminogenic. Occupied Iraq under the US-led coalition was the site of an enormous amount of criminality. This involved contract fraud committed by suppliers (see Teather 2004) as well as violations of IHL and human rights both by coalition militaries themselves and their PMC contractors. The occupation produced at least two notorious cases of human rights violation involving private security personnel: Nisour Square and Abu Ghraib.

The PMC Blackwater (now renamed), which held a US government contract to provide VIP security and close protection in Iraq, is notorious for the infamous Nisour Square massacre in 2007. This was an incident in which company operatives opened fire and killed 17 Iraqi civilians and wounded many more. It was only with great difficulty that three former Blackwater employees were finally prosecuted in the US courts – the company being subject neither to US military law nor Iraqi criminal jurisdiction. The three received 30-year prison sentences in 2015. But in August 2017, the Washington DC Federal Appeals Court overturned the conviction of one of the employees and ordered a new trial (Neuman 2017). There are two views of Blackwater's violence. One is that it was a rogue company whose employees took a delight in gratuitous violence and the shooting of civilians. David Isenberg reported an event two years before the Nisour Square massacre: 'In March 2005 Blackwater created outrage after a memo to staff was made public stating that "actually it is 'fun' to shoot some people." Bearing the name of Blackwater's president, Gary Jackson, the electronic newsletter adds that terrorists "need to get creamed, and it's fun, meaning satisfying, to do the shooting of such folk"' (Isenberg 2009: 138).

The other view is that Blackwater, as Fitzsimmons (2015) noted, had a reputation as an efficient commercial company. In a review of Fitzsimmons, Newsinger drew the implication that 'a case can be made that its readiness to shoot at Iraqis on suspicion was in fact a commercial decision that was put into effect by means of an aggressive military culture' (Newsinger 2016: 98). This raises a fundamental issue about the private sector which we shall also encounter in domestic police and penal systems. Private companies are profit-takers. It is in their interest to work closely to fulfil their contracts, especially when the latter involve some form of payment by results. In the case of Blackwater the contract involved the protection of VIPs, and fulfilment of the contract involved transporting VIPs safely between two points. Wildly shooting at any civilian who appeared to get in the way was one way of fulfilling the contract. Where Iraqi civilians were not regarded as citizens with any status or rights then the moral pressure against shooting anyone who came near the convoy was arguably weakened.

But regular military patrols faced very similar situations and developed similar attitudes towards the civilian population. Some caution is therefore necessary in making too firm a distinction between the behaviour of soldiers and that of PMC employees. A contrast between professional soldiers – who are aware, even in the most dangerous situations, that they are involved in winning hearts and minds – and PMC employees fulfilling contracts by the shortest route can be exaggerated. This is particularly so where the civilian population is not taken seriously as conditional citizens in need of help and rehabilitation but rather as potential insurgents. A more plausible interpretation is that the military leads the way and lays down the parameters of acceptable behaviour in similar situations for the private sector. And as we have said, in new wars the situations for regular military and PMCs are often indeed very similar. An account by a US soldier who served in Iraq arguably reveals the behaviour of Blackwater employees in Nisour Square as not too far from standard operating procedure for at least some regular military: 'we had a pretty gung-ho commander, who decided that because we were getting hit by IEDs a lot, there would be a new battalion SOP [standard operating procedure]. He goes, "If someone in your line gets hit with an IED, 360 rotational fire. You kill every motherfucker on the street"' (Lopez 2010). There is of course a difference. If the above account is reliable, the regular soldiers had to wait for an IED attack before unleashing a massacre on civilians, whereas for the Blackwater employees it was just a question of clearing the route to get the job done.

Alongside Nisour Square, the other indelible stain on US behaviour in Iraq is the case of Abu Ghraib prison from where graphic photographs of the torture and humiliation of Iraqi detainees by US personnel went viral on global media in April 2004. This occurred in the context of a US doctrine of the time that IHL, in particular the Geneva conventions regarding treatment of prisoners, did not apply in the case of Iraq. This massive violation of human rights is of course nothing to do with an overreaction to the unpredictable risk of attack. It rather resulted from a high-level policy decision by the US following the 2001 terrorist atrocities in New York that in the hastily declared war on terror, US forces and agencies such as the CIA were authorised 'to use all necessary and appropriate force' against terrorist suspects. This amounted, in effect, to the legalisation of torture. Although subsequently overturned, the doctrine is further evidence that the US was not inclined towards the view that it was at war with another state, which would necessitate that captured Iraqi soldiers and detained civilians had to be treated in accordance with IHL. Rather, the US saw itself as engaged in a generalised war on terror ungoverned by any prior existing rules, and that somehow Iraqi detainees were terrorist suspects (see Cohen 2012).

Some of the torture was carried out by private contractors working for the CIA. In 2013 a total of 71 former detainees of Abu Ghraib and other US detention facilities were awarded $5.8 million against the contractor concerned, L-3 services Inc., which provided linguists and interrogators to the US military in Iraq (Cockburn 2013). What became clear was that the private contractors were under pressure to recruit personnel rapidly for deployment in Iraq and failed to apply adequate background checks in many cases (Isenberg 2009). But the behaviour of private contractors was no different to the behaviour of the military interrogators. Several of the latter subsequently convicted by court martial were US National Guard reservists with civilian jobs in the US as prison guards in both public and private sector prisons. At least one individual had similar convictions for abuse of inmates (see Gordon 2006a; 2006b).

This episode further underlines the dangers of too firm a contrast between the behaviour of the state and that of the private sector to which it outsources. It is all too easy to fall into the trap of seeing the private sector – driven by cost-cutting and profit-taking – as responsible for failure and a decline in standards, while the state remains committed to high standards in those services for which it has retained responsibility. Our position is different. In the military and in other areas of outsourcing, it is the prior change in state behaviour, and in particular the lowering of standards, which make possible the entry of the lower-cost private sector in the first place. The empirical consequence is that we should not always expect to encounter different behaviour by state and private sector institutions. In the case of Iraq, the US had abandoned the notion of that country as a legitimate state and Iraqis as citizens entitled to IHL protection. The US had thereby weakened the sanction against war crimes by state military and at the same time cleared the ground for the employment of lower-cost, lower-standard employees by private contractors and PMCs.

That is not to say that private companies do not have an added incentive to fulfil their contract in the cheapest way possible and are more prone to cut corners or engage in criminal negligence than the state. The private sector can be expected to take advantage of situations where it is possible to deploy a lower-quality and lower-paid workforce. In situations involving sustained combat, PMCs prefer to employ trained ex-soldiers, usually from special forces such as the UK SAS or the US Green Berets. But for some security purposes – guarding embassies for example – cheaper, less well-trained personnel can be deployed. This has its predictable consequences. In 2009 ArmorGroup (now part of G4S) sustained reputational damage arising from its $187 million contract to guard the US Embassy in Kabul (Afghanistan): 'The Kabul embassy scandal broke ... when a watchdog group accused ArmorGroup of jeopardizing security at the embassy by understaffing the facility and ignoring lewd, drunken conduct and sexual hazing by some guards – and provided graphic photos as evidence' (Quinn 2009; see also Leander 2012).

The end of the (official) coalition occupation of Iraq after 2011 meant a reduction in funds and subcontracting. For the private sector this placed an emphasis on cost reduction, and in particular finding sources of lower-paid employees. According to a documentary aired by Al Jazeera in May 2017, one British PMC was bringing former employees of mercenary organisations in Sierra Leone to work in Iraq. Some of these, though the number is unknown, were former child soldiers (Ellesoe 2017). A reduction in the quality of the labour force made sense in terms of the changing role of the private sector. Armed combat subsided and 'the biggest market for British PMSCs in Iraq ... [became] ... the provision of security for private corporations seeking to invest in the country' (War on Want 2016: 4). For many private providers there was a move towards the type of role that private security companies play in the stable societies of the global north, albeit with a more precarious edge and with armed force never far away. More typical now is G4S handling security at Baghdad International Airport, as well as 'providing protective security, stabilisation and post-conflict reconstruction services to government and commercial organisations' (G4S Iraq 2019). There is no suggestion that G4S was ever involved in the child soldier issue. One important service that private security companies provide to commercial organisations in such environments as Iraq is of course intelligence and threat assessment. Much of this work is outsourced to specialist private intelligence companies.

All this needs effective regulation. The fact that, during the occupation of Iraq, Blackwater and similar PMCs appeared liable neither to US military law nor to Iraqi domestic criminal law was a scandal. But even in the case of UN outsourcing to PMCs, regulation has left much to be desired in the way it sifts out the cowboys from providers with a high sense of corporate responsibility. To date the main attempt to regulate the PMCs has been at the level of voluntary self-regulation by the industry itself. This is common practice in domestic private security. Across the spectrum of private coercion – from private military to private prisons and security – self-regulation is the neoliberal panacea.

On the face of it such an orientation has a certain logic. Particularly for PMCs operating in combat zones where state regulation is non-existent – in the middle of new wars – a respect for human rights must be built into the structures of the company itself to have any chance of working. The other side of the neoliberal panacea is of course to free the competitive spirit by doing away with red tape. Too much regulation and a requirement by outsourcers that successful tenders demonstrate adherence to human rights may raise costs and reduce the number of companies capable of tendering.

Attempts at regulation in the PMC area began, as we have already noted, with the 2008 Montreux Document sponsored by the International Committee of the Red Cross. By the end of 2014, it was supported by 51 states and several international organisations including NATO, the European Union and the Office for Security and Cooperation in Europe. The problem was the reliance on states and international organisations insisting on human rights adherence at the time of tendering, rather than imposing duties on the companies themselves. This was partially remedied in 2010 by the International Code of Conduct for Private Security Service Providers (ICoC), again sponsored by the Red Cross. Critics see this as a purely voluntary code which 'does not create any new legal responsibilities for corporations and is not binding on the states that recognise it' (Whyte 2015: 50). Rather, it involves the signatories giving various affirmations to respect human rights. Indeed, according to some commentators the industry has sought to 'block attempts at more binding arrangements' (Pingeot 2014: 18). The further formation in 2013 of an industry association based on the ICoC had attracted 140 companies by 2015 (see Ralby 2015). Membership of the ICoC involves companies agreeing to abide by the principles of international human rights law (IHRL) which, deriving from the UN declaration of 1948, is more restrictive than the military orientation of IHL. This is no doubt appropriate where large numbers of civilians are constantly present in conflict zones (but see the discussion of drone warfare below). The UN issued a set of Guiding Principles on Business and Human Rights in 2011. There are also domestic industry associations, such as the Security Industry Association (SIA) in the UK, which attempt to enforce similar ethical standards on UK-based security companies irrespective of where they operate. Finally, there have been various attempts to develop more technical and detailed sets of standards derived from the ICoC to be incorporated into the operating procedures of companies.

This is a rather patchwork set of initiatives. One obvious problem of course is the existence of mercenary organisations operating in chaotic conflict zones far beyond the reach of either IHRL or IHL. But second, the nature of warfare since Iraq and Blackwater is changing rapidly, and much of the change concerns remote warfare by armed drones. New questions arise, such as 'does a contractor, employed by a state, operating a drone or weapons system, for example, have responsibility for killing civilians? These are just some of many complex and unanswered questions not addressed by regulatory initiatives to date' (Ralby 2015: 18).

WAR WITHOUT END: THE MERGING OF STATE AND PRIVATE SECTOR

Following the atrocities of 2001 (9/11), the war on terror launched by the Bush administration in the US had two components. One was the invasion and occupation of Afghanistan and Iraq. The other was the CIA-led clandestine programme of rendition bringing terrorist suspects from different countries, not by the normal legal process of extradition, but by clandestine kidnapping, to incarceration in Guantánamo Bay detention camp. With the end of the (official) occupations, US policy entered a new phase. Kidnapping and rendition have been replaced by a drone war aiming to eliminate terrorist operatives (members of Islamic State, Al Qaeda and kindred groups) in situ. Meanwhile, military action on the ground has largely abandoned full-scale invasions in favour of activity involving mobile special forces operating in a number of locations, particularly in the Middle East and sub-Saharan Africa, aimed mainly at blocking the spread of Islamic jihadism. As Paul Rogers has pointed out, this jihadism is simply one manifestation of a 'revolt from the margins' based on poverty, climate change and socio-economic marginalisation (Rogers 2017). Both elements of policy have in common the discarding of respect for the legitimacy of other states. Drone strikes take place in countries with which the US is neither at war, nor has the permission of the sovereign state authorities (e.g. Pakistan, Syria, Somalia, Yemen). Clandestine military activity in Syria is in violation of the sovereignty of that state. In both cases this ignoring of state sovereignty then facilitates a growing involvement of the private sector.

Drone killings involve a number of issues concerning both IHRL and IHL. In the case of IHL there is frequently insufficient effort put into identifying the targets as actual combatants as opposed to simply civilians or fighters wishing to surrender or rendered *hors de combat* (Lee 2015; Boyle 2015). Target selection on the basis of video and satellite surveillance is subject to error. A farmer carrying a spade might be taken for a terrorist with a weapon, a wedding party for an armed insurgent group. Second, the US seems to have abandoned the strategy of attempting to ascertain the actual personal identity of the target in favour of a risk-based approach using '"signature strikes" approved even if the personal identity of the target is unknown. These are authorised on the basis of evidence such as "pattern of life" and documented suspicious or hostile behaviour of potential targets' (Barela 2015: 262).

The number of drone strikes accelerated markedly after the US withdrew from Iraq in 2011 and ended combat in Afghanistan formally in 2014. From then on the emphasis shifted to the drone war against Islamic State in Iraq and Syria. The number of strikes accelerated so rapidly that the US Air Force, which led the drone programme, ran out of pilots and began to call on the private sector to make up the deficit (Porter 2018). Apart from actually piloting drones the private sector has become embedded in drone warfare in two ways. First, the selection of targets, unlike situations where there are troops and intelligence officers on the ground in the conflict zone, relies heavily on an army of intelligence officers analysing intelligence reports, satellite and video from surveillance drones. The US has massively outsourced this to an expanding 'intelligence-military-corporate apparatus' (Priest and Arkin 2012: 25) of specialist companies – such as Booz Allen Hamilton, the company for which Edward Snowden worked at the time of his revelations in 2012.

These private contractors then become incorporated into the 'kill chain' in which the gathering and interpretation of intelligence and the actual selection of targets becomes blurred (Porter 2018). Although the armed drone launches its missile on the command of a military officer, there is a continuous risk that intelligence gathering by private contractors can step over the boundary into target acquisition and the decision to kill (Fielding-Smith et al. 2015). Drone warfare thus blurs the boundary between the private sector and the military in a new way. In Iraq the generalisation of armed conflict over the whole occupied terrain put PMCs and the military in essentially the same combat conditions. In drone warfare, combat capabilities become increasingly dependent upon and integrated with support roles. The mass of data and interpretation required for target selection and the decision to fire puts the private contractors and the military pilots on the same blurred continuum.

Meanwhile, evidence of the clandestine war on the ground in the Middle East and further south has begun to build up. What was important about this type of military action was that it was largely hidden both from public gaze and political control. This was not only the classic advantage of deploying PMCs and mercenaries but also of the form increasingly taken by military action – the deployment of special forces organised in small groups and engaged in highly mobile warfare. By the time the media arrives, the conflict has moved on. Thus in 2013, the UK Parliament prohibited the government from participating in US-led illegal military action in Syria against the Assad regime. But in 2016 UK special forces were pictured on the ground in Syria (Sommerville 2016), and there have also been reports of private military activity in the region (Chase and Pezzullo 2016). The present war in Syria is subject to a double process of delegitimation. First, the US and its allies see the government of that country as an illegitimate regime towards whom a policy of regime change has been the preferred option until very recently (late 2018). Second, the major military conflict has been with a non-state force, Islamic State, which itself operates in both Iraq and Syria. Islamic State, in attempting to build its own version of an Islamic caliphate, negates the secular legitimacy of both Iraq and Syria.

In October 2017, a group of US special forces working with the local military were ambushed, with several fatalities, in the West African state of Niger while in action against Islamic State. The survivors were rescued by a combination of French air force jet fighters and helicopters, and other US forces. Casualty evacuation from the combat zone was handled by a private contractor, Berry Aviation, which was apparently on call as the ground operation progressed. Another survivor from the ambush was allegedly a private intelligence contractor (Trevithick 2017). The US intervention was with the collaboration of the Niger military in the battle against local Islamic State offshoots, and to that extent respected the legitimacy of Niger as a state. But from the point of view of Niger the situation is very similar to that in which Nigeria employed mercenaries against Boko Haram (discussed above). Questions of the legitimacy of private force or, in the Niger case, a mixture of US and PMC forces, are easily backgrounded where the very survival of the state itself is the main issue.

These examples illustrate two developments. First, until media reports of the ambush, the American public had no idea its troops were on active service in Niger, and certainly Berry Aviation was nowhere on the public radar. Secondly, this small battle group contained a highly integrated mix of military and private sector operatives. This reveals what may be a new, closer integration of special forces and PMCs and the face of the current phase of the ground war against Islamic State, at least as far as US forces are concerned. Some confirmation of this future might be seen in recent US plans for military organisation which give a much greater prominence to special forces. US special forces in recent years, particularly since the Iraq occupation, have expanded massively, to a considerable extent at the expense of conventional forces (Kalman et al. 2019). The US is of course not the only powerful state now on the ground in sub-Saharan Africa. The Russian PMC known as the Wagner Group is also reported to have substantial forces in the Central African Republic in a training role with UN permission. Whether Wagner is a PMC on the US and European model or more integrated into the official state military is, however, debatable (see Grossman 2019).

CONCLUSION

In this chapter we have very briefly plotted the main features of the return of the private sector, whether as mercenary or PMC – assuming these are not just different terms for the same entities – to modern armed combat. Our object has not been to provide a detailed overview of the military policies of the US or the UK, or a detailed documentation of the private military sector itself, but simply to illustrate that the main tendency of the period before the two world wars and the establishment of the welfare state has been decisively reversed. In the following chapters we shall plot similar developments in other areas which involve the state in its coercive activities: policing and the penal system. Our aim is to draw some parallels.

What we have stressed in this chapter and will stress further in subsequent chapters is the central role of the legitimacy of the state. As we saw in Chapter 2, it was the consolidation of the view that the sovereign state was the unique agent of legitimate international force – warfare – just as it was the unique agent of legitimate domestic coercion. It was this that delegitimised private force, both between states and within the territory of the state. But we also stressed that this legitimacy is not some inherent quality. The state as the unique sovereign power emerged historically as a result of sustained conflict over centuries, as Tilly (1985) demonstrated. There is absolutely no reason why it should not fracture in the future. In plotting the growth of the private sector, we may be witnessing the beginnings of this fracture. We have tried to show that what has created a space for the return of the private sector in international armed force is the increasingly contested nature of the legitimacy of the sovereign state. We argued that this had occurred in the weakest states of the global south and also as an arm of the foreign policies of the US and its allies as the powerful states of the global north. Where the legitimacy of another state is disregarded then the legitimacy of the type of force used against it – private or public – is simply a matter of pragmatic choice.

We made another observation that will become important in the following chapters. Granted that the decision to use private or public force, or a mixture of the two, becomes a pragmatic decision only when the legitimacy of the opponent as a sovereign state has been disregarded, the decision to deploy the private sector is not simply a matter of financial resources. In new wars in weak states, we briefly noted, the use of private force in the form of foreign mercenaries was in some cases part of a deliberate attempt by outside forces to arrest the process of colonial independence. In other cases it was a matter of the survival of the ruling elite. In other words, it was a matter of political choice. In the deployment of PMCs by the US and its allies, private force became legitimate, not simply as a cheaper alternative to the state, but because the type of war the state itself was fighting made possible the use of private force. We shall see this latter argument repeated in subsequent chapters. The deployment of private policing, prisons or probation is made possible by virtue of the fact that the state itself has changed the way it polices or treats its convicted prisoners, and thereby makes outsourcing to the private sector both legitimate and feasible. Only at that point does a debate about the private sector being the cheaper option make sense.

4
Private Security and Policing

The resurgence of private military force in international armed conflict since the end of the cold war has been paralleled by a reappearance of private security within nation states. In the UK, by 2015 there were 232,000 private security guards. This was considerably greater than the number of police officers which (in 2016) stood at 151,000 after a period of substantial decline. On an international scale, in 2017 an international survey revealed that in 44 out of 81 countries private security employees outnumbered police (Provost 2017; see also Button and Stiernstedt 2018).

This 'rebirth of private policing' (Johnston 1992) within the national state is part of the same process which underlay the resurgence of private military discussed in Chapter 3. The failure of post-Second World War economic growth to sustain the conditions for a peaceful community of sovereign states was also a failure to sustain the conditions for the welfare state and its project of social cohesion within the UK. As we have seen, internationally the fragmentation of the post-Second World War world enabled the most powerful states to ignore the sovereign legitimacy of other states, while many weak states remained embroiled in internal conflicts. In both cases the private sector could re-emerge without raising any insuperable problems over the relative legitimacy of state and non-state actors in armed conflict.

In the same way the ending of the period of economic expansion in the UK and many other industrial countries led the ruling elite to adopt neoliberal policies aimed at the demolition of the Keynesian welfare state and the associated power of the organised working class (Roberts 2016). The result was a decline in manufacturing industry and strong working-class communities based around well-paid, secure industrial jobs and, at the same time, the rise of a new wealthy elite concentrated in the global financial sector. Social and economic inequality increased dramatically (Dorling 2018; Piketty 2014), and this created new opportunities for the development of the private security industry. The most powerful sections of the elite were able to make their own private security arrangements, both for their housing and for the areas of urban commercial space that they increasingly dominated. At the other end of the social structure the fastest growing sections of the working class became the low-wage, insecure 'precariat' (Standing 2011) alternating between employment at below-poverty wages in the 'gig economy', bouts of unemployment and various forms of petty crime. Meanwhile the middle classes, formerly secure in lower managerial and white-collar employment, felt increasingly politically and economically anxious and 'squeezed' (OECD 2019). These developments mark the end of *corporate liberalism* (van der Pijl 2013), in which the ruling elite had accepted the working and middle classes as legitimate political actors just as it had accepted other states as legitimate sovereign entities.

THE SECURITISATION OF PUBLIC SPACE

These developments have strong implications for the organisation of urban space and policing. As far as the elite is concerned, the poorest sections of society appear less as 'fellow citizens' and joint participants in a multi-class public space and increasingly as a risky 'dangerous class'. In this respect there is something of a return to the urban class relations of the eighteenth and early nineteenth centuries (Lea 2015). The aim of much social policy has shifted away from guaranteeing the inclusion and participation of working-class citizens in public space and towards the management of the risks presented to the middle classes and the elite by the very proximity of the precariat. Coercive power, rather than something that has to be made to appear as *legitimate* authority to all citizens as part of social and political cohesion, has become simply part of the tool box of techniques for managing the disenfranchised and marginalised poor. Such a tool box can be outsourced to the most efficient provider, which might well be a private security company. Problems of legitimate authority have evaporated, along with the status of the precariat as full citizens in a post-welfare state society.

In the UK, citizens are increasingly likely to encounter private security guards not just when entering mass private property such as leisure parks or shopping centres, but also in public space in town centres. They will find private security employees equipped with certain 'police' powers such as the right to demand that a person provide their name and address and to issue them with a fixed penalty notice for the infringement of various regulations – enacted by the local authority – regarding consumption of alcohol in public, walking a dog in a dog-exclusion zone, rough sleeping or other varieties of antisocial behaviour.

The police were initially firmly opposed to such developments. In 2012, the year in which transnational private security giant G4S spectacularly bungled its contract to provide security staff for the London Olympic Games, Lynne Owens, then chief constable of Surrey, said that 'any suggestion that a private sector company will patrol the streets of Surrey is simply nonsense' (Peachey and Lakhani 2012). In the same year Peter Fahey, chief constable of Greater Manchester, reacted to a proposal by city centre retailers to employ Securitas – another large security transnational – to patrol public space adjacent to shops: 'We do not think that the public would be happy with private company employees patrolling the streets wearing body armour and camera equipment' (quoted in Scheerhout 2012). These remarks had been preceded a few years earlier, in 2008, by a forthright statement from Simon Reed, then chair of the Police Federation of England and Wales, representing rank-and-file police officers, that: 'the Federation has concern about the presence of an ill-equipped and poorly trained second layer of law enforcement ... [which] ... undermines the special covenant between the police and the public who rightly expect policing functions to be performed by fully trained, independent and accountable officers of the Crown' (Police Federation 2008).

These sentiments can easily be dismissed as simply a reaction to a jealously guarded monopoly being threatened. The 'special covenant' referred to by Reed might be dismissed as opportunist nostalgia. But even so, it clearly refers back to the notions of policing, discussed earlier, in which the mass of citizens accepted the legitimate authority of the police as the 'state on the street', while the majority of police officers understood the need to reproduce that legitimacy through their behaviour. On the other hand, the reference to 'ill-equipped and poorly trained' private security is perhaps a failure to recognise that the task of managing risky populations no longer requires the type of paternalistic authority associated with traditional British policing. Police leaders eventually came to recognise this fact. In the words of former Metropolitan Police Commissioner Sir John Stevens, the private security sector was 'no longer seen by the police as the enemy' (quoted in Thumala et al. 2011: 294). This process of acceptance required three sets of changes: in the private security industry itself; in police organisation; and in prevalent notions of the governance of public space.

For the private security industry, the crucial development was the emergence of licensing and regulation. The establishment in 2003 of the SIA aimed to separate out the competent and reliable companies – suitable recipients of police outsourcing contracts – in a way not dissimilar to that whereby legitimate PMCs had come to be distinguished from mercenaries. This was something that the UK Home Office had initially resisted because it did not see any role for an elite of private sector companies in the policing area (White 2018). Unregulated cowboy outfits were less of a problem when the role of private security was largely restricted to guarding warehouses and nightclubs, rather than tasks which place it in direct interaction with the general public. But the other changes – in police organisation and in notions of public space – made such interaction appear inevitable and acceptable.

Changes in police organisation facilitating the entry of the private sector (to the annoyance of Simon Reed) were authorised by the 2002 Police Reform Act, which enabled chief constables to delegate a subset of police powers to non-police persons. This enabled police forces to create their own quasi-police in the form of Police Community Support Officers (PCSOs). Their powers with regard to the public include the issuing of fixed penalty notices (see below), demanding names and addresses and moving people on in a public place. They are also empowered to detain members of the public for a short time pending the arrival of police officers. The next stage in the development was the extension of similar powers, minus the power of detention, to non-police agents who may be neighbourhood wardens, hospital security guards, park wardens, shopping centre guards and train guards. Some of these roles in the new 'extended police family' will be filled by private security employees who obtain their cut-down police powers as officers in police-authorised Community Safety Accreditation Schemes (CSAS) under the 2002 legislation. At this point it is important to understand that it is not the appearance on the scene of accredited private security that somehow undermines the police – which appeared to worry Simon Reed. Rather, the 2002 Act empowered police chiefs themselves to start the ball rolling in the creation of a 'second layer of law enforcement' by means of the creation of PCSOs. This is another example of state agencies changing their behaviour in such a way as to facilitate the entry of the private sector, rather than competition from the private sector forcing the state agencies to change. The state is the leading sector in the privatisation process. We shall encounter further examples of this dynamic in the penal sector, but none of this would have made any sense in the absence of a third set of much more fundamental changes governing public space.

As we have already noted, the welfare state ideal of the access of all classes as citizens to public space, albeit governed by a gendered 'moral economy of place and space' (see Chapter 2) and with the police as its symbolic upholders, is in decline. A neoliberal determination to replace the last residues of Keynesian planning with the rigours of the free market has created in its place a highly surveilled and securitised space, traversed by CCTV and a variety of crime and disorder prevention measures which we shall elaborate presently. The overriding aim is to force communities, cities and regions to take responsibility for making their areas attractive to consumers and investors by keeping the poor and unemployed as far out of sight as possible. Public space increasingly becomes space fortified against the poor, even while police still talk about community policing and governments still talk about community cohesion. However, some time ago the latter became 'less about socially integrating those who live at the margins of society and more about guarding the boundaries between the established and the outsiders' (Rodger 2008: 165). The decline of police patrols in English cities is often explained as a misguided response to reductions in street crime during the 1990s, a decline now reversed (House of Commons 2018). More important in the long run may be the lack of a perceived necessity for the presence of symbolic authority in public space. All this has been common knowledge for some years, but what is important is the way in which the securitisation and fragmentation of public space has enabled even Simon Reed's 'ill-equipped and poorly trained second layer of law enforcement' to play an increasingly integral role in its governance.

The police officer as 'the state on the street' possessed a reservoir of intervention strategies, including those now decentralised to PCSOs and private security, but, crucially, they had other strategies, ranging from arrest to a good talking to, which were highly dependent on the status and authority of the officer, who could use discretion as to which strategies to deploy in a particular situation. There were also, of course, a number of other natural authority figures such as bus conductors, park-keepers and parents, who deployed their informal status to deal with trouble. These have been in decline for some considerable time.

Private security employees, by contrast, carry neither clear arrest powers (although see below) nor any semblance of natural authority. In more elaborate terminology they lack the capacity to emit 'control signals' (Jackson et al. 2013; Rowland and Coupe 2014), or to participate in a 'legitimacy dialogue' whereby their authority is established towards the people with whom they interact (Bottoms and Tankebe 2012). Their discretion is generally limited to deciding whether or not to attempt a limited procedure, such as threatening a fixed penalty notice, demanding a name and address or simply 'looking the other way'. What is important therefore is that diffuse notions of trouble and public antisocial behaviour have been broken down by recent legislation into precisely delineated categories – such as noise, dropping litter, dog mess, aggression, consuming alcohol in public, throwing stones – each carrying a penalty. All that is required of the agent is to identify the infraction and (attempt) to impose the penalty notice.

This introduces a tick-box character to the regulation of antisocial behaviour in public space which enables its management to be outsourced to relatively unskilled operatives. This is in fact very similar to the way in which – as we shall see in Chapter 5 – tick-box procedures for assessing the risk to the public by, for example, an offender on probation also enables their management to be outsourced to relatively unskilled practitioners. The decline of the traditional probation officer, whose job it was to 'advise, assist and befriend' – in other words, to get to know their client as a person – mirrors the decline of the other natural authority figures mentioned above who, like traditional patrolling police officers, would get to know and look out for old people, by checking if they have been recently seen by anyone (see Jones and Newburn 1999; Minton and Aked 2013) and would talk to members of the local community as a useful source of intelligence about crime. This was part and parcel of a community life in which the residents themselves knew each other. The low-paid, bored, private security employee who will probably be employed in a totally different location next week, can never replace these people. But if the aim is simply to keep the lid on certain forms of antisocial behaviour by handing out penalty notices, then private security may suffice.

The move of private security into public space – normally town centres – has gathered pace, particularly in smaller towns, where police presence has been steadily reduced. For example, 2014 saw the town centre of Boscombe in Dorset being patrolled by a small private security company called Guarding UK Ltd. The company is licensed by the SIA and its town centre patrol holds accredited CSAS status as community safety patrol officers granted by the Dorset chief constable. Powers include issuing fixed penalty notices, demanding names and addresses and requiring people to move on. Duties focus on issues such as street begging, drinking alcohol or using drugs in public (Frampton 2014). Things can, of course, go wrong. In 2016, in Maidstone in Kent, a private security patrol, employed by the local authority in a similar role, attempted to fine a woman for feeding ducks (Gazet 2016).

The increase in tick-box regulation of public space which enables private security to function as a quasi-police presence has also occurred in larger cities. In 2012 the Manifesto Club, a London-based campaigning organisation, identified 435 'special zones' in the capital which included 'no-dog zones; no-leafleting zones; alcohol-confiscation zones; and dispersal zones' (Appleton 2012). More recently, the 2014 Anti-Social Behaviour, Crime and Policing Act brought together a variety of powers regarding the control of antisocial behaviour of various types by the police, local authorities and other agencies. In particular the legislation introduced the Public Space Protection Order (PSPO) under which local authorities may enact orders, covering a defined space, banning any activity they deem to have a 'detrimental effect on the quality of life of those in the locality' for a maximum duration of three years. PSPOs are frequently directed at the banning of busking, loitering, begging, rough sleeping, litter, street drinking, leafleting and cycling on the pavement. By the end of 2017 over 40 per cent of English local authorities had used PSPOs since 2014. According to a Freedom of Information request by the Manifesto Club the average monthly number of PSPOs issued by local authorities rose from 8.1 during the period November 2014–February 2016 to 15.3 during the period August 2017–January 2019. The number of fixed penalty fines issued rose from 470 in 2015 to 9,930 in 2018 (Manifesto Club 2019).

Of the 2018 fines, 6,010 were issued by CSAS-accredited private security employees working for four large English local authorities, three of which employ a particular company, Kingdom Services Group. It should be emphasised that the company is licensed by the SIA, and according to its website operates 'under some of the tightest legal guidelines, which are robustly quality managed by an experienced and well-resourced team and infrastructure with exceptional customer service skills' (Kingdom Services 2018). The same web page reveals that

'Kingdom's costs are covered by the Fixed Penalty Notices (FPNs) we issue'. This could of course establish a perverse incentive to maximise the imposition of fixed penalty notices. Indeed, a whistleblower claimed that some of the company employees 'would target certain age groups, like over-60s, as they were law-abiding and if issued with a fixed penalty notice they would pay it' (Marsh and Greenfield 2019). If true, such allegations identify an important tendency built into the role of the private sector. If the aim is revenue collection then the perverse incentive to target those who can pay would widen the scope of antisocial behaviour control beyond unemployed youth and rough sleepers and other groups with little money to pay fines even if imposed on them.

In this context we might agree that 'it is surprising that there has been little controversy surrounding the Community Safety Accreditation Scheme given that it involves the potential for private security officers to secure special statutory powers' (Button and Wakefield 2018: 137), and despite the fact that 'profit-making is widely seen as being incompatible with the ideals of impartial justice and universal service intrinsic to modern policing' (Button and Wakefield 2018: 156). The lack of controversy, however, is probably concentrated in the wealthy and middle classes who, in the fragmenting city, are less concerned with who has legitimate authority than with who provides effective security. The 'culture of control' (Garland 2001) has replaced the guaranteeing of rights with the management of risk and the provision of security as the predominant concern. The middle classes are therefore prepared to tolerate private security on the streets – although not happy about being fined for feeding the ducks. There is also the fact that the majority of CSAS schemes have been local authority-initiated schemes rather than private security directly taking over police work (Crawford 2013: 3). Those who regard private security in public space as controversial are more likely to be on the receiving end – the precariat, in particular the young, the poor and the homeless. But they may well regard the local authority, private security and the police themselves, who turn up when things get agitated, as all part of the same machinery of control.

Such developments are certainly not limited to the UK. Numerous studies document similar developments in the US (see for example Beckett and Herbert 2010). But in many states in the global south the relations between state police and private security in public spaces may be quite different. We noted in Chapter 3 that optimistic assumptions about global economic growth and socio-political assimilation of former colonial territories to northern social and political structures proved utopian. Many countries in the global south have remained poor and unstable. They suffer severe levels of urban inequality and poverty and have states that lack both competence and legitimacy. The marginalised urban poor make up the vast majority of the population and are frequently scarcely regarded as citizens by ruling elites. The middle classes want security against the urban poor, but not in the relatively timid form of fixed penalty fines for antisocial behaviour. Rather, they want an aggressive – if possible, armed – response. If the state police cannot provide this then private security is available. Furthermore, in countries like South Africa the police never symbolised social cohesion but rather the racist regime of apartheid or similar situations in other colonial territories. Under apartheid, public space in South Africa was strictly racially segregated: the antithesis of the multi-class welfare state. The state police were in effect the private security of the white elite, with the task of keeping the black working class and poor out of white-reserved areas. The lack of a contrast between the roles of police and private security as such makes it easier to combine them. Recent research on private security found that 'South Africans repeatedly expressed how they regarded private security, particularly the armed response sector, as similar, or even identical, to the state police' (Diphoorn 2016: 324).

South Africa is one of the more powerful states on the African continent. But further north, state machineries in many cases not only lack legitimacy with the population as a whole but are relatively unconcerned with the issue because their power is based on support and finance from global corporations. Again, the combination of police and private security is easier, particularly if the private sector has superior technology and organisation – vehicles, communications, facilities for criminal intelligence analysis, etc. In Nigeria global private security companies are 'not simply a "junior partner" to the state ... [but rather] ... a key component in the operations of state forces' (Abrahamsen and Williams 2011: 143) and are able to compete with the state for legitimacy in the provision of core policing tasks 'in the symbolic market of security' (Abrahamsen and Williams 2011: 206). The private sector competes directly with the state for legitimacy in policing a public space that never approached the secure multi-class public space ideal of the welfare state era in the global north nor the supremacy of the public (state) police implied by that ideal.

SECURING PRIVATE RESIDENTIAL SPACE

Returning to the global north, we find a strong connection between social inequality and the rise of private security. 'When we look across advanced industrialised countries, we see the same pattern: the more inequality, the more guard labor' (Bowles and Jayadev 2014). In the UK the dismantlement of multi-class public space is paralleled by the increasing tendency of the wealthier sections of the population to make their own security arrangements. Legitimate state authority is outsourced to the authority of the property owner to protect their property, and this authority extends de facto to the immediately adjacent public space.

We can start with the wealthiest in the UK, one of the most unequal societies in Europe. The financial elite is heavily concentrated in London and the south-east and much of this group has in recent years been of Eastern European origin. London is well known as the money-laundering capital of Europe (Barrington 2019). In her recent essay on the London housing market, Anna Minton (2017) described a bus tour around some of the richest residential areas of the city which 'wended its way past Belgrave Square in Kensington, where a business tycoon, formerly the richest man in Russia, owned number 5, while oligarch Boris Berezovsky, who died in 2013, had several flats at number 26' (Minton 2017: 3). These global financial oligarchs are the least likely section of the population to adhere to notions of membership of a community for which issues such as the legitimacy of the state and the authority of the police in public space have any real meaning. London is simply a convenient place to park money and buy real estate. Although gated communities are on the rise in the UK, the wealthy have often been content with more subtle processes of rises in rents and housing costs to engineer a social cleansing whereby the poor and risky are simply priced out of the area (Minton 2017). The decline of the last remnants of multi-class public space simultaneously removes the incentive for police patrolling and opens the area more clearly for private security arrangements.

These are not in short supply. In August 2018 the press reported negotiations between the Duke of Westminster's Grosvenor Estate and other landlords of wealthy properties in the Belgravia area – on the route of Minton's bus tour – and a private security force aptly named My Local Bobby run by ex-police officers and owned by a private security company, TM-Eye (Roundtree and Middleton 2018). This company provides very nearly the same services as those provided by the old eighteenth-century

Association for the Prosecution of Felons, and employs not only a body of private detectives to investigate burglaries but apparently has access to the police national computer. It has demonstrated a willingness to use citizen's arrest powers (see below) and to devote resources to private prosecution. The My Local Bobby scheme, launched in 2017, involves operatives patrolling micro-beats of around 250 houses. Householders pay variable fees depending on the frequency with which their property is checked (Gilligan 2018). A resident of Belgravia reported: 'I live in Belgravia and was robbed in the early hours while returning home. The police were unable to attend. I called the team from My Local Bobby and within hours a highly experienced detective attended and commenced an investigation. Additional high-visibility patrols were put in to support me' (quoted in Harris 2018). The scheme plans to expand to a national scale (Powell 2018).

If the wealthy are able to afford the most elaborate private provision, the decline of police street patrols in England and Wales in general has encouraged the general expansion of private security patrols. In smaller towns local residents, including those in less affluent areas, may pay for private security patrols largely against burglary, vandalism and antisocial behaviour. These usually involve smaller local security companies such as Sparta Security in Darlington, Atraks in Southampton and Garde UK in various parts of Essex. There are similar arrangements in numerous other smaller towns (Davis 2010). These resident-funded patrols may become general patrols of public space, very similar to, but not necessarily the same as, those having the CSAS accreditation enjoyed by police- and local authority-sponsored schemes. In 2015 in Frinton-on-sea in Essex (population 4,000), 300 local residents were employing AGS, a small local company, to drive around the town during the hours of darkness (Khomami 2015). In Martock in Somerset (population 4,700), Atlas UK Security Services provides a night patrol which pays particular attention to the shopping parade, with a focus on noise, criminal damage and antisocial behaviour (Harris 2018).

PRIVATE OWNERSHIP OF PUBLIC SPACE

The fact that private security employees do not have police powers is only an issue when it comes to dealing with crime and antisocial behaviour in public space. In larger towns and cities the growth of mass private property in the form of shopping centres, leisure parks and entertainment centres has long been known as a driver for the expansion of private security (Shearing and Stenning 1983). Consumers entering a shopping centre may not be aware, or understand the significance, of the fact that they are leaving public and entering private space. As consumers they may not object to the security guards expelling young, dishevelled skateboarders who have no money to spend and are a noisy nuisance as far as shoppers are concerned. In such spaces the authority of private security is not outsourced from the police or local authority but rather derives from commercial property owners who have the right to secure their property and to determine – within the law – how it is to be used. The lack of full police powers is not an obstacle to this type of enforcement of private definitions of antisocial behaviour.

There is of course no reason why police should not patrol large commercial shopping malls, though they will normally require payment – as they do for event security such as policing football matches. In Chapter 2 we noted the continuation of the tradition of paid policing into the modern period. The owners of the large Bluewater Centre near Dartford in Kent originally paid Kent police to patrol the centre, but reduced it in the early 2000s. The issue was not simply that private security was cheaper, but rather that drawing the police into the paid service of commercial property owners potentially compromises the operational independence of the police. 'By clinging on to notions of "operational independence" the police may undermine their own capacity to compete effectively with private providers who have no such wider concerns' (Crawford and Lister 2016: 67). But this operational independence was not so much a question of refusal to be competitive with private security, rather than being crucial to the status of the police as the impartial guardians of public space, something ultimately incompatible with the enforcement of privately determined norms. This is particularly so when these take the form of 'an entire code of conduct for entry, not to mention a dress code. No hoods, no baseball caps, no swearing, even' (Hatherley 2012). Such forms of behaviour the police would not normally exclude from public space (see Wakefield 2005).

In such a context, things can go wrong, just as they did with feeding the ducks in Maidstone. In March 2019, Bluewater was 'urgently re-training' staff after a security guard instructed someone with a guide dog to leave the centre (Rider and Smolen 2019). This 'poorly trained second layer of law enforcement' is, however, encountered in a more complex form in some cities in the global south. Sobia Kaker (Forthcoming) reports on the retreat of middle-class residents in Karachi to fortified housing enclaves, smart hotels and other facilities employing private security guards: a process she calls 'enclavisation'. Paradoxically, the process 'actually intensifies urban interactions between the rich and the "potentially dangerous" poor. This is especially since private security guards from the city's "dangerous slums" come in to work in shifts to secure affluent enclaves ... by exacerbating existing inequalities and urban marginality in a city that is already highly polarised, practices of enclavisation in fact work to perpetuate urban insecurity' (Kaker Forthcoming: 6).

Returning to South Africa, another example of demanding that private security guards act like the state police – when the state police itself, as we have said, was traditionally the private security of the white ruling elite – is the use of private security to enforce the colonisation of public space by wealthy private residents:

> South Africa's private security industry was thrust into the spotlight in December 2018, when guards from Cape Town's PPA Security company were accused of moving people off Clifton Beach at the request of the area's wealthy homeowners. But the Clifton incident is just the tip of the iceberg. The private security industry dwarfs the South African Police Service in size, with well over twice as many private security officials as police officers. The industry argues that it is providing a vital social service – but critics say that it is increasingly, and illegally, usurping the powers of police. (Davis 2019)

PRIVATELY OWNED PUBLIC SPACE

In the UK a private security company moving sunbathers off Brighton beach to preserve the area for wealthy residents would hardly be tolerated. But there has developed a corporate equivalent in which private security may enforce regulations in public space not dissimilar to those in private shopping centres discussed above. The private enclosure of public land has a long history in Britain (Christophers 2018). The economic slowdown from the late 1970s saw local authorities in many cities investing in commercial property themselves, and also selling off prime public land to private financial institutions and corporations in an attempt to offset falling government funding. The result was the creation of what has come to be known as 'privately owned public space' (POPS).

The result was that 'the ownership of an ever-increasing number of urban centres has been relinquished by elected city authorities to international property developers and investment companies' (Macleod and Johnstone, 2012: 21). At the same time, neoliberal-inspired economic policy sought to encourage inward investment into deprived urban areas by creating special deregulated zones administered by local authorities, such as 'enterprise zones' and 'business improvement districts' (BIDs) (see below). The key neoliberal strategy was that, rather than relying on public state investment in areas to create jobs and incomes, it is the responsibility of the people of an area, through their local authorities, to make their area an attractive one for investors.

This encroachment of private ownership or special regulation into public space combines with the development of special zones governed by PSPOs to undermine older ideas of multi-class public space occupied by 'citizens'. Rather, different types of people are welcome or unwelcome in different zones. PSPOs exclude, as we have seen, the marginalised poor, skateboarders, beggars, rough sleepers, street-drinkers and any groups seen as risky. These categories will also be excluded by POPS but with added regulations devised by the private landowners covering such activities as taking photographs, consuming food, gathering in groups or handing out leaflets. The aim is fundamentally to treat areas of non-enclosed public space essentially as if they were private shopping centres on the Bluewater model. Regulations, which normally have to be approved by the local authority, may include the explicit repression of activities traditionally associated with the exercise of citizenship rights such as public gathering, public meetings, leafleting, eating or even taking photographs. Again, these are not activities that would normally attract the attention of the police but are enforced by private security acting on behalf of the landowners. If an attempt to enforce such private regulations results in public disturbance then the police might be called and in effect become the guarantors of private regulation.

The early stages of these developments during the 2000s in the UK were generally characterised by the sale of land to a large single owner with no interest in erecting the types of obstacles to traffic characterised by private urban landownership in the nineteenth century discussed in previous chapters. In one of the largest developments in Europe in the early 2000s, Liverpool City Council chose a single private landlord, Grosvenor Estates, owned by the Duke of Westminster, to lease and develop 35 streets in the city centre. The Liverpool One project created anxieties about the role of private security 'who, it is feared, will prohibit access to "undesirables" such as *Big Issue* sellers, beggars ... and young people skateboarding or hanging out with friends. Alcohol and food consumption will be allowed only in designated areas' (Carter 2008; see also Minton 2006). The role of private security was one aspect of a more general 'governing through crime' initiative involving massive use of CCTV and access control, and an overwhelming focus on the criminal labelling of the young and poor (Coleman et al. 2005; Kinsella 2011).

POPS expanded rapidly during the early years of the present century. London examples include More London, a large territory along the South Bank of the Thames, which in 2013 was sold off to a property company based in Kuwait in one of the largest such property deals in British history (Garrett 2015). This process of shrinking public space in central cities has been a growing subject of controversy highlighted by such architectural activists as Anna Minton and Bradley Garrett (see Garrett 2017) and the *Guardian* newspaper. The *Guardian* Cities Investigation conducted in 2017 in collaboration with Greenspace Information of Greater London (CiGL) (Cox 2017) revealed the studied secrecy and reluctance of local authorities and the private corporations concerned to reveal the actual extent of POPS in major cities (Shenker 2017). Part of the *Guardian*/GiGL initiative was an attempt to map the substantial growth of the phenomenon.

Private regulation is in fact quite precarious in POPS. The public enter the areas freely and indeed may not notice that they are entering 'private' space. They may be unaware of the regulatory powers of private owners and may feel they have the right to behave as free citizens in what they regard as free public spaces. This is a recipe for conflict between members of the public and private security guards attempting to enforce the extra powers of the property owners. A couple of London examples convey the flavour; on the Thames South Bank

> the transformation of the area outside City Hall into a POPS meant that it was no longer possible to protest outside the headquarters of the mayor and the Greater London Authority. Or to take photos, apparently: when I was filming with Channel 4 there in 2015, we were swiftly removed from the property. This is nothing new. In 2010, during a London Assembly planning and housing committee meeting, Jenny Jones, from the Green Party, said: 'It has taken us eight years

> to negotiate with More London so that we politicians can do a TV interview outside our own building.' (Garrett 2015)

Further east, a journalist reported his experiences in Stratford:

> On Wednesday I covered a protest for a news agency outside Stratford underground station, I climbed some stairs to get a wide shot of the crowd. Within seconds I was surrounded by five Westfield security guards telling me I couldn't film there, I was on private property. One put his hand on my camera and told me not to film him, despite him then filming me on his seriously inferior camcorder ... A police officer later confirmed to me that the steps and bridge that Westfield claim to be private are on top of public land ... To hell with these multinational corporations that would tax the air we breathe given half a chance. It's time for the public to reclaim public space. (Mendez 2017)

The journalist was eventually able to complete his work, but the particular restrictions on taking photographs or handing out leaflets have been commonplace regulations in the management of POPS (see Hadaway 2009). In its 2011 guide to private security companies, established in coordination with the Home Office, the British Security Industry Association (BSIA), the private security trade association (not to be confused with the SIA) felt it necessary to remind its members that 'It is not an offence for a member of the public or journalist to take photographs/film of a public building' (BSIA 2011). The security operatives at Stratford but also on the Thames South Bank had, it might appear, yet to assimilate this guidance. In 2017 the London mayor proposed to establish a Public London Charter regarding rights and responsibilities for users and owners of POPS. The outline of this charter is still awaited.

Photography is just one aspect of the extra-regulation of POPS by private management and enforced by private security. Other regulations may impede political demonstrations. In 2011 the Occupy demonstrators in the City of London had to move their encampment out of Paternoster Square onto the adjacent steps of St Paul's Cathedral where the Church of England, a more liberally minded institution than the owners of the square, allowed them to stay. Paternoster Square is in fact POPS owned by the Mitsubishi Estate Company who successfully obtained an injunction which stated: 'The protestors have no right to conduct a demonstration or protest on the Square, which is entirely private property' (Vasagar

2012). Meanwhile, while citizens are prohibited from taking photographs, the property companies themselves are starting to use the latest facial recognition CCTV systems. These are currently controversial even when used by the police. In August 2019 the mayor of London, Sadiq Khan, wrote to the owner of the Kings Cross development POPS which had admitted its use of facial recognition technology 'in the interests of public safety' (Sabbagh 2019).

BIDS AND KEEPING OUT THE POOR

Closely analogous to POPS are BIDs. Originating in the US during the 1970s, in the UK they can be created under the Local Government Act 2003. In London they began to be created in 2005 and by 2016 numbered around 50 (FOLRS 2016). BIDs involve local businesses funding extra services such as environmental improvements to make the area attractive to consumers and investors. These extra services may include private security which, as in both POPS and the various local authority measures such as PSPOs discussed above, attempt to secure their area against populations likely to engage in antisocial behaviour deemed bad for business. As such they make further impositions on the old idea of free public space. As they are technically, unlike POPS, still public space, their private security patrols are normally CSAS accredited.

The Victoria BID is in central London in the area adjacent to Victoria station, a busy thoroughfare. Private security patrols are currently (2018) provided by Land Securities, a property management company, which in turn subcontracts to Ultimate Security Services whose CSAS-accredited employees patrol areas with high levels of antisocial behaviour and rough sleeping. The company, it is interesting to note, also provides a range of back-office services to police forces (see below), as well as security solutions for the retail trade and for software and internet companies. This is a large and well-established company and a long way from the cowboy outfits that may still exist in some of the smaller towns. As such it is well placed to develop a sophisticated relationship with the police. Rather than, as in some of the examples discussed earlier, taking over the policing of forms of antisocial behaviour which the police might well not bother with, there is close liaison between private security and the police. As part of its Safe and Secure programme, London Victoria BID has close relations with British Transport Police – near a busy railway station – and the Metropolitan Police. The BID-sponsored CSAS organises private security patrols which involves 'BID Security officers ... collecting intelligence to pass on to the Metropolitan Police under our Information Sharing Agreement; for counter-drug and illegal immigration operations' (VBID 2018: 6). The BID also participates in the London-wide Employer Supported Policing which provides police training – in crime prevention – for staff who may also apply for selection as part-time police special constables who, unlike PCSOs, are fully warranted police officers.

Involvement in intelligence gathering on drug and immigration crime lifts private security out of a focus on low-level antisocial behaviour and moves it towards a more equal partnership with the police. The idea of the private sector as an 'ill-equipped and poorly trained second layer' is consigned to the history books, as the relationship between police and private security moves towards a partnership of equals. Police, private business and private security (both static security and CSAS patrols) are being brought together into a single 'extended police family' or 'assemblage' (see Abrahamsen and Williams 2011), reinforced through joint participation in numerous networks with names such as the Community Security and Resilience Network, the National Association of Business Crime Partnerships and West End Security Group (see VBID 2018: 6). Meanwhile, in addition to SIA accreditation, the elite of private security companies have established professional and trade associations to reinforce their public profile of competence and legitimacy. These include the BSIA, mentioned earlier, and the Pacesetters Approved Contractor Scheme (ACS) made up of the top 15 per cent of SIA-approved companies. From private security *replacing* the police in street patrolling there is a shift towards *co-policing*. This shift is reinforced by several developments.

THE EXTENDED POLICE FAMILY

The collaboration between police and private companies generally in crime prevention and detection is considerable. It is important to distinguish between private companies as the potential and actual victims of crime and the private security industry itself. As regards the former, many companies at all levels implement sophisticated crime-prevention measures ranging from access control to cybersecurity. They have their own security experts who have their own lines of communication with the police. In addition, private companies sponsor the police financially. At one end of the spectrum, local traders may pay to have their logo on a police vehicle. At a more organised level, private companies may donate money to police specialist criminal investigation units, especially in complex financial crime, the investigation of which demands extensive police time and resources. Many of these initiatives in the UK date from the 2002 Proceeds of Crime Act (see Lea 2004) which inaugurated an era of closer collaboration between the police and the banking and finance sector. For example, in 2012 the City of London Police established an Insurance Fraud Enforcement Department with a start-up donation of £9 million from the Association of British Insurers (Barrett and Mendick 2012). The question may arise as to whether a particular investigation would have been viable without private sector financial contributions.

Payment by a private company for a direct police investigation is another matter. In 2009, Virgin Media found an individual allegedly importing and selling TV set-top boxes which enabled the user to receive Virgin Media channels without a subscription. In order to gain evidence for a private criminal prosecution, but themselves lacking powers of investigation, Virgin persuaded the London Metropolitan Police to apply to magistrates for, and subsequently execute, search warrants. When applying for search warrants the police omitted to inform magistrates that the action was to assist Virgin in a private criminal prosecution. Subsequently Virgin contracted to pay the Metropolitan Police Authority 25 per cent of any money obtained through asset confiscation upon conviction of the illegal importer. There were technical legal issues concerning whether a civil action would have been more appropriate in this and similar cases. But the advantages for a private individual or company of having a major police force acting on their behalf as an investigator are obvious (see Cape 2014).

Such incidents may, however, be indications of a creeping privatisation in the sense that a lack of police resources for complex investigations increases police dependence on private donations. In a similar way, police dependence on the private security sector as an ancillary investigation arm appears to be growing. TM-Eye, the company that owns My Local Bobby, specialises in intellectual property theft and counterfeit goods, an area in which, besides the police, local authority trading standards officers have a surveillance and investigative role. TM-Eye works rather like the latter. The company website lists a number of high-profile clients in the retail trade for whom it offers 'a complete package from gathering intelligence and evidence through to supporting raids and the completion of evidential statements for court'. The conclusion of an investigation leads to the identification of suspects 'for Trading Standards and Police enforcement action or to bring private criminal prosecutions' on behalf of clients (see TM-Eye 2019). The company website details a recent case (November 2018) in St Albans in which a seller of counterfeit goods was successfully prosecuted by the company itself. The company carried out the normal investigation work such as undercover operatives making covert test purchases to establish the illegal selling of counterfeit goods and then, in the final stage, 'Police Officers together with TM-Eye detectives [*sic*] obtained the correct details allowing the criminal summons to be served for three trade mark offences' (TM-Eye 2018). Case preparation for private prosecution was handled by a firm of solicitors with whom the company was in partnership. In the context of declining police resources, particularly in local fraud squads, there is increasing collaboration between police and the private sector in this area. TM-Eye appears to be a fairly small and recently established UK company with a productive relationship with the police. It might be thought that such private investigation systems, since they may call in the police at some stage to make arrests, exercise an undue influence on police resources. On the other hand, the House of Commons Home Affairs Committee 'heard that investigators often take up cases that are very important to the public, but too small or too complicated for the police to deal with' (House of Commons 2012: para. 13).

Action against counterfeit goods on sale in local street markets is small fry compared with the activities of large international private sector organisations. Thus Cerberus Investigations Ltd, based in Cyprus, has a global sphere of operations which includes: 'locating large wholesalers and manufacturers of counterfeit goods and liaising with local authorities in the countries to conduct inspections against them ... With a strong infrastructure in the United Arab Emirates, Africa and India we at Cerberus Security and Investigations can offer our clients on the ground, real time work in any country in the regions' (Cerberus 2019).

The methodology seems clear: the company conducts the investigations, identifies suspects and then contacts local law enforcement agencies with the evidence. This is also evident in the work of another UK-based company, Blackhawk Intelligence, working in the area of general fraud prevention. In a case study dated January 2016, the company acted for a global banking client operating in Africa where 'the organisation and its employees are potentially at risk from a variety of criminal activities, particularly bribery and corruption'. The resources that Blackhawk was able to mobilise to enhance the security of its client were substantial:

> Through its considerable base of contacts and local operatives, Blackhawk was able to collect and analyse a wealth of local intelligence data that helped our client make informed decisions in regard to business transactions and employee security. These sources included the local police force, Interpol, counterterrorism experts and intelligence sources within a particular country's police force or within which the client has its HQ, also local embassies. (Blackhawk 2016)

Here the relationship between the intelligence company and local law enforcement seems to conform to the relationship between private security and the police outlined by Abrahamsen and Williams (2011) and mentioned above. It seems to have been a case of utilising local police as an intelligence source for private security rather than the other way round. Whatever the capacities of local law enforcement it is clear in this case that the private security company is the hub of intelligence gathering and risk assessment.

In the UK itself a further driver of close collaboration between police and private security – a shift towards *co-policing* – has in recent years, particularly since 2001, been that of adaptation to the threat of terrorist attack. This has operated on two levels. First, the private sector as a whole – businesses, estate agents, banks, shops – become part of the eyes and ears of the police and security services. This was established early on in the fight against organised crime and money laundering, when the duty to report suspicious transactions was imposed on banks and financial institutions (see Lea 2004). These organisations are expected to become the eyes and ears of the criminal justice agencies in a sort of war effort involving most sectors of the economy.

As anti-terrorist strategies have become more elaborate and comprehensive so more institutions have been drawn in. The latest iteration of the strategy, known as CONTEST (HM Government 2018), includes event organisers, communications service providers (telephone companies and internet service providers) and passenger and freight services as part of a comprehensive surveillance system, aspects of which, in particular the role of Government Communications Headquarters (GCHQ) in the interception of internet and mobile phone metadata, have become highly controversial and regarded by many as a threat to civil liberties. In this general context it is hardly surprising that the private security industry has achieved growing prominence.

The CONTEST strategy aims to

> enhance collaboration with academia and the private sector to ensure we can access and exploit the most advanced technology, advice and solutions for counter-terrorism ... Wherever possible, we will co-design our approach on cross-cutting issues with the private sector, including building joint platforms for taking the work forward. JSaRC is a collaboration between and staffed by both Government and the security industry that drives innovation. (HM Government 2018: 80–1)

The acronym JSaRC refers to the unit within the Home Office known as the Joint Security and Resilience Centre. Established in 2016, it brings together civil servants and private security companies to develop solutions and expertise. On the industry side is the Security Commonwealth established in 2015 to coordinate the various private security organisations in their response to government initiatives. Similar well-funded projects involving state and private security industry collaboration have developed across the European Union (see Jones 2017). London, for example, as a key hub for global finance, is currently refining its terrorist preventative capacity in the Secure City Programme which involves, in the words of the Commissioner of the City of London Police, a reworking of prevention strategies towards terrorism:

> We will completely remodel our approach to CCTV and Automatic Number Plate Recognition, make use of facial recognition capabilities and link in with smarter city technology, such as smart street lighting. We have visited locations in the UK and across the globe to gain an insight into how other control rooms support the provision of wide-ranging security arrangements that protect people, places and buildings in the most effective way. (Dyson 2019)

Meanwhile the Security Commonwealth urges companies to coordinate action and share best practice. But in the development of the 'militarised city' (Graham 2011), what does the private security industry do apart from research and implement what are essentially forms of crime prevention? Is there a tendency for the sector to become involved at the level of determining the content of risk profiles and identification of targets for police action? Some security industry spokespeople are certainly claiming a parallel importance to that of the police as part of a seamless urban security and surveillance regime:

> The profile and professionalism of the security industry needs to be deemed as an extension of the way that the emergency services are respected by government, the public and by business leaders. Looking at most large crowded spaces, shopping centres, sporting locations, business districts, education and healthcare environments, the private security industry offers a far greater level of resource carrying out very similar observations, incident management and visual deterrence duties that can be found within the emergency services. Notwithstanding Powers of Arrest, are these duties so different? Are we not, as an industry, protecting the nation in our everyday security roles at no cost to the taxpayer? (Catton 2018)

It is obvious that private companies that are running CCTV schemes, intruder-detection systems and access control to buildings and even streets, and their being linked to police-led anti-terrorist security projects, may come to exercise influence, as would be expected in any collaborative activity. In the wake of the 2005 London bombings, Project Griffin coordinated (Metropolitan and City of London) police forces and private security such that the latter 'provided much needed support by carrying out external patrols of premises and by reassuring the communities most directly impacted by the terrorist attack. Similarly, private security guards actively assisted in the evacuation of the West End's Tiger Tiger Night Club when an explosive device was found outside the club's premises in June 2007' (NCTSO 2016).

The successor to Project Griffin is Project Servator, which since 2018 has involved a police-led eyes-and-ears security strategy in which 'our officers engage with a range of community partners, from the barista in the coffee shop to staff at major corporations, to encourage them to be our eyes and ears when we're not there, and report anything that doesn't feel right … The effect is the creation of a network of vigilance that creates an uninviting environment for potential terrorists considering their targets and individuals looking to commit crime' (Dyson 2019). Just as private security becomes part of the 'extended police family' it becomes a key part of the 'network of vigilance' against terrorism. Police come to depend on private security; even at a mundane level, 'police are welcoming corporate security officers patrolling beyond their front entrance, in the name of "extra eyes and ears" and making the most of "assets" in an era of public sector austerity' (Servator 2014). Similar projects have been rolled out in various cities in the UK. The aim of such 'eyes-and-ears' strategies is to link up police, business, private security, local government and public in a seamless end-to-end surveillance system. Private security has an influence on what is reported and therefore worthy of attention, but so of course do the general public.

THE PRIVATE SECTOR IN THE STATE: THE POWER TO ARREST

Under ever closer cooperation between police and private security, the leading sectors of the private security industry inevitably come to think of themselves as also being first responders to incidents alongside the police. For example, in the context of a growing concern about gun crime in London and a declining number of police officers, a senior executive of Churchill Security, a reputable ACS member company, wrote about the potential role of private security employees: 'With crime victims waiting up to 50 percent longer for 999 calls to be answered, security staff are increasingly relied upon to provide an effective first response. Trained to take charge in an emergency, help people stay safe and detain suspects, security officers can prevent crises escalating and minimise additional harm' (Melling 2017).

In fact, as we have already seen, the situation is blurred. The My Local Bobby company, discussed earlier, understands the availability of citizen's arrest powers. In common law jurisdictions there is a traditional power of any citizen to make an arrest in a case of breach of the peace. In England and Wales this has been elaborated by more recent legislation such as section 24A of the Police and Criminal Evidence Act of 1984 which enables a person 'other than a constable' to effect an arrest of anyone 'who is in the act of committing an indictable offence; or whom the person has reasonable grounds to suspect is committing an indictable offence' (see Myers 2011). An indictable offence is one that would be tried in the Crown Court in front of judge and jury. But this is only allowed if it does not seem reasonably practicable for a police officer to make the arrest. If private security and the police are collaborating closely then the implication is that the police themselves will be readily available in situations where an arrest is likely. In other jurisdictions, private security, using nothing more than citizen's arrest powers, do indeed make a considerable number of arrests. A private security officer told a journalist in South Africa: 'Sixty percent of the time, when police arrive we've already arrested a suspect ... Then police just come and do paperwork' (Davis 2019).

In England and Wales there are in fact a number of ways in which civilians – possibly, but not necessarily, the employees of private security companies – can acquire quasi-police powers. Other state agencies besides the police, notably customs and immigration, have arrest powers. As in other jurisdictions, the courts employ agents to enforce their decisions, for example to collect fines. The enforcing agents may be police officers, court officials and also civilian enforcement officers, who are traditionally civil servants with powers of arrest and detention on the basis of a warrant issued by a magistrate to collect fines or detain individuals in breach of community penalties. In 2017 the government proposed making cost savings by outsourcing this service to the private security company, G4S. This was, it should be noted, a considerable period of time after the 2012 Olympics fiasco and illustrates a point we shall dwell on in Chapter 5: the ability of some security companies to secure government contracts despite previous failure or even criminality.

Other sources of the diffusion of quasi-police powers derive from the 2002 Police Reform Act. We have discussed the CSAS schemes made possible under that legislation. There are other aspects of the spread of police-like powers. Many police forces in England and Wales have for some time employed civilian investigators, usually former police officers, to work on cold (long-unsolved) cases. At one point G4S saw this as a potential source of income, and by 2012 was able to claim 20,000 former police officers on the company books with between 300 and 600 employed at any one time to meet the demand from police forces for investigators (Warrell and Plimmer 2012). But that year the monumental chaos surrounding the attempts of G4S to fulfil its contract to provide security for the 2012 London Olympic Games led the company to suffer considerable reputational damage (Neate 2013). This probably reinforced a trend for civilian investigators to be employed directly by police forces rather than subcontracted from private security companies.

The trend in deploying civilian investigators, however, has continued. By August 2018, the Metropolitan Police, the UK's largest force, had 42 civilian investigators, up from 21 six years previously (Burgess 2018), though this was in the context of an overall fall in resources. The work of civilian investigators is covered by schedule 4 of the 2002 Act, which specifies considerable police powers relevant for criminal investigation which may be delegated to civilian investigators. They include entry to premises and seizure of evidence, but in particular the power of 'arrest at a police station for another offence' (of someone already arrested and in police custody) quite clearly extended the powers of civilian investigators into terrain hitherto reserved for police officers. This partial arrest power may well have been seen as a step too far as it seems to have been removed in the more recent modification of delegated policing powers by the 2017 Policing and Crime Act (see Rathmell 2017). Nevertheless, once the principle of delegating police powers to non-police persons on pragmatic grounds of efficiency and effectiveness has been conceded, it can easily be extended. Older notions of the monopoly of legitimacy and authority of the police as a state agency will have been further marginalised. This is all the more likely considering how far the police have allowed themselves to be privatised from within.

Ultimate Security Services, the company that provides private security patrols for the London Victoria BID also provides services to police forces including civilian detention officers who, according to the company website, assist police custody officers 'by carrying out checks on detainees, and conducting any other delegated tasks such as conducting swabs, finger-printing and cleaning cells'. Call handlers have the task of 'determining the response to emergency and non-emergency telephone calls … and log calls using the incident grading methods, in accordance with local and national quality and performance standards'. Finally, station enquiry assistants perform tasks including 'dealing with members of the public who call at stations, directing enquiries to other police departments and recording and maintaining records' (Ultimate Security 2018). This range of services is very similar to the major 25-year contract signed in 2012 between the private security giant G4S and Lincolnshire police. G4S provides a 'street to suite' service in which, once arrested by a warranted police officer, G4S drives the detainee to the custody suite in the police station which it runs. There, G4S civilian staff take DNA and fingerprints and manage the cells. The custody sergeant remains in overall control, but some way up the chain of command.

In fact, of course, the distinction between front-line police work (basically arresting suspects) and back-office work (managing custody, responding to calls from the public either by emergency phone calls or visits to the police station) is blurred. Responding to emergency calls from the public involves crucial decisions regarding the eventual police response to calls for assistance. Most of these roles were initially 'civilianised' by the employment of non-police officers by the police forces themselves. Increasingly they are subcontracted out to private security companies who bring the added dimension of the necessity of financial profitability to such work. In a detailed account of the early years of this contract, Adam White (2014a) gives some interesting examples. For example, G4S had to cancel a cost-cutting scheme to answer emergency calls with an interactive voice response system in which the caller selects numbers on the phone keyboard in accordance with the nature of the service required. It was soon realised that many calls to the police are from members of the public either in a state of distress resulting from criminal victimisation or who are unsure precisely which service they require. Either way, real time interaction with a skilled operator able to ascertain the details of the incident and direct resources accordingly is essential. Similar problems have occurred with other services such as health care where an unskilled operator may not detect signs of a particular serious illness. But it is clear in which direction the pressures of financial profitability lead. In any case, what is obvious from this example is not just that the operation of emergency call systems by private sector operators may lead to mistakes and inefficiency. The linking of citizens to the state, by requesting the assistance of the police as public authority, has become mediated by the concerns of private profit. As we shall see in Chapter 5, some would regard this as illegitimate per se.

Most important of all from the standpoint of the person detained, the arrest by a police officer, the trip to the police station, the taking of fingerprints and DNA and being locked in a cell prior to delivery before a magistrate are simply different stages of a single coercive process, all involving a suspension of freedom. In other words, from the standpoint of the detainee, the security employees indeed have the power of arrest by virtue of their activity in sustaining this coercive process.

The traditional view that for just this reason the different stages of the coercion of citizens should all be performed by a police officer or legal official of the state has come to be seen as archaic and largely displaced by the view that legitimate coercion can be outsourced. The point is not that the private security employees are not themselves governed by legal rules of conduct prescribing civilised treatment of detainees. It is rather that they are the employees of a profit-making private company. That such an argument might be dismissed as fuss about nothing shows just how far we have travelled towards the notion of a legitimate private component to the state itself.

CONCLUSION

In this chapter we have argued, mainly in the UK context, that the growth of private security in a policing role is the result of several factors. First, the fragmentation of public space such that the role of the traditional police officer as the symbolic presence of the 'state on the street' becomes marginalised in favour of a practical 'fire brigade' response to incidents of crime and security. The security of public space has become a predominant concern irrespective of who provides it, and a mix between police and private security is increasingly seen as acceptable. Much public space is subject to outright private ownership or special regulation by local authorities which focus on the exclusion and regulation of particular populations, mainly the young and poor, and this has opened opportunities for private security. This has been complemented by growing social inequality in cities and the tendency of (especially) wealthy residents to provide additional private resources for their security.

Second, the private security sector itself has matured and grown in status. We shall return to this theme later but it can be said here that the increasingly close working relationship between police and the leading sectors of the security industry has enabled the latter to begin a movement from the status of subcontractors for particular tasks towards that of full members of the 'extended police family'. The acquisition of arrest powers by private security would be the completion of this process. On the one hand, this is probably presently considered a compromise too far on the state monopoly of legitimate force. On the other hand, the English system in particular provides a tradition of citizen's arrest powers supplemented in recent years by various delegated quasi-police powers relating to the extraction of information from citizens and the imposition of penalty notices. It will be interesting to see how the situation develops in the next decade.

Finally, the police themselves – having trimmed their role to that of efficient security provider, and increasingly governed by government-imposed financial constraint – have allowed the private sector to play a growing role in their own organisational structure. By this we mean not just car parks, canteens and vehicle maintenance, which have always been handled by civilians, but rather the incursion of the private security industry into the coercive tasks associated with the arrest process and the allocation of resources in response to public calls to the police. The police role as the monopoly of legitimate force has been effectively concentrated on the act of arrest itself. This is the most important form the division between core competences and outsourceable ancillary operations has taken in domestic policing. Its possibility is linked to the decline in the role of the police as a general symbolic authority in public space. In Chapter 3 we noted similar developments in the military and how this was related to the changed nature of warfare. In Chapter 5 we shall see very similar dynamics at work in the penal sector.

5
The Private Sector in the Penal System

The return of the private sector to the penal system – the building and management of prisons, and the management of probation and other forms of constraint such as immigrant detention – has similarities to, and differences from, the growth of private policing. There are, as we have seen, a number of avenues whereby private security has been able to insert itself into various police-like roles without directly challenging the police organisation or its monopoly over the power of arrest. In a similar way the extension of penal control beyond the prison has created opportunities for private security in areas such as immigration, detention and removal and the management of housing accommodation for asylum seekers.

The difference from policing is that the private prison is performing an identical role to the state or public prison: incarcerating offenders for periods of time determined by the courts. There may be slight differences between the captive populations of the two sectors: high-security prisons holding terrorists and other dangerous offenders may remain entirely in the public sector. Nevertheless, the tasks of the prison and, importantly, the powers of prison managers over their inmates, remain the same in the two sectors. There is no area, analogous to the growth of private urban space, in which private prisons could gradually emerge alongside the state sector. The decision by UK governments to allow the private sector into the prison estate was therefore much more of a centralised policy decision than in the examples from policing. This means that the issues surrounding both the legitimacy of private coercion as well as the relative cost and efficiency of the two sectors tend to be more politicised and clearly posed.

THE LEGITIMACY OF PRIVATE INCARCERATION

There is one important analogy between the privatisation of prisons and one particular element in the privatisation of policing. As we noted in

Chapter 4, the outsourcing of various parts of the police organisation itself, in particular the management of custody, presupposed that the essence of the police role is focused on arrest. Once an arrest has been made then the arrested person, as 'police property', can be handed over to a private company to be transferred to the police station and processed. We noted that from the standpoint of the arrested person, the transport to the police station and subsequent custody may appear very much as a continuation of the coercive process that began with arrest.

A similar issue arises with prison privatisation. The doctrine which justifies the re-entry of the private sector into the prison estate is the disconnecting of the initial determination of punishment by the courts from its allocation by the prison. The idea here is that – just as once a person has been arrested it no longer has to be a police officer who administers custody – once the courts have convicted an individual then the sentence need not be carried out by the state itself. However, just as the arrested person will see custody as part of the chain of events that began with arrest, so the sentenced offender arriving in prison will see incarceration as part of the same chain of events that began with the sentence of the court.

The traditional argument against privatisation concedes that the prisoner's view is the correct one. The sentence of the court is not simply 'five years' imprisonment' as warehousing, but 'five years' rehabilitation' and re-education. The prisoner as conditional citizen has the right to expect this. Among the reasons for which the state during the nineteenth century took over and centralised the prison system (see Chapter 2) was the enforcement both of consistency of punishment and its effect as rehabilitation.

Thus, on the one hand, imprisonment as rehabilitation through re-education is implied in the sentence of the court. On the other hand, rehabilitation involves the direction – indeed the coercion – of the prisoner in the interests of re-education (see Genders 2002; Moyle 2001). Because it is both implied in, and a continuation of, the sentence, it must be carried out by the same authority and not outsourced to any organisation which may act according to *additional* motives to those of the state. The prison governor and his or her advisers will decide on parole, and on the system of rewards and punishments inside the prison which not only regulate the progress of rehabilitation but guarantee the orderly functioning of the prison institution. This power cannot be exercised by anyone driven by any extraneous motive, such as private profit, but only by those directly in the service of the state. Any notion of a dichotomy between determination and allocation of sentence is vacuous (see Sparks 1994).

This argument for the illegitimacy of prison privatisation was rehearsed at the level of jurisprudence by a well-known ruling of the Israeli Supreme Court in 2009. In 2004 the Knesset (the Israeli parliament) had responded to prison overcrowding problems by authorising the construction of a private prison. This decision was challenged in 2005 and resulted in the eventual judgement by the court that 'the very existence of a prison that operates on a profit-making basis reflects a lack of respect for the status of [prisoners] as human beings' (*Prison Legal News* 2013).

This judgement has given rise to much jurisprudential and philosophical argument (see for example Dorfman and Harel 2013; Feeley 2013; Simmons and Hammer 2015; Jacovetti 2016). Two closely connected themes in the discussion can be detected: one concerning the motivations of private contractors and the other concerning the status of prisoners. The first theme is that private contractors are by definition motivated by profit and thus, even if seeking to carry out the instructions of the state – in this case, the court sentence imposed on the prisoner – will invariably proceed from their own conceptions mediated by issues of commercial profitability (Dorfman and Harel 2013). The state may decree a term of imprisonment while the private prison administrators will interpret this from the standpoint of profit maximisation by, for example, varying or minimising recreation or rehabilitation activities. No private company is likely to bid for a contract that does not allow it to make a profit.

The second theme goes further, noting that the Israeli Supreme Court ruling implies 'that it was not the often deleterious consequences of privatisation that violated the rights to liberty and dignity, but that privatisation of prisons by itself was a violation' (Simmons and Hammer 2015: 488). This is because, irrespective of whether treatment of inmates is better or worse in private prisons, 'privatisation commodifies inmates – they are treated as a means to an end, the profits of a corporation' (Simmons and Hammer 2015: 496). In short, they are not being treated as conditional citizens, and even in the best case – a well-run private prison with plenty of rehabilitation facilities – their right to rehabilitation is subordinated to, and a by-product of, profit making. Other commentators have provided similar formulations, relating commodification to indignity: 'the additional harms that accompany being legally coerced or legally detained – the disruption, the harms to family life, the conditionality of one's choices and aspirations – become indignities when they are facilitated by those with no simple interest in the discharge of justice but with mixed motives' (Riley 2017).

There are two possible resolutions to this problem. The first is that the private security company relinquishes all concern with profitability. In such an unlikely circumstance, it would in reality cease to be a private company and become de facto part of the state. It would rapidly lose the interest of investors. The other possibility is that the state forces its own institutions to behave as if they were private companies in competition with the profit-seeking private sector by creating a level playing field on which the public and private sectors can compete in terms of costs and profitability. The state prison system becomes in effect part of the private sector – a variety of state capitalism. This of course requires the effective abandonment of rehabilitation as the only goal of the prison. The requirements of profitability are allowed an influence. The distinction between the determination and allocation of punishment then becomes a convenient rationalisation for this state of affairs. The consignment of the convicted prisoner into the hands of those – state or private – whose motives will include commercial profitability implies an eventual abandonment of the notion of the prisoner as conditional citizen with the right to a rehabilitation process unmediated by other motives. With these debates in mind we now turn to developments in the English prison system.

FROM REHABILITATION TO WAREHOUSING

When the issue of the re-entry of the private sector into the building and management of prisons was posed in the 1980s, the initial reaction was hostile. Most politicians and academics probably opposed private prisons with some version of the arguments outlined above. Douglas Hurd, the Conservative home secretary from 1985 to 1989, said in a parliamentary debate in 1987: 'I do not think that there is a case, and I do not believe that the House would accept a case, for auctioning or privatising the prisons or handing over the business of keeping prisoners safe to anyone other than Government servants' (House of Commons 1987).

In a letter to *The Times* in 1988 the respected criminologist Sir Leon Radzinowicz argued similarly:

> In a democracy grounded on the rule of law and public accountability the enforcement of penal legislation ... should be the undiluted responsibility of the state. It is one thing for private companies to provide services for the prison system but it is an altogether different matter for bodies whose motivation is primarily commercial to have coercive powers over prisoners. (Quoted in Shaw 1992: 31)

Yet two years later, Hurd had taken the opposite position. In a very different parliamentary speech he argued that

> the introduction of the private sector into the management of the prison system ... offers the prospect of a new kind of partnership between the public and the private sector ... We should not be scornful of new ideas which, if successful, will make an important contribution to the government's programme of providing decent conditions for all prisoners at a reasonable cost. (House of Commons 1989)

Quite rapidly, the older view moved from settled consensus to the margins, where it has since remained as an infrequent oppositional critique of private prisons. Its deployment, however, has sometimes been followed by hypocritical shifts of policy. In 1993, Tony Blair, then shadow home secretary, reading out Douglas Hurd's 1987 statement to the House of Commons, said: 'it is fundamentally wrong in principle that persons sentenced by the state to imprisonment should be deprived of their liberty and kept under lock and key by those not accountable primarily and solely to the state' (House of Commons 1993). When Labour formed the government in 1997 this did not stop them from immediately proceeding with the funding of private sector prisons.

The resurgence of private prisons in the UK was a case of policy transfer from the US, where the private sector was well organised (McDonald 1994). The first UK private prison, HMP Wolds in Humberside, was established in 1992, but the late 1990s and early 2000s were the growth years for the private sector. By 2015, 14 private sector prisons (out of a total of 121 in England and Wales) held around 18 per cent of the prison population. This was in fact a higher proportion than in the US, where the private sector holds around 10 per cent of inmates. Australia is the highest, with 19 per cent, although, of course, the number of prisoners in the US is much larger. The management of the sector in England and Wales is currently dominated by three large global private security corporations: G4S, Serco and Sodexo. In 2019 G4S ran five prisons, Serco also ran five and Sodexo ran four. Institutions for children and young people include three Secure Training Centres, two of which are currently run by G4S (see Brown 2018; Institute for Government 2018).

The most important practical reasons for allowing the private sector into the penal system during the 1980s were to relieve prison overcrowding while reducing costs, and as part of this to break the power of the Prison Officers' Association, the trade union of prison staff (see Ryan 1994). But there was little by way of critique of the old position or defence of the new. On the contrary, 'complex arguments about the ethical risks of punishing for profit, as well as arguments over variations in, and measurement of, performance in the public sector, were sidestepped' (Liebling and Ludlow 2017: 474). The market, it was argued, could handle the issue and guarantee efficiency, effectiveness and value for money.

However, in the early days of private prisons in England and Wales there was one crucial concession to the older view of the state's monopoly of legitimate coercion. Under the 1991 Criminal Justice Act, the directors (as they were titled) of private sector prisons were prohibited from conducting disciplinary hearings, imposing solitary confinement or applying special measures of control or restraint. These powers, obviously deemed necessary to the management of any prison, were instead exercised by a state-appointed controller tasked with monitoring the private management's compliance with its contract (see Liebling and Ludlow 2017). In other words, there was a recognition both that the distinction between determination and allocation of punishment was not watertight – because the administration of the prison may involve additional punitive decisions – and also that the state should remain the legitimate authority for such decisions, or at least monitor them closely. But if the directors of private prisons lacked the full powers of governors then they would be at a competitive disadvantage in managing their institutions, and so the 2007 Offender Management Act obligingly enabled the director to conduct disciplinary hearings, segregate prisoners or apply special measures of control or restraint.

What had happened to marginalise the older views concerning the legitimacy of coercion? If the overriding aim of penal policy was the rehabilitation of the prisoner as conditional citizen then, as we have argued, the role of the state as legitimate superintendent of that rehabilitation would have remained the main focus. But arguably the aim of imprisonment was gradually shifting under the impact of changed socio-economic conditions and neoliberal political ideology. The direction it was taking was towards a more straightforward strategy of containment or warehousing of difficult and dangerous individuals who were seen as holding a much greater personal responsibility for their own rehabilitation and were barely to be regarded as citizens at all. 'Punishment is now being used not upon those who are thought to be conditional citizens with a view to reintegration but against those who are thought to be non-citizens to disable or exclude them' (Vaughan 2000: 36).

The general drivers of this shift – growing social inequality, slowing economic growth, deindustrialisation and the neoliberal attack on the welfare state – have been mentioned already. As far as penal welfare and rehabilitation were concerned, these changes acted in two ways. First, the fragmentation of poor communities and the decline of stable, well-paid, working-class jobs made the whole prospect of rehabilitation, culminating in stable social resettlement, increasingly problematic. Today this is of course felt acutely by those, such as probation officers, whose task it is to help ex-prisoners back into 'non-criminogenic' social relations (Fitzgibbon 2011). Meanwhile, financial austerity reduces the resources for education and rehabilitation within prisons. At a certain point any serious strategy of rehabilitation is fatally undermined by rising chaos inside prisons. Drugs, violence and self-harm increase among inmates who understand perfectly well that there is no route out of their predicament. Prisons become 'warehouses of suffering and death' (Scott 2017). As we shall see, there is little reason to believe that there is much difference in this respect between private and public prisons.

It is obvious that the private prison sector is a minority enterprise, accounting for approximately 12 per cent of the prison estate and 18 per cent of the inmate population. This does not, of course, preclude future growth. Meanwhile much debate focuses on the question of whether private prisons are better or worse than public prisons by reference to such issues as treatment of inmates, rehabilitative activities and reoffending rates after release. But such comparisons are not the main issue. Searching for faults in the private sector – of which there are many and specific to the focus on profit-taking – can easily become a process of letting a failing public sector off the hook. But further, expecting to find major differences misunderstands the purposes of privatisation – of driving down costs for the sector as a whole, by substituting expensive rehabilitation schemes with lower-cost warehousing.

The creation of a level playing field on which the private and public sectors can compete for contracts for prison building or management (or both) enables a mutually reinforcing process. On the one hand, the private sector can demonstrate cost-cutting through, for example, a lower-paid labour force of prison staff, a higher ratio of prisoners to staff and more profitable exploitation of prisoners as a low-wage workforce for private companies. Through the process of competition for outsourcing contracts, this regime can be imposed on the sector as a whole. For this process to take place, the private sector does not have to be large. Once the demonstration effect is established then the public sector follows the private sector in the creation of new prison regimes. On the other hand, prior changes in the public sector may be required to make it worthwhile for private companies to compete for tenders in the first place. We shall presently see this dynamic as a central element in the privatisation of probation in England. If the state sector insisted on high standards, prioritising trained staff and well-funded education and rehabilitation programmes, then the private sector would hesitate to compete.

It is these changes in the nature of the target of state repression that make the entry of the private sector possible. As we have seen, it is the changed nature of armed conflict that makes possible the resurgence of private military. Likewise, it is the changed nature of public space and social citizenship that enables the resurgence of private policing and security. In the penal system it is the shift from rehabilitation towards straightforward warehousing that makes possible the entry of the private prison and probation sectors. Only within the context of these more fundamental changes is discussion about the relative costs and performance of private and public solutions able to take place. And even in this context, the aim of privatisation is to facilitate and speed up cost-cutting changes which have already been initiated in the public sector and which enable the entry of private companies. It is hardly surprising, therefore, that comparison between the public and private sectors is difficult and controversial. At a particular moment in time, crucial flaws in the private sector may be identified – only for them to appear later in the public sector. Both sectors are caught in a downward spiral of deteriorating conditions and crisis.

There are of course some technical obstacles to comparing private and public prisons. Inmate populations differ between the sectors. High-security prisons holding dangerous offenders are public sector. Many public sector prisons are local and old, whereas private sector prisons tend to be newer and larger. Until recently the top three largest prisons were all in the private sector: G4S-run Oakwood (1,600 inmates) and Birmingham (1,436) (although this is now back in the public sector – see below), and Sodexo-run Forest Bank (1,348). There are also perverse effects such as the character of the private sector prison guards (inexperienced, lower paid, fewer per prisoner, higher turnover) who are more fearful of the inmates – hence the prisoners report higher satisfaction. As a result, researchers are reluctant to pronounce on the superiority of either sector: 'there has been no conclusive evidence to suggest that public and private prisons can be distinguished in terms of key outputs (e.g. keeping prisoners in custody, providing decent conditions and reducing the re-offending rate). This means that claims are often made about the superiority of each sector on the basis of little empirical evidence' (Panchamia 2012: 4). Alison Liebling summed up the then current research, in a talk to the UK All-Party Penal Affairs Parliamentary Group in 2012: 'when private sector prisons are good, they are very good, and when they are bad they are very poor' (Prison Reform Trust 2012).

The tendency of the level playing field to transmit the characteristics of one sector into the other can be illustrated by reference to staffing. By the early 2000s the private sector had achieved lower staffing costs. By 2004 the average basic wage for a public sector prison officer was 43 per cent higher than for the private sector. But by 2014, wage differences were narrowing (Tanner 2013). Staff turnover for a long time was higher in the private sector, and this reflected at the same time a success in breaking down the old public sector 'macho' prison officer culture by recruiting a new type of prison officer who then found the job too demanding: '"You got people who'd worked in Wetherspoons [the pub chain] thinking 'I'll give that a whirl for the extra few grand', and finding it was much more challenging than they were prepared for," said one prison boss' (Ford and Plimmer 2018).

The positive consequence was a more customer service-oriented culture among prison staff, which produced higher rates of satisfaction among inmates. Research by Crewe et al. (2011) found that lack of staff experience and confidence determined how authority was exercised and experienced by prisoners. However, high staff turnover and lack of experience may also undermine the functioning of the prison. In 2013, an inspection of the new G4S-run large capacity (1,600 inmates) HMP Oakwood, found that 'Prisoners had little confidence in the staff to act consistently or get things done. Many staff were passive and compliant, almost to the point of collusion, in an attempt to avoid confrontation, and there was clear evidence of staff failing to tackle delinquency or abusive behaviour' (HM Chief Inspector of Prisons 2013: 5).

The negative consequences of a low-paid, unskilled labour force can be severe. To take an example from the global south, G4S was employed by the South African Department of Corrections from 2000 onwards to manage the 3,000-inmate high-security Mangaung Prison near Bloemfontein. In 2013, following a strike, G4S dismissed 350 prison guards and then brought in untrained staff who, it was alleged, were using forcible administration of heavy drugs and even electric shocks to subdue inmates illegally (Hopkins 2013). The Department of Corrections took control of the prison from G4S following an investigation which concluded: 'The contractor has lost effective control of the facility' (*AllAfrica* 2013). The prison was returned to G4S management in August 2014. Since then, in subsequent court cases, the company has allegedly attempted to prevent the publication of inmate medical records relevant to allegations of torture (Hopkins 2018).

Back in the UK we should note the murder of Jimmy Mubenga by G4S operatives in 2010 (see below). More recently however, in January 2016, a BBC *Panorama* programme documented serious abuse by G4S guards at Medway Secure Training Centre (STC) for young people (Travis 2016). Their exposé led to the suspension and arrest of G4S staff for violent behaviour. However, despite an inquiry which 'highlighted initial concerns about the efficacy of monitoring arrangements and about whether G4S staff had sufficient understanding and training in relation to the safeguarding of children in their care' (Holden et al. 2016: 8), no attempt was made to go beyond prosecution of the employees involved in order to attribute responsibility to the company itself. This, as we shall see, is a recurring theme in relation to the accountability of private security companies.

By 2018 the prison sector as a whole – public and private – was in crisis. This was reflected in rising rates of violence, drugs, suicide and self-harm, deteriorating security and sanitary conditions and rising assaults on staff. In January 2019, Ministry of Justice statistics showed record levels of self-harm, assaults and deaths, all having increased over the previous twelve months (Ministry of Justice 2019). This is in the context of reduced spending across the sector – by 2018 it was 16 per cent below 2009–10 levels (Institute for Government 2018).

Government had responded to the gathering signs of crisis with a rapid recruitment of new prison officers in the public sector, but staff turnover rates increased. The character of public sector staff was mirroring the private sector. By June 2018 a third of public sector prison officers had under two years' experience, compared with 7 per cent in March 2010 (Institute for Government 2018: 6). By that time no one was talking about the emergence of a friendly customer service culture and more respect for prisoners, but rather about a system on the edge of collapse. For example, HM Inspectorate of Prisons concluded that the 'inexperience of many staff' underpinned the problems it encountered at the public sector Nottingham prison in January 2018, where conditions were so poor that an 'Urgent Notice' was invoked, making the secretary of state directly accountable for improving performance (Institute For Government 2018: 6). An inspection of a private sector prison, HMP Birmingham (run by G4S), in 2018 revealed that

> staff–prisoner relationships had deteriorated markedly ... At times, it was difficult to find staff on the wings, and we found some locked in their office. We also found staff asleep in wing offices during patrol periods ... We regularly saw evidence of open drug taking, prisoners expected to endure intolerable living conditions, and some vulnerable prisoners being openly bullied, with staff failing to take action. (HM Chief Inspector of Prisons 2018a: 14)

The prison was subsequently returned to the public sector. But at around the same time in HMP Liverpool (public sector), prison inspectors found 'squalid conditions' in which 'many cells had broken windows with dangerous jagged glass ... broken or blocked toilets ... [and] many communal areas were in a decrepit state and there was a significant problem with cockroaches and rats throughout the prison' (HM Chief Inspector of Prisons 2018b: 14).

Thus to agree that 'some of the weaknesses originally characteristic of the lower-cost private sector are now being replicated in the much reduced cost per place public sector' (Liebling and Ludlow 2017: 489) is simply to recognise that the general crisis of the prison system tends to obliterate private/public differences, and reveal both as varieties of low-cost warehousing of inmates. The key issue is falling spending and decline in conditions across the sector. Problems no sooner break out in private prisons than they recur in public prisons.

Recent commentary on the state of prisons in England and Wales has suggested that private prisons are 47 per cent more violent in terms of assaults, and that three of the ten most violent adult prisons are in the private sector (Grierson and Duncan 2019). But this means that seven of the ten most violent prisons are in the public sector! According to the July 2019 Ministry of Justice Annual Prison Performance Ratings, all of the 16 prisons or young offender institutions given the lowest rating were in the public sector. A further 28 prisons rated 'of concern' were public sector (Ministry of Justice 2019).

Negative inspection reports and the return of Birmingham prison from G4S to the public sector has not resulted in a rejection of the private sector in plans for further prison building. The private sector, with its investment and managerial expertise, is very much a partner, and in 2019 plans for prison expansion included two private sector prisons – at HMP Glen Parva in Leicestershire and HMP Wellingborough in Northamptonshire.

However, the penetration of the private sector into the penal system is not simply a question of taking over and running whole institutions. The private sector has made considerable headway in organising the provision of services within public sector prisons. The planned expansion of HMP Berwyn at Wrexham, announced in 2015, will be public sector, but will outsource about a third of its services to the private and charity sectors, including a large industrial workshop. These developments have to be seen in the context of falling spending on the type of rehabilitation associated with the penal welfare period, in particular on education. Reductions in general staffing levels are also important obstacles to prisoners being out of their cells and able to make use of any services provided.

In 2018 the prison inspectorate found that only 16 per cent of prisoners were unlocked for the recommended ten hours per day. It is hardly surprising then that by 2018 the number of prisoners who completed 'accredited programmes', designed to improve thinking skills, had fallen by 22 per cent since 2014–15 (from 6,994 to 5,479). In addition, by 2018 there had been a decline from 2011 in the number of prisoners achieving GCSEs – 43 per cent in English and 38 per cent in Maths (Institute for Government 2018). The number of prisoners doing Open University degrees fell from 1,722 in 2010 to 1,079 in 2015 (Allison and Sloan 2015). Funding has been so tight that even private sector suppliers of education and training services turn down contracts. In 2014 the private sector welfare-to-work provider A4e pulled out of a £17 million contract to deliver education and training to prisoners in twelve London prisons on the grounds that it was unable to run the contract at a profit (Gentleman 2014). Meanwhile, for teachers themselves, the constant retendering and changes in private sector employers operating within prisons has disrupted continuity (Rogers et al. 2014).

The spread of cheap labour regimes, largely run by private companies, into the prison itself increasingly functions as a substitute for education. From April 2017, prison governors in both sectors were granted autonomy to organise work and training regimes to respond to the needs of the local labour market (see Webster 2017). This might be seen as a positive development, and indeed by no means all commercial work in prisons comes under the category of low-wage captive labour. The opening of restaurants run by prisoners and organised by the voluntary sector charity, Clinks, was a media focus a few years ago: some have won gastronomy awards in competitions with top restaurateurs (Young 2017; Williams 2019). But more characteristic may be the following:

> G4S has 400 prisoners working 40 hours a week in its six prisons, being paid next to nothing. At Altcourse prison in Liverpool, G4S works with Norpro, an engineering firm that has converted three former metal workshops into a factory floor using 25 prisoners to produce high-quality office furniture 'at an economic price'. The enterprise has apparently been 'so successful', or so cheap, that work previously done in India has been brought back to the UK and done in the prison. (Corporate Watch 2012)

The expansion of this type of 'work experience' has to be seen in the context of funding reductions for prison education in general. Of course, low-paid captive labour can be regarded as rehabilitation in the sense that it is attempting to adjust prisoners to the actual situations they will face on release, given the collapse of stable, well-paid manufacturing employment, particularly in the deprived areas where many prisons are located. This only reinforces the fact that rehabilitation as part of penal welfare was previously based on the assumption of an expanding economy of well-paid jobs. A former prisoner described the effects of the replacement of education by this type of commercial labour:

> If you are in prison and you want to get educated you will find yourself at a financial disadvantage compared to those who agree to do the mind-numbing 'work' of private companies in the prison workshops. The average wage for those partaking in full-time education is around £7 per week; whereas spending your days fitting washers onto bolts can earn you up to £30 per week. The message this sends to prisoners, a lot of whom have had very little, or no, education, is that education is pretty worthless, when, I believe, education should be a top priority in prisons. (Smith 2016)

In this case the prisoner was able to secure funding for a journalism course from a private charity. Voluntary sector groups and charities are doing their best to offset the decline in education in prisons. The system is precarious. As a recent report on the charity sector concluded: 'The relationship between the charity sector and the state has deteriorated in this area to the extent where some independent funders have pulled out of funding criminal justice charities entirely. We are at risk of losing a valuable resource to society: it cannot be taken for granted that charities will always be there to pick up the slack' (Wyld and Noble 2017: 47).

We have seen that the decline of old privatisation saw the private charity sector being taken over and modernised by a state dedicated to expanding penal welfare. In the present period, the charity sector struggles to compensate for the dismantling of penal welfare by a state devoted to neoliberal austerity.

COMPANY POWER

We have stressed that the main issue is not the different regimes of private and public sector prisons but rather their mutual reinforcement of common features as part of a regime of general decline in conditions across the prison estate. Nevertheless, the private sector has certain advantages. Obviously the opening up of the prison estate as an area for private security companies is a pure gain for private capital in terms of expanding the range of investment opportunities. To what extent the private sector is able to wield direct political power on government to expand such opportunities, particularly in the UK, is hidden as far as possible from media scrutiny. All that is directly visible is the steady movement onto the boards of private companies of retired senior police, military officers and politicians with connections in defence or criminal justice ministries.

In the US, where political lobbying is less secretive than in the UK, there is evidence of much more direct pressure. In 2009, two judges in Pennsylvania were convicted of sentencing 2,000 young people to prison in return for bribes from private prison companies (Monbiot 2009). Anita Mukherjee, referring to this and similar cases, notes that in the US private prisons are usually paid for each occupied bed, 'creating a potentially perverse incentive for them to maximize the number of occupied beds' (Mukherjee 2017: 1). She contrasts this payment system with the 'pay for performance' contracts more characteristic of the UK. Such contracts (better known in the UK as payment by results), based on indicators such as reoffending rates and inmate satisfaction, avoid such perverse incentives. However, such contracts have their own problems, as we shall see presently in the case of English probation services.

There are various other ways in which private power can be exercised. In 2011 there was evidence to suggest that the competitive tendering for new private prisons was artificially skewed in favour of the private sector by the public sector bidders being 'forced to increase the total cost of their bids by more than 21 per cent' (Doward 2011). If true, this would have given an innovative meaning to the idea of a level playing field between public and private sector prisons. It would have been clear evidence of the lobbying power of the private sector companies and an indication that the real purpose of privatisation was to carve out new areas of profitability for private capital, and would explain the apparent pressure on the public sector to increase their bid costs.

The private sector also arguably has an advantage in the way it is able to deal with failure. When, in April 2019, HMP Birmingham was returned from private management by G4S to the public sector, the company suffered some short-term reputational damage. However, apart from some financial penalties, there are advantages to the company in returning failing prisons to the public sector. In the long run, the company, unlike the state, is no longer associated with failing institutions. The result is the 'empirical fact' that many private institutions appear better than public ones, as though this was somehow the outcome of competition between the two sectors or better management on the part of the private sector.

A further factor here is that the private prison sector involves some of the biggest global security companies, whose criminal justice outsourcing work is a significant but minor part of their total global security portfolios (see Chapter 6). This gives them the flexibility to rationalise their investments by withdrawing from areas where they appear to be failing without unduly affecting their global profitability. Following the Medway STC scandal mentioned above, G4S decided to pull out of this particular area of work (see Fitzgibbon and Lea 2017). This flexibility is the other side of the coin to the process of 'lock-in' (Menz 2011), by which the state continues to issue contracts to private companies despite their previous failures because there is simply no other provider available. Both aspects testify to the enormous power of the companies.

PRIVATE PROBATION IN ENGLAND AND WALES: A STEP TOO FAR?

The part privatisation of the probation service in England and Wales is now widely regarded as a costly mistake: a privatisation too far. Our previous discussion of probation noted its emergence out of the private charity sector and gradual absorption through professionalisation and state regulation as part of the penal welfare system. The limits of the prison as a site of rehabilitation have always been acknowledged. By contrast, the image of the probation officer, under the banner of 'advise, assist and befriend', helping prisoners released on licence or sentenced directly to probation by the courts – by getting them into employment, finding them accommodation and steering them into non-criminogenic social networks and environments – was the very essence of rehabilitation. Far more offenders are placed on probation in England and Wales than go to prison: in 2018, just over 260,000 compared with 83,000 sent to prison (Ministry of Justice 2018).

The decision by the UK government in 2013 to privatise 70 per cent of the probation service in England and Wales (Scotland and Northern Ireland are devolved jurisdictions) came as something of a shock and was widely regarded as an irrational leap in the dark motivated purely by neoliberal ideology and unrelated to the solution of any conceivable problem faced by the service. Furthermore, probation officers and other experts almost unanimously predicted the failure of the project (Fitzgibbon and Lea 2014).

However, the notion of irrational, politically motivated destructive changes has limited explanatory power. There are of course differences with prison privatisation, notably that there are no private and public sector organisations dealing with the same group of offenders. The state-run National Probation Service (NPS), created at the same time, deals exclusively with high-risk offenders (around 30 per cent of the total), while the 21 privatised Community Rehabilitation Companies (CRCs) deal with the remaining 70 per cent of (lower-risk) offenders.

Practitioners and administrators alike were perplexed by the fact that the existing system appeared to be fulfilling all the tasks required of it by government. In 2011 it had been awarded the British Quality Foundation's Gold Medal for Excellence and was publicly praised for meeting all its targets (Fletcher 2013). What fewer critics grasped was that the changes which probation had undergone in the previous decade were precisely those that made the entry of the private sector possible.

Probation had changed since the 1970s in two main ways. First, penal welfare – increasingly considered 'soft' – had been replaced by tougher community sentences and a neoliberal orientation, with less emphasis on social relations and helping clients back into work, and more on individualised guidance to help them make the 'right choices' through management of 'criminogenic needs' (Fitzgibbon 2007; Hannah-Moffat 2005). Second, probation had been cut back and slimmed down through deskilling – the labour-intensive social work skills of traditional probation officers were systematically replaced by those of the offender manager. The main task of the latter was monitoring the client's risk to public security. This was increasingly done by formulaic tick-box assessments administered by semi-skilled, lower-grade probation service officers – in some ways akin to the PCSOs discussed in Chapter 4.

Insofar as the management of criminogenic needs required specialist help – such as support with drugs or alcohol addiction – this could be outsourced to charity and voluntary sector agencies which still had a repository of social work and therapeutic skills. These tasks were no longer part of the core surveillance and risk management elements of the probation service. Later they could be dispensed with altogether. That probation was already in effect making way for privatisation is illustrated by the adoption not just of tick-box assessment, but the type of technological fixes that are second nature to a Serco or Sodexo. In 2012 London probation was piloting electronic kiosks which enabled clients to log in to a terminal and respond to a series of questions to determine if their risk level had changed and whether they therefore need a face-to-face meeting with a human (Doward 2012).

But if this was already happening, what were the reasons for privatisation? Most of the early criticism of the privatisation proposals contained in the government document 'Transforming Rehabilitation' (Ministry of Justice 2013) conformed to the 'irrational ideologically-motivated' view. The House of Commons Justice Committee (House of Commons 2014a) focused on the rushed nature of the government's plan and the lack of clarity about the proposed system of payment by results for the private probation companies. Others focused on how such payment methods would combine with the fact that CRC employees would no longer have to be trained probation officers, in effect undermining the working relationship between offender managers and their clients (see Evans 2016). Such criticism was of course based on the assumption that the government intended the CRCs to provide – albeit at lower cost – existing systems of probation, rather than being oriented to the quite different goals that private profit-taking companies would prove more able to achieve.

Two such new goals can be plausibly identified. One is that of breaking the professional culture of probation. In prison privatisation a motive had certainly been to weaken the power of the union, the Professional Trades Union for Prison, and achieve wage and cost reductions. In probation the target was less the probation officers' union, the National Association of Probation Officers (NAPO), than the whole culture of professional autonomy that characterised the service. Probation, despite the breaking of the old church missionary links (see Chapter 2), never became part of the state apparatus in the same way as the police or the prison system had become, but retained strong autonomy both in terms of methods of work with offenders and relations with other criminal justice agencies (Whitehead and Crawshaw 2013; Fitzgibbon and Lea 2014). Older traditions of close personal relations between practitioners and their clients tended to reassert themselves, particularly when clients committed further offences that had not been predicted by the tick-box risk assessments (Fitzgibbon 2008; 2012). Privatisation would, in the medium term, as older practitioners retired or left the service, enable a restructuring of the labour force and a clearer focus on cost-effective surveillance and risk management of clients. Other elements of this included severely undermining the voluntary sector on which much probation work had come to depend (Wyld and Noble 2017). Considerable progress has been made in achieving this aim, as we shall see. If the task of privatisation was to destroy the last resistance of penal welfare to the neoliberal paradigm of security and surveillance, then it has made great strides.

A second aim, common to most forms of privatisation, was that of opening up further opportunities for the private sector to siphon off taxpayers' money as profit was achieved for the larger private companies which came to run the CRCs. An indicator of this was the fact that the outsourcing contracts included 'a clause under which companies are paid recompense for costs and profit if [the contract] is terminated through no fault of theirs'. According to one estimate, the contracts – initially of ten years' duration – would cost between £300 million and £400 million to cancel early if the government changed its mind on privatisation (Travis and Sayal 2014). And yet, the early termination of contracts with existing CRCs has been precisely what has happened.

PAYMENT BY RESULTS

As 'Transforming Rehabilitation' rolled out in late 2014 it was clear that, despite talk about 're-invigorating the voluntary sector', the large private security companies were the main beneficiaries. It was 'unfortunate' that two of the biggest, G4S and Serco, withdrew their bids in the context of a Serious Fraud Office investigation into alleged overcharging by these companies on outsourcing contracts for the electronic tagging of offenders dating from the mid-1990s. The result was that Sodexo and Interserve took over half of the CRCs. Other private sector companies which went on to make a name for themselves included MTCnovo, a US company, and Working Links, which also runs employment training programmes in Ireland and Saudi Arabia. Only one voluntary sector organisation was successful, and then as part of a consortium led by a large private security company. Interserve (before the company collapsed) led a consortium called Purple Futures which included Shelter, the voluntary sector organisation well known in the housing and homelessness area.

We have already encountered Sodexo as a manager of private prisons. Reference to probation on the company website breezily reiterates the classic mantras of traditional rehabilitation: 'Our teams focus on providing prisoners with the life skills, work experience, education and accommodation on release to help equip them to successfully integrate into society. We are committed to the design and practice of more effective rehabilitation' (Sodexo 2016). Such sentiments would not have been out of place in a traditional probation office 30 years ago. The Interserve website demonstrates similar presentational skills. The company is a global multinational operating in 40 countries. A 2015 press release, as the company began its work as leader of the Purple Futures consortium running five CRCs, intoned: 'We are confident in our plans and are excited to start working with our partners and our new colleagues in the CRCs to build an integrated approach to the rehabilitation of offenders. We will provide opportunities to reform for all – but always with the safety of both the public and our staff as our priority' (Interserve Press Office 2015).

Alongside the leading role of the security companies was the method of remuneration stipulated in the outsourcing contracts. Payment by results proved to be the Achilles heel of the whole structure. The 'results' involved were the seemingly simple measurement of the reoffending rate of the clients supervised by the CRCs. Even before the CRCs went into action it was obvious that, as a mechanism that had anything to do with rehabilitation, payment by results was a charade. The system obviously involved delayed payment, since the actual offending rate would have to wait until twelve months after release to see if reoffending took place. This benefitted the larger companies like Sodexo that had the funds to carry on in anticipation of payment at the end of the period. Smaller companies, and in particular voluntary sector charities – in recent years essential probation providers – were put in the unviable position of not knowing whether or how much payment they were to receive (see Albertson and Fox 2019). They faced a perverse incentive to make money by cutting costs rather than investing substantial resources in rehabilitation using traditional probation skills.

There would also be, as early critics noted (see Mulheirn 2013), an incentive simply not to report breaches of probation conditions by offenders, since to do so would increase the likelihood of reduced payments under payment by results. Finally, if the measure of success is simply the reoffending rate, why offenders desist from reoffending is no longer relevant. It may be because they have developed a new enthusiasm for worthwhile non-criminogenic activities or it may result from imbibing exotic substances sufficient to prevent them getting out of bed. It really doesn't matter. Traditional probation, moreover, would tolerate some reoffending, hopefully less serious than the original offence, as part of the offender's journey to rehabilitation. But under payment by results it is the reoffence that is measured, not the offender's 'journey'. Most of these criticisms were voiced well before privatisation, but most were vindicated as the CRCs rolled into action.

NEGATIVE SUPERVISION

Sodexo led the way in 2015 by announcing plans both to introduce the system, piloted by London Probation in 2012, of clients reporting to electronic kiosks, and at the same time to make job cuts of around 30 per cent over the following twelve months (Travis 2015). Cost-cutting measures produced a catalogue of issues. Many were revealed in a report by Gill Kirton and Cécile Guillaume (2015) of the School of Business Management at Queen Mary University, London and commissioned by NAPO. Based on interviews with a number of probation officers working in CRCs, the authors noted that 'when it comes to workplace culture, the recurrent themes were lack of inclusion, staff feeling unvalued, uncertainty, lack of consultation and low morale' (2015: 27) while 'de-professionalisation and deskilling were words frequently used ... to describe the assault that Transforming Rehabilitation has perpetrated on probation practitioners' everyday practice as well as professional identity' (2015: 38). Much of this was a result of experienced practitioners, now working in the CRCs, having to hand over their high-risk offenders to the NPS, thereby undermining their professional identity. This deskilling process was also blurring the boundaries between probation officers and the semi-skilled (and lower-paid) probation service officers. This deskilling had, as we have noted, predated privatisation, but the distinction already existing gave the CRCs a useful guide to labour force restructuring, whereby the bulk of employees would be probation service officers, with a small number of professional probation officers retained as supervisors. This process, as Kirton and Guillaume noted, had a particular effect on female probation staff: 'Overall, the deskilling and downgrading of jobs, the end of career progression and the conversion to market forces [in the CRCs] symbolises the deterioration of a professional space that had attracted many women who found probation offered non-discriminatory working conditions and career prospects' (2015: 41). Other researchers came to similar conclusions (Robinson et al. 2016; Walker et al. 2019). Either way, the results were to be expected. As a probation officer working for a CRC told one of us in an informal interview in 2016, 'they are haemorrhaging staff as nobody wants to work there anymore. It is all grades of staff but certainly probation officers and senior probation officers.' These issues, as we have said already, are symptoms of crisis only if privatisation was aimed at continuing – at lower cost – the existing traditions of rehabilitation. But if the aim is simply to reduce recorded reoffending rates, these are not really problems. There are numerous ways of achieving statistical reductions in reoffending rates without the time-consuming and costly paraphernalia of penal welfare.

Meanwhile the CRCs, irrespective of the optimism of their websites, were honing their skills in developing an entirely new regime: what we might call 'negative supervision', or even 'social control by neglect', of the marginalised poor who had long ceased to be conditional citizens in any meaningful sense. This was becoming evident by 2016, when negative supervision was making itself felt in a number of ways. A report by HM Inspectorate of Probation (HMIP) found that offenders were in some cases not being returned to court after violating their probation conditions, such as committing a further offence. 'A number of responsible officers said that they had been told not to recommend "revoke and resentence", because it would lead to a financial penalty for the CRC' (HM Inspectorate of Probation 2016: 20). Traditional probation might have taken a similar decision, but for totally different reasons, namely that the offender was otherwise making good progress towards rehabilitation. But this would rely on high-quality supervision. As long as the existing body of relatively well-trained probation officers remained in post this could be the case. But the direction of travel was clear. In its 2017 Annual Report, HMIP noted that,

> in those cases we inspected, only a handful of individuals had received any real help with housing, jobs or an addiction, let alone managing debt or getting back into education or training ... we find that CRCs we have inspected are making little material difference to the prospects of individuals upon release, and yet this work is so important in breaking the cycle of offending. (HM Inspectorate of Probation 2017: 17)

Meanwhile, accounts emerged of offenders being 'supervised' by text message or phone calls; when they did meet their supervisors, it was in overcrowded offices with no privacy or even in public libraries (Brewer 2017).

The emergence of this new system of de facto negative supervision created friction. Despite alleged attempts by CRCs to avoid too many breach reports, the number of offenders returning to prison increased, while the loss of confidence by the courts in private probation was reflected in a decline in non-custodial sentences in England and Wales

(Bowcott 2018). The number of further offences by probation clients also increased (Morris 2017).

A further important indicator of negative supervision was the way the privatisation arrangements could not have been better designed for the task of killing off the role of the voluntary charity sector where, as we have noted, a good part of the professional expertise and patience in working with offenders now resides. Talking to us in 2016, a probation officer working for the London CRC commented on the decline in referrals to voluntary agencies:

> Not referring people because it costs money. So what exactly are they doing? I don't know what they're doing. What work are they doing? Because it's just tick boxes, people come in, are you okay? Yes, fine, bye bye, because I've got another person to see after you, I've got another person. So there's no rehabilitation, there's no ... people don't even have time to build relationships with their clients.

In its original propaganda surrounding the launch of 'Transforming Rehabilitation', the government had highlighted the role of the voluntary charity sector (or 'third sector') alongside the private security companies as a sort of partnership. But in the Foreword to a 2018 HMIP report on 'probation supply chains' the chief inspector of probation, Glenys Stacey, summed up the situation as it had actually evolved:

> with the government's 2014 Transforming Rehabilitation initiative came a new expectation: that the third sector would play a key role in probation services. Almost four years on, this expectation has not been realised. It seems that the third sector is less involved than ever in probation services, despite its best efforts ... CRCs are generally providing an insufficient range of services. (HM Inspectorate of Probation 2018: 5)

This was down to the fact that 'All CRC owners were concerned about the financial instability and viability of their own contracts with the Ministry of Justice' (HM Inspectorate of Probation 2018: 26). There is a similar dynamic at work explaining the declining role of the voluntary sector in prisons. The conclusions of the voluntary sector NGO report cited above (Wyld and Noble 2017) applies equally to both sectors.

The situation as it was developing reflected less the dysfunctional nature of a privately run system attempting to preserve older ideas of probation and rehabilitation, than the transition to a new system of negative supervision based on minimal contact between probation staff and clients. Only those who present a real threat to public security (violent offenders, traffickers, terrorists) need any type of sophisticated response. The rest – deprived of social citizenship – can be subject to occasional telephone or other technological surveillance and left to wander in the urban 'wild zones', the warehouses for the poor and marginalised. If they seriously reoffended they could be returned to the walled warehouse of the prison. But this would not be a failure of probation, more a rational reallocation of the offender to the appropriate warehouse (see Worrall 2008).

THE PROFITS CRISIS

The whole system moved rapidly towards crisis point because the profit and payment systems were not properly worked out. Payment by results, as explained earlier, is a system of delayed payment. While larger companies like Sodexo could wait for the reoffending rates of their clients to be calculated, smaller concerns ended up owing money to the government. Added to this, reoffending rates had been rising since privatisation. In fact, by 2018 only two CRCs had achieved a sufficient decline in reoffending rates to receive payments (Albertson and Fox 2019). In addition, the reduced use of community sentences by the courts (see above) meant that original workload estimates on which the private companies had based their bids were unrealistic. This fuelled a vicious circle of further cost-cutting measures to retain profitability, which then further enhanced negative supervision and further reduced the reputation of CRCs as effective probation providers.

By the beginning of 2018 it was acknowledged by the Ministry of Justice that 14 of the CRCs expected losses ranging from £2.3 million to £43 million by 2021–2. Even some of the large providers like MTCnovo and Interserve were starting to think about pulling out if the payment mechanisms were not adjusted. The head of Interserve Justice told the House of Commons Justice Committee in 2017: 'The payment mechanism is not working as was intended ... Our workload is going up, but our payment is going down ... It is not sustainable.' Pulling out 'will be an option on the table that will have to be considered' (House of Commons 2017). The CEO of MTCnovo at the same session voiced similar sentiments, but before such a move could be considered, the company collapsed.

In fact there were two collapses in quick succession. In early 2019, Working Links, which ran three CRCs in Wales and Dorset, Devon and Cornwall, and other areas of the west of England, went into administration. Financial losses had been mounting – over £2 million for Wales and £1.5 million for Devon and Cornwall (BBC 2019). The collapse followed a scathing HMIP inspection in February 2019 of the Dorset CRC, which concluded that the organisation 'is not delivering probation services to anywhere near the standards we and the public expect' (HM Inspectorate of Probation 2019a: 4). The inspectors found that 'all grades of staff believe that services delivered by the CRC are driven exclusively by financially linked contractual targets ... 94 per cent of staff surveyed stated that the CRC does not prioritise the quality of service delivered' (HM Inspectorate of Probation 2019a: 13). Alarmingly, 'in too many cases' sentence plans for offenders were 'based on little or no face-to-face contact ... In almost half of the cases, we found insufficient evidence of service user views being taken into account' (HM Inspectorate of Probation 2019a: 20). The Dorset inspection was followed by a similar report on the Gloucestershire CRC part of the Working Links organisation. Interserve went into administration in March 2019. Quite apart from its activities in the probation area, the company held thousands of government outsourcing contracts, particularly for building maintenance in local government, housing and education. Interserve was in fact the second major collapse of a government building infrastructure outsourcer, closely following Carillion in June 2018.

There are two aspects of these collapses worth noting. First, the role of overseas-based hedge funds – speculative financial organisations seeking high return on borrowed capital – in deciding the fate of CRCs. Crucial in the collapse of Interserve was the US fund, Coltrane, which owned 27 per cent of the company and vetoed a shareholder rescue plan (Brady 2019). Working Links was acquired in 2016 by a German-based financial company, Aurelius, which also invests in private healthcare in the UK. Around the same time as the Working Links collapse, Aurelius announced it was selling its remaining public sector outsourcing activities in the UK. Unlike giants such as G4S – although scale of course brings its own problems – smaller and medium-sized companies financially backed by hedge funds capable of pulling out at a moment's notice increase the vulnerability of key sections of the criminal justice system to decisions made by speculative international finance. That the treatment of probation clients from poor, marginalised communities could be so directly dependent on global finance capital seems like some sort of leftist fantasy. But here it is clearly laid out for anyone taking the trouble to look.

A second aspect of note is that, seemingly in contravention of all market logic, public sector outsourcing companies on the verge of collapse were still receiving large government contracts funded by the taxpayer despite having issued profit warnings. Such events could be interpreted in a number of ways: inadequate monitoring of public contracts by inexperienced civil servants, a malevolent desire to subsidise the companies with taxpayers' money come what may or the fact that these companies have become so essential to government activity that there are no alternatives to continue funding them even when in financial trouble. This final point parallels situations in which large private security companies – G4S and Serco, to be precise – continued to receive outsourcing contracts despite manifest incompetence and suspicion of fraud.

THE RESCUE PLAN: MORE OF THE SAME?

In 2018 the Ministry of Justice was starting to bail out the CRCs, to the tune of £342 million for the period up until 2021–2 (Travis 2018). This could not go on. In July 2018 the government announced that in Wales the entire probation system would revert to the public sector: offenders of all risk levels would be managed by the NPS. Government also announced that the existing CRC ten-year contracts would be cut short by two years and end in 2020. This, as we noted above, would carry substantial financial costs. Then, in early 2019, Glenys Stacey, in her last report as chief inspector of probation, declared the system basically unfit for purpose:

> there has been a deplorable diminution of the probation profession and a widespread move away from practice informed by evidence. This is largely due to the impact of commerce, and contracts that treat probation as a transactional business. Professional ethics can buckle under such pressures, and the evidence we have is that this has happened to some extent. (HM Inspectorate of Probation 2019b: 3)

She called for a rethink and took a swipe at the whole system of outsourced contracts: 'It will be virtually impossible to deal with these issues if most probation supervision continues to be provided by different organisations, under contract. I urge the government to consider carefully the future model for probation services' (HM Inspectorate of Probation 2019b: 17).

In May 2019, the Ministry of Justice announced a new scheme. The NPS will become responsible for the monitoring of all offenders in eleven new probation regions in England and Wales. But in each area the NPS will have an 'innovation partner' in the form of a private company or voluntary sector organisation to which various services will be outsourced, such as drug rehabilitation and supervised unpaid work. Whether this will reproduce the fragmentation which characterises the existing system remains to be seen.

As a lesson in the dangers of over-hasty, ideologically motivated privatisation, the failure of the English probation privatisation project might be clear. However, concerns remain as to how far the restoration of a unified system run by the NPS will do anything to restore the traditional relationship between probation officers and their clients. Even if private probation is to be abandoned as an unsuccessful experiment, a privatisation too far, the trend towards negative supervision is likely to continue: the social control of the marginalised poor simply no longer requires penal welfare but rather warehousing, surveillance and risk management.

THE DIFFUSION OF CONTROL

The dynamic of negative supervision becomes even clearer as we follow the expansion of the punishment system outside the traditional boundaries of the penal system to the management of wider populations increasingly surplus to the requirements of global capitalism. In the most acutely deprived urban regions of the global north, the socially and politically marginalised precariat, victims of the decline of the welfare state and of stable employment, meet the asylum seeker and illegal migrant, victims of global imperialism and ecological destruction. These populations are decreasingly controlled and socialised through the institutions of work, citizenship and penal welfare, and increasingly by the expansion of punitive risk management based on surveillance and pre-emptive criminalisation (De Giorgi 2006; Fitzgibbon 2004). The precariat is managed by the combination of a punitive 'workfare' system of social benefits conditional on adaptation to low-wage labour combined with warehousing and negative supervision in the penal system. Loïc Wacquant (2010) termed this the combination of workfare and 'prisonfare'.

The illegal migrant and asylum seeker is increasingly pre-criminalised on arrival in the UK, as trespasser rather than refugee. This tendency increased after the post-2011 upsurge in migration resulting from conflicts in the Middle East, and has continued despite a reduction in numbers by 2018 (see Matevžič 2019). It has continued to raise human rights issues (Bhui et al. 2018). Immigration, other than that specified by membership of the European Union or the acquisition of an appropriate work permit, has become something of an 'ontological crime' (De Giorgi 2006: 124), derived from the status of migrants as such, rather than any particular criminal activity. This is the extreme point of the collapse of any notion of citizenship, both legal and social. Most refugees and asylum seekers who manage to secure residence in the UK will join the precariat, while those that slip through the net of migration controls will work in the informal and illegal economies: all will live in the most insecure and deprived parts of towns and cities, the urban wild zones.

Migrants denied asylum or immigration status are destined for deportation from the UK and, as in other states with similar regulations, this extends the boundaries of the system of punishment. Punishment and migration have become interconnected in various ways as when, for example, deportation is a punishment for crimes committed by foreign nationals as well as migrants whose refugee and asylum claim has been refused. Thus, 'the punishment of foreigners seeks to return people to where they "belong"' (Bosworth et al. 2018: 43). But there is a world of difference between deporting someone from China or India who has overstayed their visa, and deporting a migrant from a state in sub-Saharan Africa or the war-torn chaos of the Middle East. Respect for the human rights of migrants is, rather like international law in general, based on the mutual interests of states. The UK will treat migrants from other states humanely on the assumption that other states will reciprocally uphold the rights of migrants from the UK. But where the area from which the migrants originate is effectively denied the status of a legitimate state, and its inhabitants not really regarded as citizens (see Chapter 3), then this reciprocity ceases to exist and migrants join the outer periphery of 'unpersons'. This 'othering' process is heavily overdetermined by the dense traditions of colonialism and racism. It is this double denial of citizenship that has aided the outsourcing of the management of migrants to the private sector and from where some of the most offensive treatment of individuals by the employees of private companies in recent years seems to have originated.

The main institutions concerned with the deportation of migrants are the immigration removal centres (IRCs). There are a total of eight of these and all but one are run by the private sector. The main centres are at Heathrow Airport, run by a company called Mitie which also runs the Campsfield House IRC in Oxfordshire; and Brook House and Tinsely House at Gatwick Airport, which are run by G4S. The contract for the IRCs at Gatwick was due to end in 2018 but has been extended to 2020. Yarl's Wood in Bedfordshire is run by Serco. Moreton Hall in Lincolnshire is run by HM Prison and Probation Service. There is no statutory limit to the length of adult detention in IRCs. There are also a number of 'short-term holding facilities'. In terms of numbers, around 2,500 people are detained, without trial or time limit, in the IRCs at any point. In 2017, a total of 27,231 people were detained, of whom 23,272 were men. In the same year, just under half of the detainees (13,173) were actually deported; the rest – over half – were bailed or released (see Corporate Watch 2018). What we have here is imprisonment without trial, a pure form of warehousing, followed either by release or deportation. The fact that such a high proportion were released or bailed attracted criticism from the House of Commons Home Affairs Committee report on Immigration Detention of March 2019, which was 'concerned about the fact that more than half of the people being detained in the year to December 2018 were simply released again, raising important questions over whether the power to detain is being used appropriately' (House of Commons 2019a: 15).

What concerns us here is the involvement of the private security companies in areas in which standards, including respect for human rights, seem to have deteriorated. There have in recent years been a number of incidents at IRCs, revealed mainly by investigative journalists, indicating serious human rights violations. This is not exactly unexpected, given what we have already said about negative supervision. Even more than probation clients, immigration detainees are literally non-citizens, destined to be removed, and therefore located at the outer periphery of permissible neglect. Just as in probation there is still a theoretical commitment to some notion of rehabilitation, so in IRCs there is a theoretical commitment to respect for human rights. Also as in probation, it is the inspectorates – assisted in the case of immigration detention by investigative journalists – who shine the light on areas of neglect that would otherwise lie beyond public knowledge. But inspectors, parliamentary committees or journalists cannot run the system; they can only expose particular injustices and sound the alarm, hoping that it will be heard.

Several cases of harm inflicted by the employees of private security companies running IRCs have achieved publicity in recent years. Three in particular stand out. In what is still probably one of the most well-known cases involving G4S, in October 2010 Jimmy Mubenga, a 46-year-old detainee, was killed by G4S guards subcontracted to the United Kingdom Border Agency (UKBA, reorganised as Border Force in 2013). He became agitated as he was forcibly put on a flight to Angola and the three guards responded by handcuffing him behind his back, which resulted in eventual cardio-respiratory collapse.

The behaviour of the G4S employees was not that surprising. It is a familiar story of a badly trained, unvetted, high-turnover labour force. The journalist Clare Sambrook, who has closely followed the global activities of the company, claimed that 'time and again racist, misogynist and otherwise dangerous people have slipped through the company's own screening process and been given power over vulnerable people. Repeatedly the company's readiness to act in response to warnings has been found wanting' (Sambrook 2016). What is interesting about this tragic case is, however, the behaviour of the authorities and the way it illustrates one of our basic arguments in this book: that the conditions created by the private security companies running outsourced coercive state activities are enabled and reinforced by the state itself.

The initial response to the Mubenga case was that the Crown Prosecution Service (CPS – the prosecutor in England and Wales) cited 'lack of sufficient evidence' as a reason not to pursue the case. During a House of Lords debate on UKBA in 2012, the former chief inspector of prisons, Lord David Ramsbotham, called such a decision 'perverse'. In the same debate the Liberal Democrat peer, Lord John Alderdice associated the behaviour of the G4S employees closely with the attitudes of UKBA itself. He said that a senior person involved with UKBA had told him: 'It's the culture of the agency. The whole approach within it is abusive and it's all about keeping people out.' Lord Alderdice continued: 'We have a serious problem. People become like those with whom they live and work. The UK Border Agency has not just employed G4S; it has become like G4S and it has the same challenge' (House of Lords 2012).

Meanwhile, in 2011, the jury at the coroner's inquest into the Mubenga death returned a verdict of unlawful killing and this – since an inquest jury operates to the same standards of proof as a criminal trial jury, namely beyond reasonable doubt – put sufficient pressure on the CPS to resume the criminal prosecution in 2014. However, rather than prosecute the company, G4S – which had been responsible for employing, vetting and training the guards whose actions led to Mr Mubenga's death – it was only the guards themselves who were prosecuted. In this way, whatever the intentions, the state acted to legitimise G4S and confirm it as a worthy subcontractor for coercive state activities. Prosecuting only the employees directly involved in the Mubenga case paralleled the efforts of the company to present itself as legitimate and competent and quite able to deal with bad apples or rogue elements that had somehow crept into its employ.

But even this attempted whitewash fell apart. In 2014, the three guards were cleared of manslaughter after a six-week trial. A feature of the trial was the refusal by the judge to admit as evidence dozens of 'grossly offensive and undoubtedly racist' text messages on the phones of two of the guards on the grounds that they did not have 'any real relevance' to the trial (Booth 2014). The evidence of racist texts – withheld from the criminal trial jury – came from a report on the inquest case by the assistant deputy coroner, Karon Monaghan QC. Among other things, she revealed not only that the Home Office accreditation of one of the guards escorting Mubenga onto the aircraft had expired, and he therefore had no authority, but also that this was not an oversight but rather 'formed part of a practice agreed between G4S and the UK Border Agency', a practice which 'had as its purpose and effect the informal authorisation of unaccredited G4S staff to carry out custodial functions and the removal of detainees from the UK' (Monaghan 2013: 11). It can be argued that the racist texts showed what sort of labour force G4S was recruiting worldwide (see Sambrook 2016), and the covert agreement between the company and UKBA illustrated the point about the symbiotic relationship between state and private security made by Lord Alderdice in the House of Lords, a point which goes to the heart of the whole issue of state outsourcing of coercive powers.

A further case which achieved a degree of media prominence concerned events at Serco-run Yarl's Wood. This IRC holds around 300 people, mainly women, with disputed immigration status who can therefore be detained without a defined time limit. The pointlessness of this is illustrated by the fact that almost three-quarters of inmates are eventually returned to the community in the UK. In March 2015, a Channel 4 undercover documentary made allegations concerning sexual abuse of female inmates by male staff. The documentary was followed by no less than five independent reviews. A 2017 review by HM Chief Inspector of Prisons (2017) indicated various improvements in conditions, yet by 2019 there were still significant levels of complaint, and demands to close the institution altogether (Parkar 2019).

Similar allegations of degrading treatment at the hands of private security employees were the main feature of the most recent high-profile case, the G4S-run IRC at Brook House near Gatwick Airport. Again, the institution came to prominence as a result of investigative journalism. On 4 September 2017, a BBC *Panorama* documentary, based on undercover reportage by a G4S detainee custody officer, revealed serious physical and verbal abuse of detainees by staff in an atmosphere of general chaos: 'people abusing drugs, dealing drugs, self-harming, fighting. And the staff, they can't cope, they can't manage with what's happening in the centre' (Holt 2017). The programme provoked a number of reports into both Brook House and the whole issue of immigrant detention, and the relationship between the Home Office and the private sector.

G4S itself commissioned an independent report which, notwithstanding company sponsorship, identified some key issues. First, a combination of failure of senior managers to visit the facility to get a clear picture of the situation, lack of proper on-the-job training and work pressures due to staff shortages leading to high levels of absenteeism and high staff turnover, with many leaving shortly after finishing training (Lampard and Marsden 2018: 120). But, as the *Panorama* investigation pointed out, it is precisely these circumstances that turn some staff in the direction of violence towards detainees. 'People can't cope and hand in their notice, but others become immune to the pain and suffering they see. Some turn to the other side and take part in the abuse' (Holt 2017).

The other theme in the G4S report, echoing the Monaghan report on the Mubenga case, was the relationship between the company and the Home Office. Although G4S staff were monitored by Home Office managers, the latter acknowledged that this 'tended to be based on consideration of the individual elements of contract performance and compliance and that they had not taken an approach that examined and questioned the wider concerns of the care and welfare of detainees, their quality of life and experience of being detained in Brook House' (Lampard and Marsden 2018: 31). For all prisons and similar facilities there exist independent monitoring boards (IMBs) of voluntary lay members who make regular inspections. Lampard and Marsden attended one such meeting at Brook House and were 'struck … by a sense of collegiality between the IMB and G4S and a tendency on the part of IMB members to over-empathise with the G4S management team and the Home Office, rather than to hold them vigorously to account' (Lampard and Marsden 2018: 235). These criticisms were endorsed by the House of Commons Home Affairs Committee Report of March 2019 on events at Brook House in particular and immigration detention in general, which concluded that: 'It is clear from the evidence we heard that the Home Office has utterly failed in its responsibilities to oversee and monitor the safe and humane detention of individuals in the UK' (House of Commons 2019a: 86). A further factor was that G4S were allegedly discussing profit levels from the running of Brook House in excess of the 20 per cent stipulated in the outsourcing contract (House of Commons 2019a: 86). In July 2019, the government National Audit Office, noting that G4S had made a gross profit of £14 million from its contract to run Brook House, reiterated concerns that 'it is worrying that the normal contract monitoring and incident reports did not communicate the gravity of what was shown by the documentary' (National Audit Office 2019).

Several issues arise out of these inquiries. A key theme in our argument has been that the decline of penal welfare is not simply the result of outsourcing to the private sector but also what makes it possible in the first place. We saw this most clearly illustrated in the case of English probation. From this standpoint the collusion of the Home Office and the private contractor in immigration detention should come as no surprise: in particular that the Home Office oversight was narrowly focused on contract compliance rather than the welfare of detainees. The process of working to the contract to the exclusion of anything not explicitly specified – such as 'behave at all times in a humane way' – is a process we have seen in a number of contexts. With immigration detention, where the outsourcing contract stipulates secure detention and removal, rather than care and welfare, the latter can become casualties. This occurs in a similar way in the last example of outsourcing in this area that we consider: asylum housing.

ASYLUM HOUSING

Migrants seeking permanent asylum in the UK as refugees are, under the 1991 Immigration and Asylum Act, eligible for support while their claim is being adjudicated. This includes housing and this is another area – and the final one we shall deal with in this book – in which the private sector is heavily involved. Even a brief glance at recent developments in the area of asylum housing in the UK clearly illustrates how privatisation provides not an alternative regime to that of the state but helps extend the latter's authoritarian management of the poor and marginalised.

Prior to the entry of the private security companies into the management of asylum housing, local authorities took the lead in liaising with both the Home Office and voluntary sector providers. Obviously, from a welfare perspective oriented towards the socio-economic integration of refugees and asylum seekers, local authorities and voluntary agencies would be expected to play the leading role. They could be expected to know more about the state of the local housing stock, the structure of the local community and how to secure welfare resources than Serco or G4S. But if the asylum population is seen simply as a potential security risk, pending expulsion from the country, to be warehoused in the same way as other risky populations, then the Home Office and a private security sector with experience in guarding and surveillance rather than welfare and social integration is a better combination. The private sector housing providers obviously have to apply to local authorities for available housing in which to place and 'manage' the asylum seeker population, though joint private sector and Home Office pressure on a local authority can be decisive (see Darling 2016a: 238).

The private sector became involved in 2012, when the Home Office outsourced the management of asylum housing under a scheme known as Commercial and Operating Managers Procuring Asylum Support (COMPASS) with G4S, Serco and Clearel. The aim was to save money. The key relationship now became that between the private security companies and the Home Office, governed by the outsourcing contracts. Asylum housing, managed by the private security sector, became the means of constructing a system of 'dispersed incarceration' of asylum seekers insulated from any local residues of welfare and socio-political integration.

The House of Commons Home Affairs Committee reported on the situation in 2018 and early 2019, and noted the complaints from local authorities regarding marginalisation from decision making regarding housing allocation. The report went on to affirm that 'local authority responsibilities for safeguarding, providing education and other public services ... managing community impacts and preventing destitution mean that they have a very clear interest in the progress of the contracting process' (House of Commons 2018: 11). It also noted the rationale of the Home Office for marginalising local government. This was firstly on the grounds of commercial confidentiality of the contracts with the private companies, and secondly because involvement of local authorities in the decision-making process would 'reduce the accountability of the Home Office and the ability to hold Providers to account' (House of Commons 2018: 15). So the marginalisation of the local democratic process is a more or less direct consequence of the organisation of outsourcing. As local authorities became marginalised so they began to lose their expertise in refugee matters and easily found themselves in the position of not wanting to be involved in asylum housing (Darling 2016b).

Meanwhile the marginalisation of the voluntary and charity sector was not surprising. As we saw in the case of privatised probation, private security companies may be reluctant to purchase any services, particularly of a social work or welfare nature, not strictly dictated by the terms of their contracts with the Home Office for the provision and maintenance of asylum housing. But how far these contracts have been adhered to in any meaningful sense is another matter. Journalists have unearthed numerous examples of atrocious rat-infested conditions of much asylum housing in various parts of the UK: conditions that would be seen as a crisis from a welfare and human rights standpoint. 'The management of the asylum housing contracts has attracted national controversy, with issues including some asylum seekers being required to wear coloured armbands in Cardiff and their homes being easily identifiable because their front doors were painted a uniform red' (Travis 2017).

Yet surprisingly little appears to have been done by the private companies, even when conditions were brought to their attention. 'Carole showed me letters from her doctor, her health visitor, her play scheme organiser, all asking Serco to move her and Nathan. "The man from Serco comes, once or twice a week. He says he reports everything but people above him do nothing"' (Grayson 2018). Such problems were given official recognition in the inspection of asylum housing by the independent chief inspector of borders and immigration in 2018, who revealed massive non-compliance with acceptable standards (see Bolt 2018), and by the House of Commons Home Affairs Committee, which concluded in the same year that 'essential improvements to accommodation are proving hard to secure, and providers who are failing in their contractual responsibilities are not being held to account' (House of Commons 2018: 21).

Under such pressure, the government announced that it was going to be 'creating a more tripartite relationship between the Home Office, local authorities and asylum accommodation providers' (House of Commons 2019b: 1). The result in 2019 has been a new Asylum Accommodation and Support Services Contract. But, as with the crisis in private probation, there is no suggestion that the private sector is to be marginalised. It is true that the configuration is changing; G4S is no longer a provider in this area. But in January 2019 Serco was awarded a £1.9 billion contract to run asylum housing in north-west England, the Midlands and the east of England. This is the largest ever such contract (Serco 2019). The details of the contracts being issued are not yet known, but it is unlikely that matters will return to the old model in which local authorities and the voluntary sector took the lead.

6

Towards a Private State?

In the preceding chapters we have tried to describe the historical and political dynamics of privatisation processes – admittedly mostly focused on the British, or even English case. Our aim has been to move beyond a perspective that sees the rise of the private sector in recent years purely as a matter of financial economy. We have sought to set current developments in a wider perspective and to understand why the earlier decline of privatisation has been reversed. The issue then becomes how to understand the social and political changes underpinning that reversal. Indeed, the focus on cost might simply reflect the political fact that the neoliberal post-welfare state wishes to spend as little as possible on the poor, who are seen increasingly as failed consumers rather than as fellow citizens.

The long lead-up to the welfare state and corporate liberalism was, as we have seen, a period of decline in private involvement, both domestically, in the process of criminal justice, and internationally, in the decline of private war. The expanding state had to seek legitimacy with regard to the mass of the population and to other sovereign states in the international order. The fact that neither in armed conflict nor criminal justice was there any place for the private sector had little to do with a financial calculation of what was cheapest, but rather was embedded in a political analysis of what was legitimate. Any discussion of costs of particular developments – expanding the army, building more prisons – took place within these constraints.

With the decline of corporate liberalism – the simultaneous decline of the welfare state and the post-Second World War system of ordered relations between sovereign states – conditions favourable to the privatisation of state coercive tasks returned. Domestically, the optimistic perspective on economic growth and social cohesion was replaced by economic stagnation, social fragmentation and growing inequality. The marginalisation of the poor has weakened the concept of social citizenship and created a space for the expansion of the private sector in the areas of policing and penal control. Neoliberalism has functioned as an ideology that both condemns the 'excesses' of the welfare state period and celebrates the necessity for private responsibility and private enterprise in the solution of social problems. It has created fertile ground for the resurgence of a private sector in welfare and criminal justice. Meanwhile, internationally, the decline in respect for the legitimate sovereignty of states, the re-emergence of non-state groups as major actors in armed conflict and the weakening economic and defence capacities of some states in the global south has created similarly fertile conditions for the resurgence of private military and mercenary groups.

But in which direction are we heading? It is clear that the private security industry is expanding and is becoming an increasingly powerful actor. First, based on our discussion in the preceding chapters, we need to draw together some of the dynamics of private sector power. Then we can attempt to assess the potential for the private sector to become an agent of the state and what form this might take – from the resurrection of the East India Company and a complete corporate sovereignty to more plausible combinations or 'assemblages' of the state and the private sector.

THE INCREASING POWER AND STATUS OF THE PRIVATE SECURITY INDUSTRY

There are two sides to the increasing power of the private security industry. One is the shrinking of the state and its increased dependence on the industry for carrying out what were previously considered state or inherently governmental functions. The other is the dominance of large private corporations such as G4S and Serco (in the UK) to the extent that they begin to exercise monopoly power in contractual relations with the state.

The general neoliberal predilection for a smaller state, more clearly focused on coercion rather than social solidarity and cohesion, has brought about a profound change in the nature of the state bureaucracy – the civil service. The reasonably competent body, capable of a degree of rational inquiry and organisation of social planning, which built and sustained the welfare state and the criminal justice reforms mentioned in earlier chapters, has been slimmed down so that this body itself is now highly dependent on, and closely interacting with, the private sector. It is interesting to note that both the early growth and recent debilitation of the civil service have had close associations with the private sector. The Trevelyan reforms, briefly mentioned in Chapter 2, were due in no small measure to the pioneering bureaucracy of the East India Company. Recent reforms have taught the civil service to emulate the 'efficiency' of the modern corporate enterprise. The difference is of course that the East India Company was indeed a state, a form of corporate sovereignty, with traditions of (colonial) public administration, whereas the private sector today is focused mainly on efficient market domination and profit-taking.

At the end of the 1970s, the Thatcher governments destroyed the older traditions of the civil service in favour of a 'new, neoliberal policy regime that was and is more brazenly willing to dissemble, more indifferent to evidence, more aggressive towards critics and distinctly less accountable ... Cynicism, we realise, is a necessary condition of neoliberal democracy' (Leys 2006: 3–4; see also Marquand 2004). Increasingly, career advancement required de facto political compliance as the Trevelyan tradition of civil service independence gave way to political control. Part of this was the rise of 'policy-led evidence' whereby civil servants and their researchers in evaluations of government policy proposals subordinated themselves uncritically to political leadership, such that 'few use available evidence that challenges the contemporary distribution of power' (Stevens 2011: 250). This might explain the evidence-free proposals for English probation privatisation in 2013 and the fact that the bureaucrats at the Ministry of Justice were incapable of preventing – despite warnings from senior practitioners – a policy that proved something of a disaster.

Under the impact of neoliberal ideology, continued into the New Labour governments of Tony Blair, the size of the civil service reduced considerably, from 534,000 in 2004 to 409,000 by December 2018 (see Civil Service Numbers 2019). At the same time secondments of civil servants to private companies, and employees from the latter to the civil service, increased. The government Civil Service Reform Plan of 2012 saw the service as becoming 'smaller and more strategic' (HM Government 2012: 11) and with a greater emphasis on secondments to 'increase dynamism and flexibility by making it easier for staff at all levels to move between the Civil Service and the private sector' (HM Government 2012: 14). This process was enormously increased by the retraction of the state sector to core competences and the turn towards outsourcing to private providers. So, for example, government departments such as the Ministry of Justice naturally have personnel seconded from criminal justice agencies such as the police, prison and probation services. As elements of these were privatised it became natural to absorb seconded personnel from the private providers. A written ministerial answer to a parliamentary question in 2016 showed there were five staff working at the Ministry of Justice on secondment from the private sector CRCs (Ministry of Justice 2017).

The debilitation of the civil service is directly relevant to outsourcing to the private sector in another way. A weak state is not in a position to drive hard bargains with the private companies to which it outsources. The incompetence of the civil servants in designing and then monitoring the outsourcing contracts to private security companies benefits the latter. As we saw in the case of prison and probation privatisation, the system of payment by results is a core ingredient of outsourcing contracts. In 2015 the UK National Audit Office reported on these payment systems – not just in the criminal justice system but across the public sector. The report concluded that:

> neither the Cabinet Office nor HM Treasury currently monitors how PbR [payment by results] is operating across government. Nor is there a systematic collection or evaluation of information about how effectively PbR is working. Without a central repository of knowledge and a strong evidence base to refer to, PbR schemes may be poorly designed and implemented and commissioners are in danger of 'reinventing the wheel' for each new scheme. If PbR is used inappropriately or is executed badly, the credibility of a potentially valuable mechanism may be undermined. (Morse 2015: 8)

The report suggests that the state did not understand the mechanisms whereby it was organising major outsourcing contracts: private companies were going to enjoy easy pickings. The reduction in the number and competence of civil service administrators obviously increases the power of the private sector both in initial negotiations and in the monitoring of contract compliance. Alongside this, the reductions in the size of the relevant state agencies, part of the concentration on core competences and outsourcing secondary aspects, automatically increase the power of the private sector, the more so when the distinction between core and secondary aspects is itself blurred.

There have been similar reductions in the particular state institutions concerned with force. Prison officer numbers have fallen in recent years

(17,000 staff left between 2012 and 2016) with an alarming number of senior managers quitting the service (Yeung 2018). The decline in police numbers in England and Wales in recent years appears to be substantial: from a peak of 144,353 in 2009 to 122,859 in 2016, although from the 1970s up to 2009 the numbers had been rising (see Garside 2015). But more interesting is the reason for cuts, namely a sharpening focus on the relations between the number of police and the crime rate. Crime statistics had shown a fall in most types of crime since the mid-1990s until quite recently, and this was the main justification for cuts. Even with recent rises in certain types of violence the argument about police numbers is still tied to crime levels. In the middle of recent rises in knife crime, causing considerable public alarm, the Prime Minister Theresa May (a former home secretary) insisted that there was 'no direct correlation between certain crimes and police numbers' (see Weaver and Pidd 2019). What this indicates, of course, is the final death of the older argument (discussed in Chapter 4) that the police exercised an important symbolic role in public space, a role that naturally, by ensuring social stability, would act as a form of crime prevention.

From time to time the desirability of police officers patrolling neighbourhoods is raised, as well as the difficulty of such activities with falling officer numbers. But this is usually seen in terms of intelligence gathering rather than contributing more generally to social cohesion. The retreat of police to the status of a 'fire brigade' response to calls from the public, together with controversial stop-and-search operations, point to a focused and narrow role for police. It will be argued that much of the patrolling and community relations work can be offloaded to PCSOs who, unlike private security guards, carry at least some residual elements of the traditional status of police officers.

Cuts in the number of soldiers are less statistically controversial. In Chapter 3 we noted reductions in military manpower in both the US and UK forces. By 2010 Peter Singer could report that as far as US military operations were concerned, 'it is becoming clear that a sort of dependency syndrome has set in, where the Pentagon cannot carry out many of its most basic public responsibilities without [private] firms' (Singer 2010). In 2018 the UK National Audit Office reported UK armed forces at '8,200 (5.7 per cent) below their requirement – the largest gap in recent years' (Morse 2018: 5). By January 2019 this had widened to a 7.6 per cent deficit, but in particular areas, notably front-line troops, there was a 20 per cent shortfall. This produced criticism of the private sector company

Capita, to which the army had outsourced its recruitment process in 2012, and whose performance had been criticised as 'shambolic and chaotic' (Perraudin 2019). Capita, it is reported, completely missed its recruitment targets and failed to deliver the financial savings envisaged in the original contract (Bond 2018). Military outsourcing to specialist private companies has tended to shift towards 'an interdependence between the state and a limited number of large companies – and a potential threat to the efficiencies being sought' (Hesketh 2018).

LOCK-IN

This brings us to the other side of the increasing power of the private security industry. It is one thing for military, police or penal systems to depend on outsourced services, but if the service providers are a small number of large companies possibly regulating the degree of competition between them, then the state becomes very dependent on them, irrespective of their behaviour and efficiency. This we can describe as 'lock-in'. The term was used by Georg Menz (2011) in a discussion of private sector management of migrant detention facilities. He recounted the incident of a fire outbreak in a migrant detention centre at Schiphol airport in Amsterdam in 2005 which resulted in the deaths of eleven detainees. The incident provoked a public outcry and the Dutch minister of justice was obliged to resign. The centre was managed by G4S; the company was blamed for inadequate safety procedures. Yet two years later, in 2007, the contract with the company was extended for another six years. In effect, the state had become so dependent on the company that even a major failure did not result in contract cancellation (see Menz 2011: 21). The question of lock-in is, as we have said, more than simply the fact that the state has become dependent on its outsourcers. It is the monopoly power of the latter which ensures the state is tied to them and renews, or continues to issue, contracts almost irrespective of their failures or even criminality. The companies become 'too big to fail' and seemingly also 'too big to prosecute'.

There are three key aspects to lock-in. First is the simple fact, as in Menz's description, that major failure or suspicion of criminal activity by a private security company is no guarantee that it will not continue to receive state contracts. This phenomenon seems to cover all the major areas of outsourcing. In 2015, observers were noting that 'despite a sordid and deadly reputation in Iraq, the mercenary army that began as Blackwater and is now known as Academi was a top recipient of Pentagon contracts for training Afghanistan's security forces from 2001 to 2014 ... The awards to Blackwater and Academi were made despite the public condemnation of the company for its brutal tactics in Iraq' (Shorrock 2015). The events of Nisour Square in 2007 (see Chapter 3) seemed to have had little impact on the suitability of the company as a recipient of US government contracts.

Returning to the UK, a close study of some of the big providers in penal services reveals a double-edged situation which gives them a great deal of power. On the one hand, the concentration of providers – for example the 'big three' of G4S, Serco and Sodexo – means that there is little room for manoeuvre or choice for the government when choosing its subcontractors. On the other hand, as we have noted already, since UK criminal justice work is often a small part of their global activities, the large companies can easily pull out of an area when they suffer reputational damage, as G4S decided to do in response to the Medway scandal. This tendency has an international aspect. Around the world, campaigns against various private security companies provoke their withdrawal from controversial forms of provision. In the UK, in response to the Medway STC incident, G4S announced its intention to withdraw from that area of provision and in another case in 2014 the company announced its intention, following international protests, to withdraw from the provision of penal facilities in Israel (Reed and Plimmer 2016; see below).

The most well-known incident in recent years, which one might imagine would have consigned the company to outer darkness, involved the inability of G4S to fulfil its contract to provide effective security for the 2012 Olympics. This was a major failure that affected large numbers of the general public rather than the 'captive population' of prisoners or probation clients. It was also the year before G4S and Serco were accused of overcharging the Ministry of Justice for services relating to the electronic monitoring of offenders, for which Serco was subject to inquiry by the Serious Fraud Office (SFO) (Travis 2013a; 2013b). Both companies received bad publicity, some senior management resigned and two English police forces decided not to proceed with proposed multi-million-pound contracts with them for outsourcing back-office work (White 2014b). Both companies were effectively barred by the Ministry of Justice from participation in initial bidding for the privatisation of most of the English probation service (Fitzgibbon and Lea 2014).

Serco was later cleared of fraud but in 2019 came to a 'deferred prosecution' agreement with the SFO involving a settlement of £19.2 million, and finally in July 2019 agreed to pay £22.9 million (Press Association 2019). G4S agreed to pay the government £108.9 million. At the time of writing (August 2019) the investigation into G4S had not yet concluded (Buckland 2019), but at the same time other contracts were continuing. In 2014 the House of Commons Public Accounts Committee found that a number of major government departments, including the Ministry of Justice, the Ministry of Defence and HM Revenue and Customs were still awarding contracts to both these companies even while under SFO investigation. The committee

> heard how there was no ban on G4S and Serco winning new work after discovery of the overcharging in July 2013 ... the fact that Government gave the impression that all discussion with Serco and G4S were halted whilst investigations took place, whilst in fact the companies have been awarded new contracts in other departments, had existing contracts extended and were in negotiation with departments over new contracts is evidence of the over reliance on these larger suppliers. (House of Commons 2014b: para. 37; see also Morse 2015: 6)

But if the government had acted against G4S and Serco as recipients of contracts in the private prisons area, as Julian Le Vay, a former finance director of the Prison Service observed, 'the government's only option would have been to give everything to Sodexo, which would have been ridiculous' (Ford and Plimmer 2018).

A second element of lock-in, which we referred to in Chapter 5 in connection with both the Jimmy Mubenga (Brook House) and the Medway STC cases, is the tendency to prosecute only the employees and not the company. There are also examples of this in the area of military outsourcing. We noted in Chapter 3 in relation to the notorious Blackwater Nisour Square case in 2007 that it was only a small number of employees who were prosecuted in the US rather than the company itself, and then only with partial success. In a UK example in 2010, Danny Fitzsimons, a former soldier employed by ArmorGroup/G4S as a guard in Baghdad, killed two of his fellow employees in a drunken brawl. He was subject to Iraqi law and in 2011 was convicted of murder and sentenced to 20 years' imprisonment. The 2014 coroner's inquiry in the UK into the death of his victims recorded a verdict of unlawful killing and noted that Fitzsimons had previous convictions that were not picked up by G4S screening and vetting procedures (Topping 2015). A G4S spokesman told the BBC that 'his screening was not completed in line with the company's procedures ... Our screening processes should have been better implemented in this situation but it is a matter of speculation what role, if any, this may have played in the incident' (BBC Scotland 2012). A charge of corporate manslaughter against the company was not contemplated.

The third aspect of lock-in is that the companies, in responding to the criminal activities of their employees, start to sound very much like government departments, stressing that 'lessons have been learned' and new procedures have been 'put in place'. For example, the G4S 2015 annual report discusses the response of the company to the Medway STC events mentioned previously. The report stresses the cooperation by the company with external inquiries into the Medway events by local authority children's services officials and the police, and notes the speed with which it put in place its own procedures to remedy such behaviour by its employees:

> We have reinforced the standards expected of all employees, reminded them of the group's whistleblowing facility 'Speak Out', implemented a series of improved processes around rotation of staff and accelerated the process to implement body-worn cameras for our employees in STCs. Refresher training for all staff on Minimising and Managing Physical Restraint (MMPR) has been conducted ... appropriate remedial action has been taken to strengthen the control environment, prevent the re-occurrence of such events and ensure that the group's values are adhered to and their importance reiterated across the organisation. (G4S 2015: 29)

In this way the view of criminal actions by particular employees as exogenous departures from the high standards insisted upon by the company is reinforced. The fact that some employees violate such standards is dissociated from the notion that the company itself does not adhere rigorously to them. Each episode is effectively insulated from all the others. There is never an overview which links the failures of the 2012 Olympics with the allegedly fraudulent tagging charges, the violence at Brook House and that at Medway STC, the Fitzsimons case – let alone the events at Mangaung Prison. Taken together these might say something about the nature of the company and how its recruitment methods, training programmes and internal cultures worldwide provide a background conducive to periodic failure. This is effectively ruled out and dismissed as a misguided attempt to link together widely dispersed and unfortunate incidents which are inevitable for a large company with a sizeable global workforce.

FROM PRAGMATIC TO NORMATIVE LEGITIMACY

The self-image of the company as an entity competent to respond appropriately to failure, rather than being itself classed as failing, raises the question of whether the company is on the way to becoming regarded as part of the state machinery rather than simply an external subcontractor. The process whereby the state continually retreats to its core competences and outsources many activities previously considered as inherently governmental is, it might be argued, paralleled by a hollowing out of state legitimacy in which the state remains as the *ultimate* repository of legitimate coercion but is able to outsource some of that legitimate authority to its subcontractors. This is so even though the private companies are driven by the concerns of profitable return on capital. On the part of the general public there will be a greater acceptability of such blurring of the boundaries between private corporations and the state if security is already itself seen as a commodity to be bought and sold (Lea and Hallsworth 2012). Those on the receiving end may of course simply experience a continuous chain of coercion, and it becomes immaterial where the authority of the state ends and that of a private company begins. The company may then begin to acquire some of the aura of legitimacy previously reserved for the state.

From time to time police officers, prison officers and other criminal justice personnel may be charged and sentenced for criminal offences – including fraud and violence – without any suggestion that such criminality demonstrates the unacceptability of the criminal justice system as such. Indeed, the vigilance of the anti-corruption investigators may enhance the reputation of the institution being investigated, demonstrating its openness and conformity to the rule of law. In response to such criminality there may be attempts at the radical reform of norms of behaviour, recruitment, mechanisms of accountability and oversight, and relations with local communities. Rarely if ever is there a conclusion that such behaviour evidences the necessity to abolish – for example

– policing as such (but see Vitale 2017). Indeed such reform will, it is usually assumed, be best handled by the agencies themselves.

Policing and the rest of the criminal justice system as part of the legitimate coercive authority of the state, possesses what some writers in the field of business management call 'cognitive legitimacy', defined as the 'acceptance of the organization as necessary or inevitable based on some taken-for-granted cultural account' (Suchman 1995: 582; see also Brinkerhoff 2005). The achievement of cognitive legitimacy is normally beyond the reach of private corporations because 'pluralist political cultures rarely go so far as to assume that only one organization can wield a given technology or pursue a given program' (Suchman 1995: 583). That is to say, the public would find it hard to accept that one large private security company should have a natural monopoly of running prisons or policing. Only the state can do this, even if it outsources management to a few companies. No one company has a legitimate monopoly.

The legitimacy of subcontractors is therefore traditionally pragmatic (Suchman 1995: 578). That is to say, it is achieved when the company 'fulfils [the] needs and interests of its stakeholders and constituents' (Brinkerhoff 2005: 4). The private subcontractor in criminal justice services, as in other areas, can aspire only to a pragmatic legitimacy by continuing to 'deliver the goods'. The legitimate authority of the director of a private prison over inmates is, from this standpoint, contingent on continued fulfilment of the outsourcing contract. This inbuilt insecurity is alleged to guarantee efficiency and its maintenance is the ostensible aim of measures such as constant monitoring and 'payment by results' (Fitzgibbon 2016). The assumption is that the private company subcontracting state activities involving coercion participates only *indirectly* in the legitimate authority of the state and only by continuing to fulfil the contract.

This situation predominates in the early stages of privatisation. There is a nervousness on the part of the private providers such that, in the conclusion of one study, 'the loud confidence that dominates the security industry's public presentation of self is accompanied by a quieter ambivalence about its credibility and recurrent efforts at self-justification and justification in the eyes of others' (Thumala et al. 2011: 286). The authors of this study discussed a variety of types of 'legitimation work' undertaken by private security companies aimed at countering negative public images stemming from 'the poor quality of industry personnel ... [and the] ... perceived dishonesty in the selling of products and services'

(Thumala et al. 2011: 287). The companies which were the subject of this study engaged in a good deal of 'symbolic borrowing' (mainly from the police) whereby private security gets as 'close' as possible to state agencies through recruiting former police officers for management positions right down to dressing employees in uniforms resembling those of police officers. The aim is to 'associate with the police in part because they wish to borrow its ethos of vocation and public service' (Thumala et al. 2011: 297; see also White 2010). Keeping close to the state is seen as the route to legitimacy in the eyes of the public. But this is in no way a strategy to become *part of* the state.

We are here talking about the sort of small and medium-sized companies to which local authorities may outsource the collection of fixed penalty notices or the patrolling of town centres (see Chapter 4). These smaller companies do not have the same powers as the police, whereas G4S, Serco and other large global security corporations running prisons or migrant detention centres exercise more or less the same powers as the state. This brings us to a third type of legitimacy, sometimes known as 'normative' legitimacy. It aims to demonstrate, independently of pragmatic issues like reliable contract fulfilment, that the corporation is a responsible 'citizen' whose activities embody 'a pro-social logic that differs fundamentally from narrow self-interest' (Suchman 1995: 579) and leads the corporation 'towards acceptable and desirable norms, standards, and values' (Brinkerhoff 2005: 4). The concept of normative legitimacy links to the theme of the social leadership duties of the corporation popularised by business gurus such as Peter Drucker (see Cohen 2009). The goal is to achieve a type of legitimacy portraying the corporation as a trustworthy recipient not only of state outsourcing contracts but the exercise of at least some of the powers of state agencies. It includes the trust that the corporation has the will, capacity and value commitments to sort out mistakes when things go wrong. In this sense it is different and more powerful than pragmatic legitimacy, which involves the constant monitoring of performance by the outsourcer.

An example of a corporation engaged in a public relations campaign to secure normative legitimacy can be seen in the self-presentation by global security conglomerates like G4S when they stress not simply their capacity to devise efficient solutions for clients, but also their commitment to human rights – a key focus of governance. The G4S Integrated Report and Accounts for 2018 states:

> We are proud of the role G4S and its employees play in society and the positive contribution they make to the protection of human rights through our range of services and the standards which we apply. However, we are clear that, as a business we have a responsibility to ensure that we are not at risk of violating human rights through the services we provide, the customers with whom we work, the suppliers we use, or through the treatment of our colleagues and others in our care. G4S' human rights policy and its related framework are based upon the United Nations Guiding Principles on Business and Human Rights. Alongside our values of Integrity and Respect, the framework reinforces the continued development of a business model which aids the realisation of the United Nations Sustainable Development Goals through the creation of employment opportunity, the global improvement of industry standards and by helping to create secure and stable communities around the world. (G4S 2018: 36)

To this end, in 2018 the company conducted human rights audits in 15 of the countries in which it operates, identified 23 countries 'as being high or very high-risk environments for human rights' and 'Conducted human rights training and awareness sessions for senior management across the Group' (G4S 2018: 36). These laudable activities and value orientations do not sit easily, it has to be said, with the incidents encountered in Chapter 5. In particular they clash with the notion of working strictly to contract, which, as we have seen, may create pressures resulting in failure. But this is the whole point: the human rights orientation of the company signals, not that things will not go wrong, but that the institution most professionally equipped to deal with them is the company itself – rather like the professional standards or anti-corruption department of a police force or government agency.

The efforts of large corporations to attain normative legitimacy coheres with neoliberalism's stress on the private sector. Indeed, the growth of 'corporate citizenship' displaces, as Emma Bell suggests, the social citizenship of the welfare state as the latter collapses into the simple individual capacity to buy and sell commodities – including security – while the corporate citizenship of the private corporation is extended and elaborated to the status of guardian of human rights (see Bell 2016).

To what extent campaigns for normative legitimacy have succeeded with regard to public opinion is difficult to assess. In the UK, a 2013 survey by the polling organisation Survation, during the period in which

G4S and Serco were placed under investigation for fraud regarding electronic tagging contracts, found 58 per cent of respondents agreed that the companies 'should pay a fine and have all their government contracts taken away and be banned from bidding again to provide public services', while only 6 per cent felt that 'they should pay a fine but be allowed to continue running the prisoner tagging service'. Also, 40 per cent of respondents felt that, in response to a private company mismanaging an outsourced public service, the service should be taken back into public ownership (Shaw 2013). Bad publicity in other areas of outsourcing affecting transport, health care and public utilities may have combined with that relating to criminal justice areas – in particular the failure of probation privatisation – to push public opinion against privatisation. In March 2019 the Labour Party proposed to ban outsourcing in 'services that deal with vulnerable people and their rights'; this might include prisons (Savage 2013).

However, assuming that the role of private corporations continues to be extended rather than restricted, it is one thing to *emulate* the state but another thing to *become* the state or even a branch of the state. The role of the East India Company in the period of old privatisation (see Chapters 1 and 2) shows that historically speaking there is no reason why private organisations should not take on state functions. It is also the case that the boundaries of the state change and are the outcome of social conflicts and class struggles. 'There is never a point when the state is finally built within a given territory and thereafter operates ... according to its own fixed and inevitable laws' (Jessop 1990: 9). New assemblages of state and private enterprises can emerge and consolidate into new forms of state power. 'What is or is not part of the state is dependent on the dominant coalitions of interests involved, the ends to which core state powers ... are being oriented and the technologies of rule being deployed' (Lea and Hallsworth 2012: 32).

With lock-in and the rise of large security corporations seeking normative legitimacy we have possibly arrived at something of a tipping point. If the functioning of state agencies has become dependent on the private sector, then it is only a matter of time before private executives from the companies come to join the core planning committees of government departments concerned with military, police and penal matters. The present system of secondment to the civil service could transform into a system of permanent representation in decision making. Under such circumstances the private companies would have become to all intents and purposes part of the state. This would of course differ from the East India Company model, in which the company *was the state* for the territories it administered. Rather, it would be a matter of the existing state apparatus expanding by absorbing private companies as de facto government departments or subdivisions of them. But there are two important factors working in the opposite direction.

The first factor is that the security industry – however powerful and successful it is in the appropriation of essential state functions as the latter retreats to its core competences – is a collection of competing companies. There is no one company that could function in the manner of the East India Company as the corporate sovereign, or even attain the stability of a government department through, for example, a long-term open-ended contract. We have returned to the issue posed by Charles Tilly's explanation (see Chapter 1) of the inability of the Sicilian mafia to become a state. However powerful and devious its clans, it remained a system of fractious competing families, with the hegemony of any one of these being temporary and precarious. In a similar way, however powerful the global private security companies, with their broadcast commitments to human rights and benevolent governance, and however closely they interface with state agencies, they remain oriented to profit making on behalf of their shareholders in a still competitive marketplace for security. If a government secured a contract with one company as its permanent agent then others – and their shareholders and bankers – would protest at being excluded from the market. If a government insisted that all the major companies amalgamated into a single corporation in order to receive a permanent outsourcing contract, then that government might have to wait a long time as well as being accused of anti-competitive practice. A radical government of the left – or conceivably of the corporatist right – might decide to solve the issue of the relationship between private capital and the state by nationalising the security industry, which would of course solve the issue as to whether it was part of the state.

The second factor is that outsourcing state services is one part of a more complex picture. As we saw in the discussion of private policing, much of its growth is associated with the protection of private space and security provided to other private corporations. In a capitalist society, private capital works closely with the state without in any sense becoming part of the state. The private security companies providing protection for business clients may work closely with state authorities, particularly on issues concerning anti-terrorist surveillance, but this does not make them part of the state. Indeed, to some extent they may use their international reach and resources to compete with states. The fact that criminal justice and state security agencies remain national gives large global security companies many advantages, but they are nevertheless dependent on information and resources secured from contacts in the policing and security agencies of national states.

In other words, there needs to be some caution in identifying a tendency towards a private state, either through private security companies becoming de facto government departments or by accumulating power and expertise sufficient to rival that of national states. There are rather developing and complex relations of interdependence – and also of conflict.

A FUSION OF PRIVATE AND STATE?

An important illustration of this complexity is found in the role of private security companies in weak states in the global south. It is here more than anywhere else that the pretensions of the large private security corporations to take advantage of the fact that, 'under the conditions of globalization, the strict division of labour between private business and nation-state governance does not hold any more. Many business firms have started to assume social and political responsibilities that go beyond legal requirements and fill the regulatory vacuum in global governance' (Scherer and Palazzo 2011: 899).

We have already noted the power relations between private security and police, in which the latter depend on the technology and organisation of global private security companies. This is a variety of lock-in that would be familiar in the global north. Urban policing simply could not take place without the role of the companies.

Also, as in the global north, a major source of growth in private security has been outside state subcontracting. Wealthy elites and businesses have been financing their own security rather than, or in addition to, overstretched and underequipped state police. In South Africa, as we have seen, the private security industry is much larger than the state police and military forces combined (Eastwood 2013). Moreover, it is itself highly militarised and has established a degree of parallel legitimacy which potentially rivals state forces. Add to this the fractured political consensus, and alleged bribery and attempts at state capture by powerful financial oligarchs (Swilling 2017; Gevisser 2019), and a certain nervousness concerning the potential power of a highly armed and staffed private security industry is understandable, more so when the ownership of local security companies is linked to larger global companies. For example, in 2007 G4S acquired a controlling interest in the large South African company Fidelity.

In the abstract, such a situation might be seen as ideal for the private security sector gradually becoming a de facto part of the state. There is a degree of ground-level collaboration with state police. Nevertheless, the industry has found itself involved in political conflict with sections of the political elite. While in the UK the regulation of the private security industry has been a relatively smooth process that enhanced the status of the big companies by separating them from the cowboys, in South Africa the process of regulation has been more complex and conflictual. In 2015 the South African parliament passed the Private Security Industry Regulation Amendment Bill, but by mid-2018 it had yet to be signed into law by the president. The main feature of the Bill is that it gives the minister of police the power to limit foreign ownership of private security companies to 49 per cent. The motives behind the legislation were ostensibly to reduce an alleged security risk from too much foreign control of the protection of key sites and strategic installations. However, critics suggest the real motive was the desire on the part of the state to capture the profitability of the fast-growing private security sector and reduce any challenge to the state police agencies (see *Daily Maverick & Chronicle* 2017).

In other areas of the African continent the relationship between private security and foreign-based transnational corporations (TNCs), particularly in the mineral extraction industry, is close. Indeed, in our brief discussion of mercenaries in Sierra Leone in Chapter 3 we mentioned the connection between mercenaries and corporations in the diamond and oil sectors. But, apart from situations of armed conflict, the role of the private security sector in servicing the needs of TNCs is a major part of their market. There are some specialist companies that perform this role. For example, Solace Global informs us that its 'VIP close protection services enable safe, controlled, proportionate and monitored movement of personnel in a country where travel poses an elevated risk, or the personnel themselves are high profile'. The company 'will mitigate risk and assist with client decisions, providing detailed journey plans, route recommendations and in-country intelligence that equip travellers with the right information pre-travel' (Solace Global 2019). These sorts of companies are also part of the revolving door of senior police, military and security on advisory boards, and this itself becomes an important component of corporate normative legitimacy. Their VIPs may also include high-ranking politicians and diplomats. Other companies in this area include Control Risks (see Chapter 3). Such companies, with their competence in risk assessment and client security and their contacts in the military and security networks of the major states, as well as local resources, begin to function as an embryonic 'global police' adequate to the global security needs of TNCs (see O'Reilly 2010).

Meanwhile, G4S is not far away. But the company tends to provide this type of specialised security service as one of a number of activities in the country to which the business traveller is headed. For example, in the Democratic Republic of the Congo (DRC), the company is able to draw on its expertise acquired in armed close protection in Afghanistan. It deploys its own Nepalese Ghurkha private military who 'work with a military strategy in mind, effective for securing high-risk environments, where there is a higher level of threat involved'. The company also 'assists its clients in the development of contingency plans to ensure the continuity of their businesses and also provides the evacuation service. G4S is equipped with armoured vehicles and speedboats.' The DRC is designated as 'an environment where the risk is permanent and where the need to reassure foreign investors is constant. For this purpose we have a professional team that provides protocol services on arrival and departure, transfers between the airport and the city as well as the Close Protection service' (G4S DRC 2019). At the same time the company provides more conventional security services such as international cash transit and deposit security, access control and static security and 'flexible service and dynamic performance ... in [the] Energy, Mining and Construction industry. We outsource security trained drivers, cleaners, gardeners to Banks, NGOs, diplomatic missions etc.' (G4S DRC 2019). The company combines elements of the PMC role with more conventional private security tasks. The company is also aware of its corporate presence in the DRC and makes an effort to stress corporate social responsibility which, as we have seen, is part of a strategy aimed at normative legitimacy. G4S demonstrates its sense of responsibility with its outreach and corporate social investment strategy oriented to local communities with core 'focus areas of health, education, welfare and support of Africa's youth' (G4S DRC 2019).

Jana Hönke (2013) criticised the notion of corporate social responsibility by foreign companies operating in the DRC, and argued that much 'outreach' work in the DRC and also South Africa fails to extend far outside the fortified mining compounds of the TNCs, such that 'community engagement can be problematic because of its narrow scope and short-term perspective' (Hönke 2013: 76). Although she was talking about the mining corporations rather than the private security companies that protect them, it might be surmised that the dynamics of working to the contract would ensure that the security companies tended to follow their clients in their own outreach activities. Thus assemblages of state and private security actors can embrace contradictions. The narrow interests of the TNCs and the security companies which organise their protection may in reality lead to a rather limited sense of corporate responsibility, certainly not one which points to taking the lead in social development in the wider community.

The state itself may be drawn into the narrow sphere of interests of the TNCs and their security providers. The TNCs themselves may pay for the state police to devote themselves to protecting company assets. Meanwhile the private security companies working for the TNCs, particularly if they have to rely on the state police to make arrests, attempt to draw the latter into their own priorities by calling for their attendance at crime incidents. The result may be that the state police, in response to payments by TNCs and time spent attending incidents involving private security, spend less time on crime-fighting priorities democratically decided by the mass of the population. This is obviously even more complex if the democratic pressure is in the direction of unearthing corrupt relations between sections of the political elite and the companies.

An important example of this type of assemblage of foreign-owned TNCs, local state police and private security comes from Peru where, in the early 2000s, a mining TNC was in conflict with local communities over access to land containing mineral resources. The private security company Forza Security worked for a Japanese-owned TNC, Santa Luisa. The latter also employed a large number of state police officers who were legally entitled to subcontract their services in this way. Forza, which also provided guarding services for important international banks and embassies, worked with the state police as a variety of 'company police' raiding the camps of protestors resisting illegal land seizures. The example of Forza 'tells a story of impunity for private security companies and public police officers working in the service of transnational mining companies in Peru' (Kamphuis 2011: 556).

However, none of these assemblages resemble the old East India Company model of a single corporation embracing all aspects of state power and commercial profit making at the same time. The epoch when this was possible or necessary has long passed. No one company could profitably take on the functions of administering a territory without suffering from the free-riding of its competitors. There is a division of labour between different types of entities – mining companies and private security companies, NGOs and already existing states and their police and military. The notion of assemblage is useful in underlining that these entities must come to an accommodation and devise new systems of rule, systems which occasionally fall apart under the weight of their own internal conflicts.

Attempts, therefore, in the present epoch to revive anything resembling the old model of the East India Company inevitably take the form of farce. A few years ago Erik Prince, the former head of the notorious Blackwater PMC, proposed a solution to the continuing stalemate and enormous cost of the US occupation of Afghanistan. Prince proposed nothing less than an entity, under his personal control, of something that sounded like the East India Company.

Observing that Afghanistan 'is an expensive disaster for America', both financially and in terms of loss of US lives (there is a curious lack of mention of Afghan lives), Prince argued in a *Wall Street Journal* article that Afghanistan should be placed under the control of 'one person: an American viceroy who would lead all U.S. government and coalition efforts – including command, budget, policy, promotion and contracting – and report directly to the president' (Prince 2017). Prince was thinking of General Douglas MacArthur's administration of Japan following the Japanese surrender in 1945. The crucial difference was that the viceroy's soldiers would not be the US military but a PMC – presumably a reincarnation of Blackwater. In an interview in the online journal *Salon*, Prince is reported as being asked whether what he had in mind was to 'replace a military occupation with the "American South Asia Company" or something like that?' Prince responded: 'Something like that, sure. If you look back in history, the way the English operated India for 250 years, they had an army that was largely run by companies – and no English soldiers. So cheap, very low cost' (quoted in Pulver 2017). The following was a typical critical response to Prince's fantasy:

> the core issue that cannot be resolved by PMCs ... is state-building in Afghanistan. State institutions like the bureaucracy and the judiciary take years to construct and require both flexibility and broad public legitimacy to survive. Private entities cannot construct state institutions in a humane, timely and cost-effective fashion; especially on behalf of foreign governments, as evidenced by the East India Company's own history ... In spite of various political reorganizations and the creation of a merit-based civil service in 1853, the Company's aggressive political-military policies sparked the Sepoy Mutiny of 1857, necessitating a massive military intervention by British troops. (Haidari and Banerji 2017)

It has to be said that state building and economic development were quite distant from the concerns of the US and its allies in both Iraq and Afghanistan (see Chapter 3), so Prince's giant PMC would only have had to be concerned with security. But that would have been its undoing. The East India Company ruled for several hundred years before being overthrown in the Rebellion of 1857; Prince's outfit would have been arguably demolished in a few weeks by an alliance of all the political factions in Afghanistan making common cause against the sudden appearance of a pretentious viceroy and his private retainers claiming to run the country. Sean McFate, a historian of mercenary warfare, summed up the flawed nature of the whole enterprise by noting that one of the features of old-style mercenary armies was changing sides in return for better rewards: 'It could go into business for itself. It could be bought out by ISIS, China, Russia' (quoted in Gray 2017).

THE AUTHORITARIAN PERIPHERY

We have encountered broadly three types of assemblage involving private security companies: with the state military and police apparatus, with the state penal system and with private sector TNCs and businesses. In the global south we encountered mercenaries and PMCs combining in various ways with states and also as the security providers for TNCs. We said less about the role of private security in the penal system except by way of brief mentions of the deliberations of the Israeli Supreme Court and the South African prison administrations. We have not had the space or time for a thorough discussion of private security in each of the regions of the globe where it is a significant player: particularly

Latin America, the Middle East and Europe – including Eastern Europe and Russia. So for our final section we attempt to draw together some of the main themes observable in the UK. Here we can see elements of all three types of assemblage but with their own national characteristics. As mentioned in Chapter 3, PMCs play a less important role in the British military than in the US, and private security companies do not attempt to demonstrate their corporate responsibility through outreach to deprived youth – unless the treatment of detained migrants at Brooke House, young prisoners at Medway STC or asylum seekers housed by Serco can be regarded as forms of outreach. Because of the high public profile of the prisons crisis, and latterly the crisis of privatised probation, the assemblage involving private security and the penal system has probably the highest profile in recent years in the UK.

In liberal democracies it is important to be aware of the effect of the private security industry on democracy. There are a number of dimensions to the issue. The private sector can be used by governments to violate the democratic decisions of parliaments as when private militaries are used in covert warfare. Private ownership of urban land confers the right to make decisions, enforced by private security, regarding CCTV surveillance. Private security is employed by local authorities to police antisocial behaviour. In each case democratic accountability requires mobilisation at different levels, from parliamentary campaigns through to demonstrations against CCTV security and campaigns to change the policies of local authorities regarding the management of antisocial behaviour. Such campaigns are easiest where the activities of private security affect the public at large, but much harder where those affected are captive populations or the very poor and marginalised.

One of the most important ways in which private security companies obstruct democratic accountability is through their profit-making interests and their rival accountability to their shareholders. It is hard enough to scrutinise government agencies, but private ownership, with its associated issues relating to the commercial confidentiality of financial accounts and internal processes, creates another barrier preventing these corporations being accountable to those who are most affected by their activity: overwhelmingly the poor and socially marginalised. Activist movements may have some effect, though how much is difficult to judge. In 2014 and again in 2015, G4S shareholder meetings in London were disrupted by activists as part of the campaign against G4S contracts in the Israeli penal system (Hickey 2015). Such action may have been a factor in the company's decision not to renew prison contracts in that country, though it was reported in 2017 that the company continued to be involved with the training of Israeli police (see BDS 2017). Meanwhile, in the UK the public–private assemblage governing the poor, spectacularly illustrated in England by privatised probation and prisons and by the treatment of migrants and asylum seekers, points to the growth of an 'authoritarian periphery' of the coercive management of the poor, harking back to the nineteenth century and the view of the poor not as citizens but as the 'dangerous classes'.

It is important to distinguish this development from any notion of the resurgence of the type of fascist regimes that developed in Europe during the interwar years. It is certainly true that far-right populism – currently undergoing a resurgence throughout Europe – contains elements of classic fascist movements. But as a political and social regime, fascism was a highly centralised system involving the seizure of key state institutions by extra-parliamentary forces. This was followed by the progressive incorporation of most areas of civil society and the private economy into the state, lubricated by an extreme racial-nationalist ideology. The end point of this was that even the family became part of the state, with children being expected to spy on their parents. Private companies were indeed required to subordinate their activities to the dictates of the state (see Neuman 2009). This is not an adequate model for current developments.

It is true that recent decades have seen the growth of highly centralised surveillance systems by police and government security agencies. This has been related to the growth of neoliberalism, which requires a strong state to enforce the repression of old ideas of the welfare state and restore the discipline of the market and the doctrine of individual responsibility for poverty and social inequality. It is also a response to global fragmentation and inequality, the return of cold war attitudes and the rise of terrorism and 'domestic extremism'. The growing apparatus of state surveillance has its own notable private dimension. Alongside surveillance by police, security agencies and government communications agencies, such as GCHQ in the UK and the National Security Agency in the US, has been the growth of the accumulation of personal data by social media, internet and mobile communications technology giants like Google, Facebook and Apple. This increasingly close relationship between the two sectors certainly evidences the emergence of a new public–private assemblage and is a growing cause for concern (see, for example, Samuels 2019). But covert surveillance and information gathering – which a lot of people may be unaware of – is not fascism. Indeed, as we shall suggest below, certain types of emerging 'control' systems which apply to the poor, and in which the private security sector is heavily involved, seem to be predicated on the absence of surveillance.

A better model for understanding the rise of the authoritarian periphery may not be classic fascism but the much older model of settler colonialism. Colonial rule by settlers pillaging land from native communities was based on the 'exclusion of the mass of the population from effective political organisation and representation of interests, a crude system of rule frozen in the transition ... characteristic of the early stages of modernisation' (Lea 2002: 65).

In other words, settler colonialism was in some ways a grotesque caricature of England during the Peterloo Massacre of 1819, celebrated in the recent film by Mike Leigh (2018). What both societies had in common was the relative freedom of the property-owning (white) elite within the rule of law, and a degree of parliamentary democracy which contrasted with the exclusion, disenfranchisement and repression of the masses. The colonial variant added the dimension of racial alongside class stratification. The modern development of the authoritarian periphery is thus in many ways a return to the early stages of industrialisation, of which settler colonialism was a 'frozen' variant. The important characteristic is, in contrast to European fascism, liberal democracy and a high degree of freedom at the centre (notwithstanding the covert surveillance noted above), and a growing repressive authoritarianism at the periphery directed at sections of the poor and marginalised – the unemployed, homeless and rough sleepers, welfare claimants, ex-prisoners and probation clients, migrants and asylum seekers. In the management of all these sections of the poor – who long ago ceased to be regarded even as conditional citizens – the private sector plays a significant role in the implementation of state policies.

The private part of the assemblage is ideally suited to the management of the marginalised poor, since it specialises in low-cost surveillance and control. And of course this is not restricted to the UK or to the industrialised countries of the north. The periphery, along with the marginalisation of the poor, is a global phenomenon (Rogers 2010; 2017), part of the fragmentation and stagnation which were the failure of the promise of post-Second World War growth and integration. The private management of the periphery is worldwide, from private operators identifying targets for drone strikes in Yemen, Syria or Chad, to private companies handling the assessment of social benefit eligibility in Newcastle, to the removal of homeless people from the city centre Business Improvement District in Vancouver (Bennett et al. 2008), to the abuse of young prisoners in Medway and the repressive administration of asylum housing in Glasgow. In each case the private sector makes a profit. In the private military and specialist surveillance sectors it profits from the recruitment of operatives that are already trained – a loss to the state which has paid the training costs – and through the employment of a deskilled, high-turnover labour force in prisons, probation and the management of public space.

We have discussed in previous chapters the relation between the rise of the private sector and the decline of the idea of welfare or social citizenship in the areas of policing public space and the management of prisons and probation. But there is an aspect of the role of private sector companies and the penal system which needs further emphasis. In the discussion of private probation in Chapter 5 we developed the concept of negative supervision, in which there is no interest in the fate of the client as long as they do not constitute a security risk and the payment by results payments can be collected by the company because the contract has been fulfilled. We noted that, strictly speaking, the reason *why* the client has not reoffended or why their risk level has not increased is not important, certainly not to the private security company working to its contract.

The next stage in the development of this paradigm is not to bother with the client at all but to place them somewhere where, even if their risk level increases or they reoffend, they are not anywhere near any person or property whose security they could compromise. Obviously, this would be the case if they were effectively warehoused in prison. However, outside, in urban space, the confinement to certain zones of the city – the most deprived and disordered – would have similar effects. Containment in certain areas of the city is the other side of the coin of exclusion from public space and private property.

As long as they stay in these 'wild zones', where inhabitants have long since failed to qualify as effective citizens, they can be entirely neglected until they come to the attention of the police, and then they can be channelled back to prison for a stretch. The 'deadly symbiosis' between prison and the urban ghetto was developed in the US urban context some time ago by Loïc Wacquant (2004). The concept of 'control by neglect' was the focus of another more recent US study by the Italian criminologist, Alessandro De Giorgi, who recently reported on his research with newly released prisoners in Oakland, California:

> I expected to return from my fieldwork documenting an extensive network of (post) carceral control, ongoing surveillance, aggressive policing, unrealistic parole and probation conditions, and that these intrusive penal technologies would emerge as the main obstacles to the successful reintegration of former prisoners ... Instead, during my three years in the field I ended up documenting widespread public neglect, institutional indifference, and programmatic abandonment of these marginalized populations by both the social and penal arms of the state. (De Giorgi 2018)

Meanwhile, back in the UK, in 2016 the HMIP inspection of HMP Bronzefield revealed that an increasing percentage – at the time almost 20 per cent – of female prisoners were leaving the institution with no fixed address, while social and local authority housing departments were regarding ex-prisoners as low priority. According to a BBC report on the inspection, prisoners on release 'were given tents and sleeping bags ... because they had nowhere to live' (BBC 2016). Research by the Howard League found that around a third of ex-prisoners were leaving without a fixed abode (Cooper 2013). One consequence of this situation is that the classic doctrine of less eligibility, whereby conditions in prison should be marginally worse than life outside – to enable imprisonment to act as a deterrent to crime – now turns into its opposite. A solicitor recently remarked in a letter to the press that 'sadly, for a lot of my clients, being sent to prison is a more attractive option than remaining in the community' (Steiner 2019).

We have said that the private sector had a special role to play in the development of control by neglect. As with negative supervision, the key is the dynamics of the outsourcing contract itself, the nature of payment by results. The system encourages a disconnection between the character and motives of the individual client as a human being and their behaviour: so long as you don't reoffend we have no interest in why, or whether, you are in any way getting your life back together. It is about as far as we can get from the old ideas of rehabilitation and assistance. As long as there is no change in behaviour there is no need for intervention. The other side of the coin is the tendency of the private sector to work to contract and not do anything which is not explicitly specified – like showing a concern for the individual as a human being. The combination of working to contract and a payment by results system prepares the ground for control by neglect. There is no interest in the individual. The final stage is to find the environment – some combination of the prison and the urban zone – which can serve as a warehouse. This dystopian theme has been widely portrayed in social science (e.g. Davis 1990; 2006) and in entertainment media. In P. D. James' novel *Children of Men* (James 2010), whole swathes of England have become effectively containment ghettos managed by private security companies and mercenaries. John Carpenter's 1981 science fiction fantasy *Escape from New York* depicts a world in which the whole of Manhattan island has been converted into a giant prison (Carpenter 1981); the United States Police Force surrounds Manhattan Island Prison, but there are no guards or soldiers inside – either private or public.

This is probably the best place to end.

References

Abrahamsen, R. and Williams, M. C. (2011) *Security Beyond the State: Private Security in International Politics*. Cambridge: Cambridge University Press.

Addison, P. (1994) *The Road to 1945: British Politics and the Second World War*, 2nd revised edition. London: Pimlico.

Agamben, G. (1998) *Homo Sacer: Sovereign Power and Bare Life*. Stanford, CA: Stanford University Press.

Akulov, A. (2016) *Private Military Contractors Fighting US Wars*. Available at: www.strategic-culture.org/news/2016/08/19/private-military-contractors-fighting-us-wars.html (accessed 12 December 2017).

Albertson, K. and Fox, C. (2019) The Marketisation of Rehabilitation: Some Economic Considerations. *Probation Journal* 66 (1): 25–42.

AllAfrica (2013) South Africa: Media Statement by the Acting National Commissioner of Correctional Services. Available at: https://allafrica.com/stories/201310281994.html (accessed 29 July 2019).

Allison, E. and Sloan, A. (2015) Prison Education Still at the Back of the Class, As Gove Takes New Course. *The Guardian*, 4 August. Available at: www.theguardian.com/education/2015/aug/04/michael-gove-prison-education-justice-secretary-jail (accessed 3 April 2019).

Anderson, C., Crockett, C., DeVito, C. et al. (2015) Locating Penal Transportation: Punishment, Space and Place c.1750–1900. In Morin, K. and Moran, D. (eds) *Historical Geographies of Prisons: Unlocking the Usable Carceral Past*. London: Routledge, pp. 148–62.

Appleton, J. (2012) Manifesto Club. *Banned in London*. Available at: www.bannedinlondon.co.uk/ (accessed 14 November 2018).

Arrighi, G. (1994) *The Long Twentieth Century: Money, Power, and the Origins of Our Times*. London: Verso.

Arrighi, G. and Silver, B. J. (1999) *Chaos and Governance in the Modern World System*. Minneapolis: University of Minnesota Press.

Atkins, P. J. (1993) How the West End Was Won: The Struggle to Remove Street Barriers in Victorian London. *Journal of Historical Geography* 19 (3): 265–77.

Auerbach, S. (2015) 'Beyond the Pale of Mercy': Victorian Penal Culture, Police Court Missionaries, and the Origins of Probation in England. *Law and History Review* 33 (3): 621–63.

Avant, D. D. (2005) *The Market for Force: The Consequences of Privatizing Security*. Cambridge and New York: Cambridge University Press.

Bailey, V. (1997) English Prisons, Penal Culture, and the Abatement of Imprisonment, 1895–1922. *Journal of British Studies* 36 (3): 285–324.

Barela, S. J. (2015) *Legitimacy and Drones: Investigating the Legality, Morality and Efficacy of UCAVs*. Farnham and Burlington, VT: Routledge.

Barlow, E. (2008) *Executive Outcomes: Against All Odds*. Alberton, South Africa: Galago Publishing Pty Ltd.

Barrett, D. and Mendick, R. (2012) Private Firms Give UK Police Forces Millions of Pounds to Investigate Crimes. *Telegraph*, 5 February. Available at: www.telegraph.co.uk/news/uknews/law-and-order/9061383/Private-firms-give-UK-police-forces-millions-of-pounds-to-investigate-crimes.html (accessed 19 January 2019).

Barrington, R. (2019) London, the Money-Laundering Capital. Available at: www.chathamhouse.org/publications/twt/london-money-laundering-capital (accessed 10 July 2019).

Bayley, B. (2016) What Does Nigeria's Use of Private Military Companies Against Boko Haram Mean for the World? Available at: www.vice.com/en_us/article/exqe9z/nigeria-pmcs-boko-harem (accessed 6 December 2017).

Bayly, C. A. (1990) *Indian Society and the Making of the British Empire*. Cambridge: Cambridge University Press.

BBC (2016) Female Inmates 'Given Tents' on Release. BBC News online, 13 April. Available at: www.bbc.com/news/uk-england-surrey-36032693 (accessed 13 April 2019).

BBC (2018) Equatorial Guinea 'Thwarts Coup Attempt'. 3 January. Available at: www.bbc.com/news/world-africa-42557638 (accessed 13 June 2019).

BBC (2019) Private Probation Firms in Wales and South West in Administration. BBC News online, 15 February. Available at: www.bbc.co.uk/news/uk-wales-47240731 (accessed 12 January 2019).

BBC Scotland (2012) In Full: G4S Response. BBC News, 1 October. Available at: www.bbc.com/news/uk-scotland-19730393 (accessed 9 August 2019).

BDS (2017) Global Security Company G4S Deepens Ties with Israeli Apartheid. Boycott G4S! Available at: https://bdsmovement.net/news/global-security-company-g4s-deepens-ties-israeli-apartheid-boycott-g4s (accessed 23 May 2019).

Beattie, J. M. (1986) *Crime and the Courts in England, 1660–1800*. Princeton, NJ: Princeton University Press.

Beattie, J. M. (2001) *Policing and Punishment in London, 1660–1750: Urban Crime and the Limits of Terror*. Oxford: Oxford University Press.

Beckett, K. and Herbert, S. (2010) *Banished: The New Social Control In Urban America*. New York and Oxford: Oxford University Press.

Bell, E. (2016) From Marshallian Citizenship to Corporate Citizenship: The Changing Nature of Citizenship in Neoliberal Britain. *Revue Française de Civilisation Britannique* 21 (1). Available at: http://rfcb.revues.org/850 (accessed 21 March 2017).

Bennett, D., Eby, D., Richardson, J. et al. (2008) *Security Before Justice: A Study of the Impacts of Private Security on Homeless and Under-Housed Vancouver Residents*. Vancouver, BC: Pivot Legal Society. Available at: http://d3n8a8pro7vhmx.cloudfront.net/pivotlegal/legacy_url/253/securitybefore justice.pdf?1345765598 (accessed 25 July 2019).

Bhui, H. S., Bosworth, M. and Fili, A. (2018) Monitoring Immigration Detention at the Borders of Europe: Report on a Pilot Project in Greece, Hungary, Turkey and Italy, 2016–2017. Oxford: University of Oxford Centre for Criminology.

Bialik, K. (2017) Where are U.S. Active-Duty Troops Deployed? Available at: www.pewresearch.org/fact-tank/2017/08/22/u-s-active-duty-military-presence-overseas-is-at-its-smallest-in-decades/ (accessed 6 November 2017).

Binder, M. (2017) *The United Nations and the Politics of Selective Humanitarian Intervention*. Basingstoke: Palgrave Macmillan.

Blackhawk (2016) Corporate Security Solution Case Study. Available at: www.blackhawkintelligence.com/case-study/case-studycorporate-security-solution/ (accessed 15 July 2019).

Blake, R. (1978) *A History of Rhodesia*. New York: Knopf.

Blok, A. (1974) *The Mafia of a Sicilian Village, 1860–1960: A Study of Violent Peasant Entrepreneurs*. Oxford: Oxford University Press.

Bolt, D. (2018) An Inspection of the Home Office's Management of Asylum Accommodation Provision February – June 2018. London: HMSO.

Bond, D. (2018) UK Savings Targets Missed in Army Outsourcing Deal. *Financial Times*, 19 January. Available at: www.ft.com/content/cec26e36-fdob-11e7-9b32-d7d59aace167.

Booth, R. (2014) Jimmy Mubenga: Judge Refused to Allow Jury to Hear About Guards' Racist Texts. *The Guardian*, 17 December. Available at: www.theguardian.com/uk-news/2014/dec/17/jimmy-mubenga-racist-texts-not-heard-case.

Bosworth, M., Franko, K. and Pickering, S. (2018) Punishment, Globalization and Migration Control: 'Get Them the Hell Out of Here'. *Punishment & Society* 20 (1): 34–53.

Bottoms, A. and Tankebe, J. (2012) Beyond Procedural Justice: A Dialogic Approach to Legitimacy in Criminal Justice. *Journal of Criminal Law and Criminology* 102 (1): 119–70.

Boutellis, A. (2019) Are Mercenaries Friends or Foes of African Governments and the United Nations? In *Think UN*... Available at: http://think-un.blogspot.com/2019/02/are-mercenaries-friends-or-foes-of.html (accessed 10 June 2019).

Bowcott, O. (2018) Decline in Community Sentencing Blamed on Probation Privatisation. *The Guardian*, 28 December. Available at: www.theguardian.com/law/2018/dec/28/decline-in-community-sentencing-blamed-on-probation-privatisation-courts-trust-justice (accessed 15 April 2019).

Bowers, P. (2003) Iraq: Law of Occupation. House of Commons Library Research Paper 03/51.

Bowles, S. and Jayadev, A. (2014) One Nation Under Guard. In *Opinionator*. Available at: https://opinionator.blogs.nytimes.com/2014/02/15/one-nation-under-guard/ (accessed 30 June 2019).

Boyle, M. J. (2015) The Legal and Ethical Implications of Drone Warfare. *The International Journal of Human Rights* 19 (2): 105–26.

Brady, D. (2019) Public Sector 'Likely to Suffer' with Collapse of Interserve. *Public Finance*, 15 March. Available at: www.bbc.co.uk/news/uk-wales-47240731 (accessed 12 January 2019).

Brewer, K. (2017) Why Are Privatised Probation Services Using Public Libraries to See Clients? *The Guardian*, 1 November. Available at: www.theguardian.com/society/2017/nov/01/privatised-probation-services-libraries-ex-offenders (accessed 15 April 2019).

Brinkerhoff, D. (2005) *Organizational Legitimacy, Capacity, and Capacity Development*. Brussels: European Centre for Development Policy Management.

Brogden, M. (1982) *The Police: Autonomy and Consent*. London: Academic Press.

Brogden, M. (1991) *On the Mersey Beat: Policing Liverpool between the Wars*. Oxford: Oxford University Press.

Brogden, M. and Ellison, G. (2012) *Policing in an Age of Austerity: A Postcolonial Perspective*. London: Routledge.

Brown, A. (2003) *English Society and the Prison: Time, Culture and Politics in the Development of the Modern Prison, 1850–1920*. Woodbridge and Rochester, NY: Boydell Press.

Brown, J. (2018) The Prison Estate. House of Commons Library Briefing Paper 05646.

BSIA (2011) Photography and Hostile Reconnaissance – A Guide for BSIA Members. British Security Industry Association.

Buckland, R. (2019) SFO Investigation of Serco and G4S Government Contracts. Letter from Robert Buckland QC MP, Minister for Justice, to Bob Neill MP. Available at: www.parliament.uk/documents/commons-committees/Justice/SFO-investigation-Serco-G4S-contracts.pdf (accessed 5 August 2019).

Burgess, K. (2018) Police Turn to Civilian Investigators. *The Times*, 20 August. Available at: www.thetimes.co.uk/article/police-turn-to-civilian-investigators-6fhv78v8z (accessed 12 January 2019).

Butt, A. I. (2019) Why Did the United States Invade Iraq in 2003? *Security Studies* 28 (2): 250–85.

Button, M. and Stiernstedt, P. (2018) Comparing Private Security Regulation in the European Union. *Policing and Society* 28 (4): 398–414.

Butto, M. and Wakefield, A. (2018) 'The Real Private Police': Franchising Constables and the Emergence of Employer Supported Policing. In Hucklesby, A. and Lister, S. (eds) *The Private Sector and Criminal Justice*. London: Palgrave Macmillan, pp. 135–60.

Calder, A. (1992) *The People's War: Britain 1939–1945*. London: Pimlico.

Canton, R. (2011) *Probation: Working With Offenders*. Abingdon and New York: Willan.

Cape, E. (2014) Virgin Atlantic, Virgin Trains, Virgin Police? Available at: www.crimeandjustice.org.uk/resources/virgin-atlantic-virgin-trains-virgin-police (accessed 19 January 2019).

Carpenter, J. (1981) *Escape from New York*. AVCO Embassy Pictures.

Carter, H. (2008) Policing the Retail Republic. *The Guardian*, 28 May. Available at: www.theguardian.com/society/2008/may/28/regeneration.communities (accessed 28 November 2018).

Catton, N. (2018) Thought Leaders from Police, Security Associations and Providers on the Increased Terrorist Threat in 2017. *City Security Magazine*, August. Available at: https://citysecuritymagazine.com/risk-management/

thought-leaders-from-police-security-associations-and-providers-on-the-increased-terrorist-threat-in-2017/.

Cerberus (2019) Investigation: Intellectual Property Rights. Available at: www.cerberussecurityandinvestigation.co.uk/service/investigation/ (accessed 15 July 2019).

Chase, S. and Pezzullo, R. (2016) *Zero Footprint: Leave No Trace, Take No Prisoners: The True Story of a Private Military Contractor in Syria, Libya, and the Worlds Most Dangerous Places*. New York: Mulholland Books.

Christophers, B. (2018) *The New Enclosure: The Appropriation of Public Land in Neoliberal Britain*. London and New York: Verso.

Churchill, D. (2014) Rethinking the State Monopolisation Thesis: The Historiography of Policing and Criminal Justice in Nineteenth-Century England. *Crime, Histoire & Sociétés/Crime, History & Societies* 18 (1): 131–52.

Civil Service Numbers (2019) Key Facts. Available at: https://civilservant.org.uk/information-numbers.html (accessed 11 August 2019).

Clement, M. (2016) *A People's History of Riots, Protest and the Law: The Sound of the Crowd*. London: Palgrave Macmillan.

Cockburn, P. (2013) Iraqis Win $5.8m from US Firm in Abu Ghraib Torture Lawsuit. *The Independent*, 9 January.

Cohen, A. (2012) The Torture Memos, 10 Years Later. Available at: www.theatlantic.com/national/archive/2012/02/the-torture-memos-10-years-later/252439/ (accessed 21 June 2019).

Cohen, P. (1979) Policing the Working Class City. In Fine, B., Kinsey, R., Lea, J., et al. (eds) *Capitalism and the Rule of Law*. London: Hutchinson.

Cohen, W. (2009) *Drucker on Leadership: New Lessons from the Father of Modern Management*. San Francisco: Wiley.

Coleman, R., Tombs, S. and Whyte, D. (2005) Capital, Crime Control and Statecraft in the Entrepreneurial City. *Urban Studies* 42: 2511–30.

Colley, L. (2009) *Britons: Forging the Nation, 1707–1837*. New Haven, CT: Yale University Press.

Colquhoun, P. (1806) *A Treatise on Indigence*. London: Hatchard.

Conway, S. (2001) War and National Identity in the Mid-Eighteenth-Century British Isles. *English Historical Review* 116 (468): 863–93.

Cooper, V. (2013) *No Fixed Abode: The Implications for Homeless People in the Criminal Justice System*. London: Howard League for Penal Reform.

Corporate Watch (2012) G4S Company Profile. Available at: https://corporatewatch.org/g4s-company-profile/ (accessed 27 July 2019).

Corporate Watch (2018) Immigration Detention Centres Factsheet: New Edition, May 2018. Available at: https://corporatewatch.org/immigration-detention-centres-factsheet-new-edition-updated-may-2018/ (accessed 20 April 2019).

Cox, J. (2017) Privately Owned Public Spaces. *The GiGLer: The Newsletter of Greenspace Information of Greater London CIC*.

Cramer, J. (1964) *The World's Police*. London: Cassel.

Crawford, A. (2013) The Police, Policing and the Future of the 'Extended Policing Family'. In Brown, J. M. (ed.) *The Future of Policing*. London: Routledge, pp. 173–90.

Crawford, A. and Lister, S. (2016) The Patchwork Shape of Reassurance Policing in England and Wales. In Goold, B. and Zedner, L. (eds) *Crime and Security*. Abingdon: Routledge, pp. 61–78.

Crewe, B., Liebling, A. and Hulley, S. (2011) Staff Culture, Use of Authority and Prisoner Quality of Life in Public and Private Sector Prisons. *Australian & New Zealand Journal of Criminology* 44 (1): 94–115.

Cusumano, E. (2014) The Scope of Military Privatisation: Military Role Conceptions and Contractor Support in the United States and the United Kingdom. *International Relations* 29 (2): 219–41.

Daily Maverick & Chronicle (2017) South Africa's R40bn Private Security Industry Under Threat. Available at: www.dailymaverick.co.za/article/2017-05-14-south-africas-r40bn-private-security-industry-under-threat/ (accessed 12 August 2019).

Dalrymple, W. (2015) The East India Company: The Original Corporate Raiders. *The Guardian*, 4 March.

Darling, J. (2016a) Privatising Asylum: Neoliberalisation, Depoliticisation and the Governance of Forced Migration. *Transactions of the Institute of British Geographers* 41 (3): 230–43.

Darling, J. (2016b) Asylum in Austere Times: Instability, Privatization and Experimentation within the UK Asylum Dispersal System. *Journal of Refugee Studies* 29 (4): 483–505.

Daunton, M. (1983) Public Space and Private Place: The Victorian City and the Working-Class Household. In Fraser, D. and Sutcliffe, A. (eds) *The Pursuit of Urban History*. London: Edward Arnold, pp. 212–33.

Daunton, M. (ed.) (2000) *The Cambridge Urban History of Britain: Volume 3: 1840–1950*. Cambridge: Cambridge University Press.

Davis, M. (1990) *City of Quartz: Excavating the Future in Los Angeles*. London: Verso.

Davis, M. (2006) *Planet of Slums*. London: Verso.

Davis, R. (2010) Security the Police Can't Provide? *The Guardian*, 28 July. Available at: www.theguardian.com/society/2010/jul/28/private-security-companies-police-housing-estates (accessed 11 November 2018).

Davis, R. (2019) The Closer Look: As SA Policing Fails, Private Security Steps In – But At a Cost. *Daily Maverick*, 15 January. Available at: www.dailymaverick.co.za/article/2019-01-15-as-sa-policing-fails-private-security-steps-in-but-at-a-cost/ (accessed 25 June 2019).

De Giorgi, A. (2006) *Re-thinking the Political Economy of Punishment: Perspectives on Post-Fordism and Penal Politics*. Aldershot: Ashgate.

De Giorgi, A. (2018) Back to Nothing: Prisoner Reentry and the 'Virtual City' of the Disenfranchised. Available at: https://thecrimereport.org/2018/03/01/back-to-nothing-prisoner-reentry-and-the-virtual-city-of-the-disenfranchised/ (accessed 6 July 2018).

DeLacy, M. (1986) *Prison Reform in Lancashire, 1700–1850: A Study of Local Administration*. Manchester: Manchester University Press.

den Blanken, W. (2012) 'Imperium in Imperio?' Sovereign Powers of the First Dutch West India Company. Masters thesis. Faculty of Humanities, Leiden

University. Available at: https://openaccess.leidenuniv.nl/handle/1887/20175 (accessed 29 June 2013).
Diphoorn, T. G. (2016) Twilight Policing: Private Security Practices in South Africa. *British Journal of Criminology* 56 (2): 313–31.
Dodsworth, F. (2004) 'Civic' Police and the Condition of Liberty: The Rationality of Governance in Eighteenth-Century England. *Social History* 29 (2): 199–216.
Dorfman, A. and Harel, A. (2013) The Case Against Privatization. *Philosophy & Public Affairs* 41 (1): 67–102.
Dorling, D. (2018) *Peak Inequality: Britain's Ticking Time Bomb*. Bristol: Policy Press.
Doward, J. (2011) Private Sector Prisons Are an Eye-Watering Scandal, Union Tells Justice Ministry. *The Observer*, 13 November. Available at: www.theguardian.com/society/2011/nov/13/privatise-prisons-scandal (accessed 6 April 2019).
Doward, J. (2012) Probation Officers to be Replaced by Electronic Kiosks in Pilot Scheme. *The Guardian*, 28 April. London.
Duffield, M. (2001) *Global Governance and the New Wars: The Merging of Development and Security*. London: Zed Books.
Duffield, M. (2012) Challenging Environments: Danger, Resilience and the Aid Industry. *Security Dialogue* 43 (5): 475–92.
Dunigan, M. (2014) The Future of US Military Contracting: Current Trends and Future Implications. *International Journal: Canada's Journal of Global Policy Analysis* 69 (4): 510–24.
Dyson, I. (2019) How Will the City of London Police Evolve in 2019? *City Security Magazine*, January. Available at: https://citysecuritymagazine.com/editors-choice/how-is-the-city-of-london-police-evolving-in-2019/.
Eastwood, V. (2013) Bigger than the Army: South Africa's Private Security Forces. Available at: www.cnn.com/2013/02/08/business/south-africa-private-security/index.html (accessed 13 August 2019).
Ellesoe, M. (2017) Child Soldiers Reloaded: The Privatisation of War. Available at: www.aljazeera.com/programmes/specialseries/2017/04/child-soldiers-reloaded-privatisation-war-170424204852514.html (accessed 7 December 2017).
Emsley, C. (1996) *The English Police: A Political and Social History*, 2nd edition. London: Taylor & Francis.
Emsley, C. (1999) The Origins of the Modern Police. *History Today* 49(4): 8–14.
Emsley, C. (2010) *The Great British Bobby: A History of British Policing from 1829 to the Present*. London: Quercus.
Evans, E. (2016) The Expected Impacts of Transforming Rehabilitation on Working Relationships with Offenders. *Probation Journal* 63 (2): 153–61.
Feeley, M. (2013) The Unconvincing Case Against Private Prisons. *Indiana Law Journal* 89: 1401–36.
Feeley, M. (2018) Privatizing Criminal Justice: A Historical Analysis of Entrepreneurship and Innovation. In Daems, T. and Vander-Beken, T. (eds) *Privatising Punishment in Europe?* London: Routledge, pp. 34–56.

Fielding-Smith, A., Black, C., Ross, A. et al. (2015) Revealed: Private Firms at Heart of US Drone Warfare. *The Guardian*, 30 July. Available at: www.theguardian.com/us-news/2015/jul/30/revealed-private-firms-at-heart-of-us-drone-warfare (accessed 7 December 2017).

Fitzgibbon, D. W. (2004) *Pre-emptive Criminalisation: Risk Control And Alternative Futures*. London: NAPO.

Fitzgibbon, D. W. (2007) Risk Analysis and the New Practitioner: Myth or Reality? *Punishment and Society* 9: 87–97.

Fitzgibbon, D. W. (2008) Fit for Purpose? OASys Assessments and Parole Decisions. *Probation Journal* 55 (1): 37–51.

Fitzgibbon, W. (2011) *Probation and Social Work on Trial: Violent Offenders and Child Abusers*. Basingstoke: Palgrave Macmillan.

Fitzgibbon, W. (2012) In the Eye of the Storm: The Implications of the Munro Child Protection Review for the Future of Probation. *Probation Journal* 59 (1): 7–22.

Fitzgibbon, W. (2016) Innovation and Privatisation in the Probation Service in England and Wales. *British Journal of Community Justice* 14 (1): 71–6.

Fitzgibbon, W. and Lea, J. (2014) Defending Probation: Beyond Privatisation and Security. *European Journal of Probation* 6 (1): 24–41.

Fitzgibbon, W. and Lea, J. (2017) Privatization and Coercion: The Question of Legitimacy. *Theoretical Criminology*: 22 (4): 545–62.

Fitzsimmons, S. (2015) *Private Security Companies During the Iraq War: Military Performance and the Use of Deadly Force*. London and New York: Routledge.

Fletcher, H. (2013) Private Sector Involvement in Probation Services. Available at: www.politicshome.com/opinion/ethos-journal/72072/private-sector-involvement-probation-services (accessed 4 October 2018).

FOLRS (2016) *The Evolution of London's Business Improvement Districts*. London: Future of London/Rocket Science. Available at: www.futureoflondon.org.uk/wp-content/uploads/delightful-downloads/2017/11/Evolution_of_Londons_BIDs_March2016_web_140316.pdf.

Ford, J. and Plimmer, G. (2018) Momentum Stalls on UK's Private Prisons. *Financial Times*, 12 February.

Foreign and Commonwealth Office (2002) *Private Military Companies: Options for Regulation*. HCP 577. London: The Stationary Office.

Forsythe, B. (1991) Centralisation and Local Autonomy: The Experience of English Prisons 1820–1877. *Journal of Historical Sociology* 4 (3): 317–45.

Foucault, M. (1977) *Discipline and Punish: The Birth of the Prison*. London: Allen Lane.

Frampton, W. (2014) Private Security Guards Given Police Powers to Tackle Antisocial Behaviour in Boscombe. *Bournemouth Echo*, 8 July.

Friedman, D. (1995) Making Sense of English Law Enforcement in the 18th Century. *The University of Chicago Law School Roundtable* 2 (Spring/Summer): 475–505.

G4S (2015) *Corporate Social Responsibility Report 2015*. London: G4S plc. Available at: www. g4s.com/en/Social-Responsibility/CSR-Reports.

G4S (2018) *Integrated Solutions in a Connected World: Integrated Report and Accounts 2018*. London: G4S plc. Available at: www.g4s.com/-/media/g4s/global/files/annual-reports/integrated-report-extracts-2018/g4s-full-integrated-report-2018.ashx.

G4S DRC (2019) G4S (DRC) SARL Provides Integrated Security Services. Available at: www.g4s.com/en-cd/content-pages/manned-security (accessed 22 June 2019).

G4S Iraq (2019) G4S SSI Operating in Iraq Since 2003. Available at: www.g4sriskmanagement.com:443/g4s-iraq (accessed 22 June 2019).

Gambino, L. (2019) Trump Designates Iran's Revolutionary Guards as Foreign Terrorist Organization. *The Guardian*, 8 April. Available at: www.theguardian.com/world/2019/apr/08/trump-designates-irans-revolutionary-guards-as-foreign-terrorist-organization (accessed 20 June 2019).

Gamble, A. (1988) *The Free Economy and the Strong State*. London: Macmillan.

Gard, R. (2012) The Creation of a 'Fully Public Service': Probation in England and Wales Between the Wars. Probation Journal 59(4): 323–38. DOI: 10.1177/0264550512458472.

Gard, R. (2014) *Rehabilitation and Probation in England and Wales, 1876–1962*. London and New York: Bloomsbury Academic.

Garland, D. (1985) *Punishment and Welfare: A History of Penal Strategies*. Aldershot: Gower.

Garland, D. (1996) The Limits of the Sovereign State: Strategies of Crime Control in Contemporary Society. *British Journal of Criminology* 36: 445–71.

Garland, D. (2001) *The Culture of Control: Crime and Social Order in Contemporary Society*. Oxford: Oxford University Press.

Garrett, B. L. (2015) The Privatisation of Cities' Public Spaces is Escalating: It Is Time to Take a Stand. *The Guardian*, 4 August. Available at: www.theguardian.com/cities/2015/aug/04/pops-privately-owned-public-space-cities-direct-action (accessed 27 November 2018).

Garrett, B. L. (2017) These Squares Are Our Squares: Be Angry About the Privatisation of Public Space. *The Guardian*, 25 July. Available at: www.theguardian.com/cities/2017/jul/25/squares-angry-privatisation-public-space (accessed 27 November 2018).

Garside, R. (2015) *Falling Police Numbers: The Longer View*. Centre for Crime and Justice Studies. Available at: www.crimeandjustice.org.uk/resources/falling-police-numbers-longer-view (accessed 15 August 2019).

Gazet, D. (2016) Wardens Suspended after Fining Woman for Feeding Ducks. *Kent Online*, 30 September. Available at: www.kentonline.co.uk/maidstone/news/firm-suspended-after-fining-woman-103324/ (accessed 14 November 2018).

Genders, E. (2002) Legitimacy, Accountability and Private Prisons. *Punishment & Society* 4 (3): 285–303.

Gentleman, A. (2014) A4e Ends £17m Prisoner Education Contract Citing Budget Constraints. *The Guardian*, 12 August. Available at: www.theguardian.com/uk-news/2014/aug/13/a4e-terminates-prisoner-education-training-contract (accessed 3 April 2019).

George, B. and Kimber, S. (2014) The History of Private Security and Its Impact on the Modern Security Sector. In Gill, M. (ed.) *The Handbook of Security*, 2nd edition. London: Palgrave Macmillan, pp. 21–40.

Gevisser, M. (2019) 'State Capture': The Corruption Investigation that Has Shaken South Africa. *The Guardian*, 11 July. Available at: www.theguardian.com/news/2019/jul/11/state-capture-corruption-investigation-that-has-shaken-south-africa (accessed 12 August 2019).

Gilligan, A. (2018) Wealthy Landlords Are in Talks to Fund a Scheme for Hundreds of Guards to Patrol Posh Areas of Central London. *Sunday Times*, 26 August.

Gordon, A. (2006a) Abu Ghraib: Imprisonment and the War on Terror. *Race and Class* 48: 42–59.

Gordon, A. (2006b) US: Supermax Lockdown. *Le Monde Diplomatique*, English edition, November. Available at: https://mondediplo.com/2006/11/09usprisons (accessed 21 August 2017).

Graham, S. (2011) *Cities Under Siege: The New Military Urbanism*. London and New York: Verso.

Gray, R. (2017) Erik Prince's Plan to Privatize the War in Afghanistan. Available at: www.theatlantic.com/politics/archive/2017/08/afghanistan-camp-david/537324/ (accessed 14 August 2019).

Grayson, J. (2018) Rodents, Bedbugs, Mould: UK Asylum Housing Still a Hostile Environment. Available at: www.opendemocracy.net/en/shine-a-light/rodents-bedbugs-mould-uk-asylum-housing-hostile-environment/ (accessed 20 January 2019).

Grierson, J. and Duncan, P. (2019) Private Jails More Violent than Public Ones, Data Analysis Shows. *The Guardian*, 13 May. Available at: www.theguardian.com/society/2019/may/13/private-jails-more-violent-than-public-prisons-england-wales-data-analysis (accessed 26 July 2019).

Grossman, E. (2019) Private Parts: The Private Sector and U.S. Peace Enforcement. *Small Wars Journal*. Available at: https://smallwarsjournal.com/jrnl/art/private-parts-private-sector-and-us-peace-enforcement (accessed 25 March 2019).

Hadaway, P. (2009) *Policing the Public Gaze: The Assault on Citizen Photography*. London: The Manifesto Club.

Haidari, M. A. and Banerjee, V. (2017) Privatization of Security Can Derail US-Led Stabilization of Afghanistan. Available at: http://thediplomat.com/2017/08/privatization-of-security-can-derail-us-led-stabilization-of-afghanistan/ (accessed 22 August 2017).

Hale, C., Heaton, R. and Uglow, S. (2004) Uniform Styles? Aspects of Police Centralization in England and Wales. *Policing & Society* 14 (4): 291–312.

Hannah-Moffat, K. (2005) Criminogenic Needs and the Transformative Risk Subject: Hybridisation of Risk/Need in Penality. *Punishment & Society* 7 (1): 29–31.

Hardman, P. J. (2007) The Origins of Late Eighteenth-Century Prison Reform in England. PhD thesis, University of Sheffield. Available at: http://etheses.whiterose.ac.uk/3037/ (accessed 13 March 2017).

Harris, A. T. (2004) *Policing the City: Crime and Legal Authority in London, 1780–1840*. Ohio State University Press.

Harris, J. (2018) The Growth of Private Policing is Eroding Justice For All. *The Guardian*, 10 September. Available at: www.theguardian.com/commentisfree/2018/sep/10/growth-private-policing-eroding-justice-for-all (accessed 11 November 2018).

Harvey, D. (1997) Contested Cities: Social Processes and Spatial Form. In Jewson, N. and MacGregor, S. (eds) *Transforming Cities: Contested Governance and New Spatial Divisions*. London: Routledge.

Hatherley, O. (2012) Bluewater Thrives by Not Alarming Shoppers with Anything New or Strange. *The Guardian*, 8 August. Available at: www.theguardian.com/commentisfree/2012/aug/08/bluewater-thrives-not-alarming-shoppers (accessed 11 July 2019).

Hay, D. (1975) Property, Authority and the Criminal Law. In Hay, D., Linebaugh, P., Rule, J., et al. (eds) *Albion's Fatal Tree: Crime and Society in Eighteenth Century England*. London: Allen Lane, pp. 17–63.

Hay, D. and Snyder, F. (1989) Using the Criminal Law 1750–1850: Private Prosecution and the State. In Hay, D. and Snyder, F. (eds) *Policing and Prosecution in Britain 1750–1850*. Oxford: Oxford University Press, pp. 3–52.

Hesketh, J. (2018) Contract or Command: An Analysis of Outsourcing in Defence. Available at: https://ukdefencejournal.org.uk/contract-or-command-an-analysis-of-outsourcing-in-defence/.

Hickey, S. (2015) G4S Meeting Descends Into Chaos, with Nine Activists Bundled Out. *The Guardian*, 4 June.

Himmelfarb, G. (1970) Bentham's Utopia: The National Charity Company. *Journal of British Studies* 10 (1): 80–125.

HM Chief Inspector of Prisons (2013) *Report on an Unannounced Inspection of HMP Oakwood*. London: Her Majesty's Inspectorate of Prisons.

HM Chief Inspector of Prisons (2017) *Report on an Unannounced Inspection of Yarl's Wood Immigration Removal Centre*. London: Her Majesty's Inspectorate of Prisons.

HM Chief Inspector of Prisons (2018a) *Report on an Unannounced Inspection of HMP Birmingham*. London: Her Majesty's Inspectorate of Prisons.

HM Chief Inspector of Prisons (2018b) *Report on an Unannounced Inspection of HMP Liverpool*. London: Her Majesty's Inspectorate of Prisons.

HM Government (2012) *The Civil Service Reform Plan*. June. London: The Stationery Office.

HM Government (2018) *CONTEST: The United Kingdom's Strategy for Countering Terrorism CM9608*. London: The Stationary Office.

HM Inspectorate of Probation (2016) *Transforming Rehabilitation Early Implementation 5*. Manchester: HM Inspectorate of Probation.

HM Inspectorate of Probation (2017) *2017 Annual Report*. Manchester: HM Inspectorate of Probation.

HM Inspectorate of Probation (2018) *Probation Supply Chains: A Thematic Inspection by HM Inspectorate of Probation*. Manchester: HM Inspectorate of Probation.

HM Inspectorate of Probation (2019a) *An Inspection of Dorset, Devon and Cornwall Community Rehabilitation Company*. Manchester: HM Inspectorate of Probation.

HM Inspectorate of Probation (2019b) *Report of the Chief Inspector of Probation March 2019*. Manchester: HM Inspectorate of Probation.

Hobsbawm, E. (1994) Barbarism: A Users Guide. *New Left Review* 206 (1): 44–54.

Holden, G., Allen, B., Gray, S. et al. (2016) *Final Report of the Board's Advice to Secretary of State for Justice*. 30 March. Medway Improvement Board. Available at: www.gov.uk/government/uploads/system/uploads/attachment_data/file523167/medway-report.pdf (accessed 24 April 2019).

Holmila, E. (2012) The History of Private Violence. In Liivoja, R. and Saumets, A. (eds) *The Law of Armed Conflict: Historical and Contemporary Perspectives*. Tartu, Estonia: Tartu University Press, pp. 45–74.

Holsti, K. J. (1996) *The State, War, and the State of War*. Cambridge: Cambridge University Press.

Holt, A. (2017) Undercover: Britain's Immigration Secrets. *BBC Panorama*. Available at: www.bbc.co.uk/programmes/b094mhsn.

Home Office (1936) *Report of the Departmental Committee on the Social Services in Courts of Summary Jurisdiction*. (Cmd. 5122). London: HMSO.

Hönke, J. (2013) *Transnational Companies and Security Governance: Hybrid Practices in a Postcolonial World*. Abingdon: Routledge.

Hopkins, R. (2013) South Africa Takes Over G4S Prison After Concerns. *The Guardian*, 9 October. Available at: www.theguardian.com/world/2013/oct/09/g4s-sacked-south-africa-prison-mangaung (accessed 29 July 2019).

Hopkins, R. (2018) Prison Company Stalls Court Actions. *The Mail & Guardian Online*, 7 December. Available at: https://mg.co.za/article/2018-12-07-00-prison-company-stalls-court-actions/ (accessed 29 July 2019).

House of Commons (1987) Debates 16th July 1987 Vol. 119 Cc 296–309. London: Hansard. Available at: https://api.parliament.uk/historic-hansard/commons/1987/jul/16/prisons (accessed 14 April 2018).

House of Commons (1989) Debates 1st March 1989 Vol. 148 Cc 277–89. London: Hansard. Available at: https://api.parliament.uk/historic-hansard/commons/1987/jul/16/prisons (accessed 14 April 2018).

House of Commons (1993) Debates 3rd February 1993 Vol. 218 Cc 431. London: Hansard. Available at: https://api.parliament.uk/historic-hansard/commons/1993/feb/03/prisons-contracting-out (accessed 14 April 2018).

House of Commons (2012) *Home Affairs Committee – Fourth Report: Private Investigators*. London: The Stationary Office. Available at: https://publications.parliament.uk/pa/cm201213/cmselect/cmhaff/100/10005.htm.

House of Commons (2014a) *House of Commons Justice Committee: Crime Reduction Policies: A Co-Ordinated Approach? Interim Report on the Government's Transforming Rehabilitation Programme*. London: The Stationary Office. Available at: https://publications.parliament.uk/pa/cm201314/cmselect/cmjust/1004/1004.pdf.

House of Commons (2014b) *House of Commons Public Accounts Committee: Twenty-Third Report: Transforming Contract Management*. London: The

Stationary Office. Available at: https://publications.parliament.uk/pa/cm201415/cmselect/cmpubacc/585/58506.htm#n48.

House of Commons (2017) Justice Committee Oral Evidence: Transforming Rehabilitation, HC 1018, Tuesday 21 March 2017. Available at: http://data.parliament.uk/writtenevidence/committeeevidence.svc/evidencedocument/justice-committee/transforming-rehabilitation/oral/49239.pdf.

House of Commons (2018) *Home Affairs Committee: Asylum Accommodation: Replacing COMPASS. Thirteenth Report of Session 2017–19*. London: The Stationary Office.

House of Commons (2019a) *Home Affairs Committee – Fourteenth Report of Session 2017–19: Immigration Detention*. London: The Stationary Office. Available at: https://publications.parliament.uk/pa/cm201719/cmselect/cmhaff/913/913.pdf.

House of Commons (2019b) *Home Affairs Committee – Asylum Accommodation: Replacing COMPASS: Government Response to the Committee's Thirteenth Report of Session 2017–19*. London: The Stationary Office. Available at: https://publications.parliament.uk/pa/cm201719/cmselect/cmhaff/2016/2016.pdf.

House of Commons Foreign Affairs Committee (2002) *Private Military Companies*. London: The Stationary Office.

House of Lords (2012) Debates 19th July 2012 Cc 381–429. London: Lords Hansard. Available at: https://publications.parliament.uk/pa/ld201213/ldhansrd/text/120719-0002.htm (accessed 14 April 2018).

Howard, J. (1777) *The State of the Prisons in England and Wales*. Warrington: William Ayres.

ICRC (2015) *The Montreux Document on Private Military and Security Companies*. Geneva: International Committee of the Red Cross. Available at: www.icrc.org/en/publication/0996-montreux-document-private-military-and-security-companies (accessed 18 June 2019).

Ignatieff, M. (1989) *A Just Measure of Pain: The Penitentiary in the Industrial Revolution 1750–1850*. Harmondsworth: Penguin.

Institute for Government (2018) Institute for Government Performance Tracker 2018: Prisons. Institute for Government. Available at: www.instituteforgovernment.org.uk/publication/performance-tracker-2018/prisons.

Interserve Press Office (2015) Purple Futures Takes Over Running of Probation and Rehabilitation Services. Available at: www.interserve.com/news-media/press-releases/press-release/2015/02/01/purple-futures-takes-over-running-of-probation-and-rehabilitation-services (accessed 14 April 2018).

Isenberg, D. (2009) *Shadow Force: Private Security Contractors in Iraq*. Westport, CT: Praeger.

Jackson, J., Huq, A., Bradford, B., et al. (2013) Monopolizing Force? Police Legitimacy and Public Attitudes towards the Acceptability of Violence. *Psychology, Public Policy and Law* 19 (4): 479–97.

Jacoby, T. (2007) Hegemony, Modernisation and Post-War Reconstruction. *Global Society* 21 (4): 521–37.

Jacovetti, S. (2016) The Constitutionality of Prison Privatization: An Analysis of Prison Privatization in the United States and Israel. *The Global Business Law Review* 6 (1): 61.

James, P. D. (2010) *The Children of Men*. London: Faber & Faber.

Jessop, B. (1990) *State Theory: Putting the Capitalist State in Its Place*. Cambridge: Polity.

Johnston, L. (1992) *The Rebirth of Private Policing*. London: Routledge.

Johnstone, P. (2015) Real Influence of Sir Robert Peel on Twenty-First Century Policing in America. In Lemieux, F., den Heyer, G., and Das, D. K. (eds) *Economic Development, Crime, and Policing: Global Perspectives*. London: CRC Press.

Joireman, S. F. (2011) *Where There is No Government: Enforcing Property Rights in Common Law Africa*. Oxford: Oxford University Press.

Jones, C. (2017) Market Forces: The Development of the EU Security-Industrial Complex. Transnational Institute, Statewatch. Available at: https://statewatch.omeka.net/items/show/13756 (accessed 18 January 2019).

Jones, C. and Novak, T. (1999) *Poverty, Welfare and the Disciplinary State*. Routledge.

Jones, T. and Newburn, T. (1999) Urban Change and Policing: Mass Private Property Re-considered. *European Journal on Criminal Policy and Research* 7 (2): 225–44.

Kaker, S. (Forthcoming) Responding to, or Perpetuating, Urban Insecurity? Enclave-Making in Karachi. In Kaldor, M. and Sassen, S. (eds) *Cities at War: Global Insecurity and Urban Resistance*. New York: Columbia University Press.

Kaldor, M. (1999) *New and Old Wars: Organized Violence in a Global Era*. Cambridge: Polity.

Kaldor, M. (2003) Beyond Militarism, Arms Races and Arms Control. In Lundestad, G. and Njølstad, O. (eds) *War and Peace in the 20th Century and Beyond: The Nobel Centennial Symposium*. Singapore: World Scientific Publishing, pp. 145–76. Available at: www.worldscientific.com/ (accessed 22 May 2014).

Kaldor, M. (2005) Old Wars, Cold Wars, New Wars, and the War on Terror. *International Politics* 42 (4): 491–8.

Kalman, B., Deiss, D. and Watson, E. (2019) U.S. Special Operations: The New Face of America's War Machine. *MintPress News*. Available at: www.mintpressnews.com/u-s-special-operations-the-new-face-of-americas-war-machine/256431/ (accessed 22 June 2019).

Kamphuis, C. (2011) Foreign Investment and the Privatization of Coercion: A Case Study of the Forza Security Company in Peru. *Brooklyn Journal of International Law* 37 (2): 529–78.

Keen, D. (2012) *Useful Enemies: When Waging Wars is More Important than Winning Them*. New Haven, CT: Yale University Press.

Kennedy, D. (2006) *Of War and Law*. Princeton NJ: Princeton University Press.

Kent, D. and Townsend, N. (2002) *The Convicts of the Eleanor: Protest in Rural England, New Lives in Australia*. 3rd edition. London and Annandale, NSW: The Merlin Press Ltd.

Khomami, N. (2015) Frinton Residents Pay Security Firm to Patrol Streets. *The Guardian*, 3 November. Available at: www.theguardian.com/uk-news/2015/nov/03/seaside-town-residents-frinton-pay-security-firm-patrol-streets (accessed 11 November 2018).

King, P. (1989) Prosecution Associations and their Impact in Eighteenth-Century Essex. In Hay, D. and Snyder, F. (eds) *Policing and Prosecution in Britain 1750–1850*. Oxford: Oxford University Press, pp. 171–210.

Kingdom Services (2018) Kingdom Local Authority Support. Available at: www.kingdom.co.uk/services/local-authority-support/ (accessed 8 July 2019).

Kinsella, C. (2011) Welfare, Exclusion and Rough Sleeping in Liverpool. *International Journal of Sociology and Social Policy* 31 (5/6): 240–52.

Kinsey, C. (2006) Corporate Soldiers and International Security: The Rise of Private Military Companies. London and New York: Routledge.

Kirton, G. and Guillaume, C. (2015) *Employment Relations and Working Conditions in Probation after Transforming Rehabilitation*. London: Queen Mary University.

Koyama, M. (2012) Prosecution Associations in Industrial Revolution England: Private Providers of Public Goods? *The Journal of Legal Studies* 41 (1): 95–130.

Lampard, K. and Marsden, E. (2018) *Independent Investigation into Concerns about Brook House Immigration Removal Centre: A Report for the Divisional Chief Executive of G4S Care and Justice and the Main Board of G4S Plc*. London: Verita Consultancy. Available at: www.verita.net/wp-content/uploads/2018/12/G4S-version-report.pdf.

Lea, J. (2002) *Crime and Modernity*. London: Sage Publications.

Lea, J. (2004) Hitting Criminals Where it Hurts: Organised Crime and the Erosion of Due Process. *Cambrian Law Review* 35: 81–96.

Lea, J. (2015) Back to the Future: Neoliberalism as Social and Political Regression. *Journal on European History of Law* 6 (1): 109–17.

Lea, J. and Hallsworth, S. (2012) Bringing the State Back in: Understanding Neoliberal Security. In Squires, P. and Lea, J. (eds) *Criminalisation and Advanced Marginality: Critically Exploring the Work of Loic Wacquant*. Bristol: Policy Press, pp. 19–39.

Leander, A. (2006) *Eroding State Authority? Private Military Companies and the Legitimate Use of Force*. Rome: Centro Militare di Studi Strategici.

Leander, A. (2012) *Cost Before Hearts and Minds – Private Security in Afghanistan*. EthZurich: Center for Security Studies. Available at: www.css.ethz.ch/en/services/digital-library/articles/article.html/152210/pdf.

Lee, S. P. (2015) Human Rights and Drone 'Warfare'. *Peace Review* 27 (4): 432–9.

Leigh, M. (2018) *Peterloo*. Entertainment One Films.

Lennon, A. T. J. and Eiss, C. (eds) (2004) *Reshaping Rogue States: Preemption, Regime Change, and US Policy toward Iran, Iraq, and North Korea*. Cambridge, MA: The MIT Press.

Lewis, J. (1995) *The Voluntary Sector, the State and Social Work in Britain: Charity Organisation Society/Family Welfare Association Since 1869*. Aldershot and Brookfield, VT: Edward Elgar Publishing Ltd.

Lewis, P., Williams, H., Pelopidas, B. et al. (2014) *Too Close for Comfort: Cases of Near Nuclear Use and Options for Policy*. Chatham House Report. London: Royal Institute of International Affairs. Available at: www.chathamhouse.org/sites/default/files/field/field_document/20140428TooCloseforComfortNuclearUseLewisWilliamsPelopidasAghlani.pdf.

Leys, C. (2006) The Cynical State. In Panitch, L. and Leys, C. (eds) *Socialist Register 2006*. London: Merlin Press, pp. 1–27.

Liebling, A. and Ludlow, A. (2017) Privatising Public Prisons: Penality, Law and Practice. *Australian & New Zealand Journal of Criminology* 50 (4): 473–92.

Linebaugh, P. (2003) *The London Hanged: Crime and Civil Society in the Eighteenth Century*. London: Verso.

Loader, I. (1997) Policing and the Social: Questions of Symbolic Power. *British Journal of Sociology* 48 (1): 1–18.

Loney, M. (1975) *Rhodesia: White Racism and Imperial Response*. Penguin Books.

Lopez, R. (2010) *Soldier's Shocking Allegation: Troops Ordered to Engage in '360 Rotational Fire' Against Civilians*. Bonn: Global Policy Forum.

MacAskill, E. (2000) UN Gets Warning Shot on Peacekeeping. *The Guardian*, 8 September. Available at: www.theguardian.com/world/2000/sep/09/sierraleone2 (accessed 21 October 2017).

Macleod, G. and Johnstone, C. (2012) Stretching Urban Renaissance: Privatizing Space, Civilizing Place, Summoning 'Community'. *International Journal of Urban and Regional Research* 36 (1): 1–28.

Mair, G. and Burke, L. (2011) *Redemption, Rehabilitation and Risk Management: A History of Probation*. London: Routledge.

Manifesto Club (2019) PSPOs – The 'Busybodies' Charter' in 2018. Available at: https://manifestoclub.info/pspos-the-busybodies-charter-in-2018/ (accessed 17 May 2019).

Mann, M. (1987) The Roots and Contradictions of Modern Militarism. *New Left Review* 162: 35–50.

Marquand, D. (2004) *The Decline of the Public: The Hollowing Out of Citizenship*. Cambridge: Polity Press.

Marsh, S. and Greenfield, P. (2019) Firm 'Uses Aggressive Tactics' to Collect Millions in Fines for Councils. *The Guardian*, 22 January.

Matevžič, G. (2019) *Crossing a Red Line: How EU Countries Undermine the Right to Liberty by Expanding the Use of Detention of Asylum Seekers upon Entry*. Budapest: Hungarian Helsinki Committee.

McConville, S. (2015) *A History of English Prison Administration*. London: Routledge.

McDonald, D. C. (1994) Public Imprisonment by Private Means: The Re-emergence of Private Prisons and Jails in the United States, the United Kingdom, and Australia. *The British Journal of Criminology* 34: 29–48.

McFate, S. (2014) The Blackwater Verdict Signals America's Growing Dependence on Wall Street to Wage War. *The New Republic*, 24 October. Available at: https://newrepublic.com/article/119975/blackwater-convictions-dont-mean-end-mercenary-war (accessed 23 September 2017).

McFate, S. (2015) *The Modern Mercenary: Private Armies and What They Mean for World Order*. Oxford: Oxford University Press.

McMullan, J. (1995) The Political Economy of Thief-Taking. *Crime, Law and Social Change* 23 (2): 121–46.

McMullan, J. L. (1996) The New Improved Monied Police Reform, Crime Control, and the Commodification of Policing in London. *The British Journal of Criminology* 36 (1): 85–108.

McWilliams, W. (1983) The Mission to the English Police Courts 1876–1936. *The Howard Journal of Criminal Justice* 22 (1–3): 129–47.

McWilliams, W. (1985) The Mission Transformed: Professionalisation of Probation Between the Wars. *The Howard Journal of Criminal Justice* 24 (4): 257–74.

Meiksins Wood, E. (1992) Custom Against Capitalism. *New Left Review* 195: 21–8.

Melling, J. (2017) #GiveUpYourGun: Can Security Guards Help Tackle Gun Crime in London? Available at: www.churchillsecurity.co.uk/2017/02/09/giveupyourgun-security-guards-tackle-gun-crime-london/ (accessed 29 November 2018).

Mendez, Y. (2017) 5 Westfield Security Guards Try to Stop Journalist from Filming in Public Space. Available at: www.youtube.com/watch?time_continue=73&v=-kLUWaoptOc (accessed 27 November 2018).

Menz, G. (2011) Outsourcing, Privatization and the Politics of Privatizing Migration. Paper presented at the International Studies Association Conference, Montreal, 2011.

Ministry of Justice (2013) *Transforming Rehabilitation: A Strategy for Reform*. Cm 8619. London: The Stationery Office.

Ministry of Justice (2017) Ministry of Justice: Secondment: Written Question – 70955. Hansard (House of Commons Written Questions). Available at: www.parliament.uk/business/publications/written-questions-answers-statements/written-question/Commons/2017-04-13/70955/.

Ministry of Justice (2018) *Offender Management Statistics Bulletin, England and Wales*. London: Ministry of Justice.

Ministry of Justice (2019) *Annual Prison Performance Ratings 2018/19*. London: Ministry of Justice.

Minton, A. (2006) *The Privatisation of Public Space*. London: Royal Institution of Chartered Surveyors.

Minton, A. (2013) *Common Good(s) — Redefining the Public Interest and the Common Good*. London: How To Work Together. Available at: http://howtoworktogether.org/wp-content/uploads/htwt-think_tank-anna_minton-common_goods.pdf (accessed 18 April 2017).

Minton, A. (2017) *Big Capital: Who Is London For?* London: Penguin.

Minton, A. and Aked, J. (2013) 'Fortress Britain': High Security, Insecurity and the Challenge of Preventing Harm. Prevention Working Paper. London: New Economics Foundation.

Monaghan, K. (2013) Report by the Assistant Deputy Coroner Karon Monaghan QC: Inquest into the Death of Jimmy Kelenda Mubenga. Available at: http://

iapdeathsincustody.independent.gov.uk/wp-content/uploads/2013/12/Rule-43-Report-Jimmy-Mubenga.pdf.

Monbiot, G. (2009) George Monbiot: This Revolting Trade in Human Lives is an Incentive to Lock People Up. *The Guardian*, 3 March.

Morris, S. (2017) Increase in Serious Crimes by Offenders on Probation, Figures Show. *The Guardian*, 1 August. Available at: www.theguardian.com/society/2017/aug/02/increase-serious-crimes-offenders-probation-figures-show-plaid-cymru (accessed 15 April 2019).

Morse, A. (2015) Outcome-Based Payment Schemes: Government's Use of Payment by Results. Report by the Comptroller and Auditor General. HC 86 SESSION 2015–16, 15 June. London: National Audit Office. Available at: www.nao.org.uk/wp-content/uploads/2015/06/Outcome-based-payment-schemes-governments-use-of-payment-by-results.pdf.

Morse, A. (2018) Ensuring Sufficient Skilled Military Personnel. Report by the Comptroller and Auditor General. HC 947, 17 April. London: National Audit Office. Available at: www.nao.org.uk/wp-content/uploads/2015/06/Outcome-based-payment-schemes-governments-use-of-payment-by-results.pdf.

Moyle, P. (2001) Separating the Allocation of Punishment from its Administration: Theoretical and Empirical Observations. *The British Journal of Criminology* 41 (1): 77–100.

Mudlark (2016) Today in London History: Duke of Bedford Closes His Private Road, 1798. Available at: https://pasttenseblog.wordpress.com/2016/09/29/today-in-london-history-duke-of-bedford-closes-his-private-road-1798/ (accessed 5 November 2018).

Muenkler, H. (2005) *The New Wars*. Cambridge: Polity.

Mukherjee, A. (2017) Impacts of Private Prison Contracting on Inmate Time Served and Recidivism. ID 2523238, SSRN Scholarly Paper, 20 August. Rochester, NY: Social Science Research Network. Available at: https://papers.ssrn.com/abstract=2523238 (accessed 13 March 2019).

Mulheirn, I. (2013) *Paying for Results? Rethinking Probation Reform*. London: Social Market Foundation.

Murray, C. (2009) *The Catholic Orangemen of Togo and Other Conflicts I Have Known*. London: Atholl Publishing.

Musah, A.-F. and Fayemi, J. K. (1999) Africa in Search of Security: Mercenaries and Conflicts – An Overview. In Musah, A.-F. and Fayemi, J. K. (eds) *Mercenaries: An African Security Dilemma*. London: Pluto Press.

Myers, R. (2011) A Legal Guide to Citizen's Arrest. *The Guardian*, 9 August. Available at: www.theguardian.com/law/2011/aug/09/guide-to-citizens-arrest (accessed 15 July 2019).

National Audit Office (2019) Home Office's Management of its Contract with G4S to Run Brook House Immigration Removal Centre – National Audit Office (NAO) Report. Available at: www.nao.org.uk/report/home-offices-management-of-its-contract-with-g4s-to-run-brook-house-immigration-removal-centre/ (accessed 28 July 2019).

NCTSO (2016) Project Griffin Guidance. Available at: www.gov.uk/government/publications/project-griffin/project-griffin (accessed 16 July 2019).

Neate, R. (2013) G4S Profits Tumble on Olympics Failings. *The Guardian*, 13 March. Available at: www.theguardian.com/business/2013/mar/13/g4s-profits-tumble-olympics-failings (accessed 12 January 2019).

Neocleous, M. (2000) Social Police and the Mechanisms of Prevention: Patrick Colquhoun and the condition of poverty. *British Journal of Criminology* 40: 710–26.

Neuman, S. (2017) U.S. Appeals Court Tosses Ex-Blackwater Guard's Conviction in 2007 Baghdad Massacre. Available at: www.npr.org/sections/thetwo-way/2017/08/04/541616598/u-s-appeals-court-tosses-conviction-of-ex-blackwater-guard-in-2007-baghdad-massa (accessed 21 June 2019).

Neumann, F. (2009) *Behemoth: The Structure and Practice of National Socialism, 1933–1944*. Chicago: Ivan R. Dee.

Newsinger, J. (2016) Review of Fitzsimmons (2015) *Private Security Companies during the Iraq War: Military Performance and the Use of Deadly Force. Race & Class* 58 (2): 96–9.

O'Brien, K. (1999) Private Military Companies and African Security 1990–98. In Musah, A.-F. and Fayemi, J. K. (eds) *Mercenaries: An African Security Dilemma*. London: Pluto Press, pp. 43–75.

O'Reilly, C. (2010) The Transnational Security Consultancy Industry: A Case of State-Corporate Symbiosis. *Theoretical Criminology* 14 (2): 183–210.

OECD (2019) *Under Pressure: The Squeezed Middle Class*. Paris: OECD Publishing.

Østensen, Å. G. (2013) In the Business of Peace: The Political Influence of Private Military and Security Companies on UN Peacekeeping. *International Peacekeeping* 20 (1): 33–47.

Panchamia, N. (2012) *Competition in Prisons*. London: Institute for Government.

Parkar, N. (2019) Life as Immigration Detainee 'Like Hell'. *BBC News*, 5 April. Available at: www.bbc.com/news/uk-england-beds-bucks-herts-47802425 (accessed 24 April 2019).

Parmar, I. (2018) The US-Led Liberal Order: Imperialism by Another Name? *International Affairs* 94 (1): 151–72.

Pattison, J. (2014) *The Morality of Private War: The Challenge of Private Military and Security Companies*. Oxford: Oxford University Press.

Paul, J. and Nahory, C. (2007) *War and Occupation in Iraq*. Bonn: Global Policy Forum.

Peachey, P. and Lakhani, N. (2012) A Force for Good? The Rise of Private Police. *The Independent*, 12 March. Available at: www.independent.co.uk/news/uk/crime/a-force-for-good-the-rise-of-private-police-7561646.html (accessed 12 November 2018).

Perraudin, F. (2019) UK Army Combat Units 40% Below Strength as Recruitment Plummets. *The Guardian*, 9 August. Available at: www.theguardian.com/uk-news/2019/aug/09/uk-army-combat-units-40-below-strength-as-recruitment-plummets (accessed 11 August 2019).

Peters, H., Schwartz, M. and Kapp, L. (2017) Department of Defense Contractor and Troop Levels in Iraq and Afghanistan: 2007–2017. Washington, DC:

Congressional Research Service 7-5700, R44116. Available at: www.crs.gov (accessed 15 July 2017).

Petersohn, U. (2014) The Impact of Mercenaries and Private Military and Security Companies on Civil War Severity between 1946 and 2002. *International Interactions* 40 (2): 191–215.

Pfotenhauer, D. (2016) The Case for Private Contractors in Northern Nigeria. Available at: www.africandefence.net/case-for-pmcs-in-nigeria/ (accessed 6 December 2017).

Piketty, T. (2014) *Capital in the Twenty-First Century*. Cambridge, MA: Harvard University Press.

Pile, S., Mooney, G. and Brook, C. (1999) *Unruly Cities? Order/Disorder?* London: Routledge.

Pingeot, L. (2014) *Contracting Insecurity: Private Military and Security Companies and the Future of the United Nations*. Bonn: Global Policy Forum.

Polanyi, K. (1957) *The Great Transformation: The Political and Economic Origins of Our Time*. Boston, MA: Beacon Press.

Police Federation (2008) Extension of Police Powers to Civilian Roles. Available at: www.policeoracle.com/news/Extension-Of-Police-Powers-To-Civilian-Roles_17125.html (accessed 12 November 2018).

Porter, G. (2108) America's Permanent-War Complex. Available at: https://johnmenadue.com/gareth-porter-americas-permanent-war-complex-the-american-conservative-15-11-2108/ (accessed 21 November 2018).

Powell, I. (2012) Private Firm Flouts UN Embargo in Somalia. Available at: www.globalpolicy.org/pmscs/51323-private-firm-flouts-un-embargo-in-somalia.html?itemid=id#1455 (accessed 22 October 2017).

Powell, T. (2018) UK's First Private Police Force to Go Nationwide after London Success. Evening Standard, 6 May. Available at: www.standard.co.uk/news/uk/britains-first-private-police-force-to-go-nationwide-after-success-in-londons-wealthiest-a3832321.html (accessed 15 July 2019).

Press Association (2019) Serco Fined £22.9m over Electronic Tagging Scandal. *The Guardian*, 3 July. Available at: www.theguardian.com/business/2019/jul/03/serco-fined-229m-over-electronic-tagging-scandal (accessed 10 August 2019).

Priest, D. and Arkin, W. M. (2012) Top Secret America: The Rise of the New American Security State. New York: Back Bay.

Prince, E. D. (2017) The MacArthur Model for Afghanistan. *Wall Street Journal*, 31 May. Available at: www.wsj.com/articles/the-macarthur-model-for-afghanistan-1496269058 (accessed 15 September 2017).

Prison Legal News (2013) Israeli Supreme Court: Private Prisons Violate Human Dignity. Available at: www.prisonlegalnews.org/news/2013/mar/15/israeli-supreme-court-private-prisons-violate-human-dignity/ (accessed 4 March 2018).

Prison Reform Trust (2012) Public or Private Sector Prisons? March 2012. Available at: www.prisonreformtrust.org.uk/Press Policy/Parliament/AllParty ParliamentaryPenalAffairsGroup/PublicorprivatesectorprisonsMarch2012 (accessed 25 July 2019).

Provost, C. (2017) The Industry of Inequality: Why the World is Obsessed with Private Security. *The Guardian*, 12 May. Available at: www.theguardian.com/inequality/2017/may/12/industry-of-inequality-why-world-is-obsessed-with-private-security (accessed 25 June 2019).

Pulver, M. (2017) Erik Prince's Dark Plan for Afghanistan: Military Occupation for Profit, Not Security. Available at: www.salon.com/2017/06/03/erik-princes-dark-plan-for-afghanistan-military-occupation-for-profit-not-security/ (accessed 15 September 2017).

Pyman, M. (2013) *Corruption and Peacekeeping: Strengthening Peacekeeping and the United Nations*. London: Transparency International.

Quinn, A. (2009) U.S. to Drop Contractor in Kabul Embassy Scandal. *Reuters*, 8 December. Available at: www.reuters.com/article/us-afghanistan-usa-embassy/u-s-to-drop-contractor-in-kabul-embassy-scandal-idUSTRE5B75F420091208 (accessed 16 October 2017).

Ralby, I. (2015) Accountability for Armed Contractors. *Fletcher Security Review* 2 (1): 15–19.

Rathmell, A. (2017) Power to the Police Staff? Big Changes to Police Powers. Available at: www.ukpolicelawblog.com/index.php/9-blog/112-power-to-the-staff-big-changes-to-designated-powers (accessed 12 January 2019).

Rawlings, P. (1999) *Crime and Power: A History of Criminal Justice 1688–1988*. London: Longman.

Reed, J. and Plimmer, G. (2016) G4S Close to Selling Israeli Business. *Financial Times*, 16 August.

Reiner, R. (2010) *The Politics of the Police*. Oxford: Oxford University Press.

Ricks, T. E. (1997) The Widening Gap Between Military and Society. Available at: www.theatlantic.com/magazine/archive/1997/07/the-widening-gap-between-military-and-society/306158/ (accessed 20 June 2019).

Rider, W. and Smolen, B. (2019) Shopper with Guide Dog Ordered to Leave Bluewater by Security Guard. Available at: www.essexlive.news/news/essex-news/bluewater-responds-after-shopper-guide-2613237 (accessed 11 July 2019).

Riley, S. (2017) Private Security: Twin Indignities. *Critical Legal Thinking*. Available at: http://criticallegalthinking.com/2017/11/13/private-security-twin-indignities/ (accessed 23 April 2018).

Roberts, M. (2016) *The Long Depression*. Chicago: Haymarket Books.

Robins, N. (2006) *The Corporation that Changed the World: How the East India Company Shaped the Modern Multinational*. Hyderabad: Pluto Press.

Robinson, G., Burke, L. and Millings, M. (2016) Criminal Justice Identities in Transition: The Case of Devolved Probation Services in England and Wales. *The British Journal of Criminology* 56 (1): 161–78.

Rock, P. (1983) Law, Order and Power in Late Seventeenth and Early Eighteenth Century England. In Cohen, S. and Scull, A. (eds) *Social Control and the State*. Oxford: Blackwell, pp. 191–221.

Rodger, J. R. (2008) *Criminalising Social Policy: Anti-social Behaviour and Welfare in a De-civilised Society*. Cullompton: Willan.

Rogers, L., Simonot, M. and Nartey, A. (2014) *Prison Educators: Professionalism Against the Odds*. London: Institute of Education.

Rogers, P. (2010) *Losing Control: Global Security in the 21st Century*. London: Pluto.

Rogers, P. (2017) *Irregular War: The New Threat from the Margins*. London and New York: I.B.Tauris.

Rostow, W. W. (1962) *The Stages of Economic Growth: A Non-Communist Manifesto*. Cambridge: Cambridge University Press.

Roundtree, C. and Middleton, J. (2018) Wealthy Landlords Consider Funding Largest Private Police Force. *Mail Online*, 26 August. Available at: www.dailymail.co.uk/news/article-6099477/Duke-Westminsters-estate-landlords-consider-funding-largest-private-police-force.html (accessed 11 November 2018).

Rowland, R. and Coupe, T. (2014) Patrol Officers and Public Reassurance: A Comparative Evaluation of Police Officers, PCSOs, ACSOs and Private Security Guards. *Policing and Society* 24 (3): 265–284.

Ryan, M. (1994) Some Liberal and Radical Responses to Privatising the Penal System in Britain. In Biles, D. and Vernon, J. (eds) *Private Sector and Community Involvement in the Criminal Justice System*. Canberra: Australian Institute of Criminology, pp. 9–18.

Sabbagh, D. (2019) London Mayor Writes to King's Cross Owner over Facial Recognition. *The Guardian*, 13 August. Available at: www.theguardian.com/technology/2019/aug/13/london-mayor-writes-to-kings-cross-owner-over-facial-recognition-concerns (accessed 13 August 2019).

Sambrook, C. (2016) British Security Company G4S Confirms that Florida Shooter is One of Their Own. *openDemocracy*. Available at: www.opendemocracy.net/en/shine-a-light/british-security-company-g4s-confirms-that-florida-shooter-is/ (accessed 31 July 2018).

Samuels, D. (2019) Is Big Tech Merging with Big Brother? Kinda Looks Like It. *Wired*, 23 January. Available at: www.wired.com/story/is-big-tech-merging-with-big-brother-kinda-looks-like-it/ (accessed 14 August 2019).

Sarre, R. (1994) The Legal Basis for the Authority of Private Police and an Examination of their Relationship with the 'Public' Police. In Biles, D. and Vernon, J. (eds) *Private Sector and Community Involvement in the Criminal Justice System*. Canberra: Australian Institute of Criminology.

Savage, M. (2013) The British Class System is Becoming More Polarised between a Prosperous Elite and a Poor 'Precariat'. *British Politics and Policy at LSE*. Available at: http://blogs.lse.ac.uk/politicsandpolicy/mike-savage-placeholder/ (accessed 15 May 2015).

Scheerhout, J. (2012) Manchester Police Chief Blasts Plan for 'Private Police Force'. *Manchester Evening News*, 15 June. Available at: www.manchestereveningnews.co.uk/news/greater-manchester-news/manchester-police-chief-blasts-plan-689684 (accessed 12 November 2018).

Scherer, A. and Palazzo, G. (2011) The New Political Role of Business in a Globalized World. *Journal of Management Studies* 48 (4): 899–931.

Scott, D. (2017) *Building Warehouses of Suffering and Death: The Case Against the New Prison in Wellingborough*. Community Action On Prison Expansion: Fighting Prison Expansion in England, Wales and Scotland. Available at: https://cape-campaign.org/building-warehouses-of-suffering-and-death/.

Sengupta, K. (2008) An African Adventure: Inside Story of the Wonga Coup. *The Independent*, 12 March. Available at: www.independent.co.uk/news/world/africa/an-african-adventure-inside-story-of-the-wonga-coup-794470.html.

Serco (2019) Serco Awarded UK Asylum Support Services Contracts with an Estimated Value of £1.9bn; Serco's Largest Ever Contract Award. Available at: www.serco.com/news/media-releases/2019/serco-awarded-uk-asylum-support-services-contracts-with-an-estimated-value-of-19bn-sercos-largest-ever-contract-award (accessed 12 July 2019).

Servator (2014) Servator around St Paul's. Available at: www.professionalsecurity.co.uk/news/interviews/servator-around-st-pauls/.

Shameem, S. (2010) UN and Africa to Discuss Mercenaries and Private Military and Security Companies. Office of the UN High Commissioner for Human Rights. Available at: https://business-humanrights.org/en/ethiopia-un-working-group-on-the-use-of-mercenaries-to-meet-34-mar-with-representatives-from-25-african-states#c29878.

Shaw, F. (2013) Private Sector Mismanagement and Public Opinion. Available at: www.survation.com/public-sector-mismanagement-majority-agree-defrauding-companies-should-have-contracts-taken-away/ (accessed 29 July 2019).

Shaw, M. (1991) *Post-Military Society: Militarism, Demilitarization and War at the End of the Twentieth Century*. Cambridge: Polity.

Shaw, S. (1992) The Short History of Prison Privatisation. *Prison Service Journal* 87: 30–2.

Shearing, C. D. and Stenning, P. C. (1983) Private Security: Implications for Social Control. *Social Problems* 30: 493–506.

Shenker, J. (2017) 'It's Really Shocking': UK Cities Refusing to Reveal Extent of Pseudo-Public Space. *The Guardian*, 26 September. Available at: www.theguardian.com/cities/2017/sep/26/its-really-shocking-uk-cities-refusing-to-reveal-extent-of-pseudo-public-space (accessed 27 November 2018).

Shorrock, T. (2015) Blackwater: One of the Pentagon's Top Contractors for Afghanistan Training. *The Nation*, 31 March. Available at: www.thenation.com/article/blackwater-still-top-pentagon-contractor-afghanistan-training/ (accessed 8 August 2019).

Shubert, A. (1981) Private Initiative in Law Enforcement: Associations for the Prosecution of Felons 1744–1865. In Bailey, V. (ed.) *Policing and Punishment in Nineteenth Century Britain*. London: Croom Helm.

Simmons, W. and Hammer, L. (2015) Privatization of Prisons in Israel and Beyond: A Per Se Violation of the Human Right to Dignity. *Santa Clara Journal of International Law* 13 (2): 487.

Singer, P. W. (2007) *Corporate Warriors: The Rise of Privatized Military Industry*. Ithaca, NY: Cornell University Press.

Singer, P. W. (2010) The Regulation of New Warfare. Available at: www.brookings.edu/opinions/the-regulation-of-new-warfare/ (accessed 8 August 2018).

Smith, E. B. (2002) The New Condottieri and US Policy: The Privatization of Conflict and its Implications. *Parameters* 32 (4): 104–19.

Smith, N. (2016) There Is No Rehabilitation Without Education. Available at: www.prisonerseducation.org.uk/stories/noel-smith (accessed 25 April 2017).

Sodexo (2016) What We Do and Why. Available at: https://uk.sodexo.com/home/services/on-site-services/justice/what.html.

Solace Global (2019) VIP Close Protection Services. Available at: www.solaceglobal.com/services/protect/journey-management-executive-protection/ (accessed 9 August 2019).

Sommerville, Q. (2016) UK Special Forces Pictured in Syria. *BBC News*, 8 August. Available at: www.bbc.co.uk/news/uk-37015915 (accessed 3 December 2017).

South, N. (1988) *Policing for Profit: The Private Security Sector*. London: Sage Publications.

Sparks, R. (1994) Can Prisons Be Legitimate? Penal Politics, Privatization, and the Timeliness of an Old Idea. *British Journal of Criminology* 34 (1): 14–28.

Spierenburg, P. (1991) *The Prison Experience: Disciplinary Institutions and Their Inmates in Early Modern Europe*. New Brunswick, NJ: Rutgers University Press.

Standing, G. (2011) *The Precariat: The New Dangerous Class*. London: Bloomsbury Academic.

Steiner, K. (2019) When Prison is Preferable to Life on the Streets. *The Guardian*, 11 April.

Stern, P. J. (2012) *The Company-State: Corporate Sovereignty and the Early Modern Foundations of the British Empire in India*. Oxford: Oxford University Press.

Stevens, A. (2011) Telling Policy Stories: An Ethnographic Study of the Use of Evidence in Policy-Making in the UK. *Journal of Social Policy* 40: 237–55.

Storch, R. (1976) The Policeman as Domestic Missionary: Urban Discipline and Popular Culture in Northern England 1850–1880. *Journal of Social History* 9: 481–509.

Suchman, M. (1995) Managing Legitimacy: Strategic and Institutional Approaches. *The Academy of Management Review* 20 (3): 571–610.

Swilling, M. (ed.) (2017) *Betrayal of the Promise: How South Africa is Being Stolen*. Stellenbosch: Stellenbosch University, State Capacity Research Project.

Tanner, W. (2013) *The Case for Private Prisons*. London: Reform.

Teather, D. (2004) Halliburton Staff Sacked 'For Taking Bribes'. *The Guardian*, 24 January. Available at: www.theguardian.com/world/2004/jan/24/usa.iraq (accessed 21 June 2019).

Thompson, E. (1967) Time, Work-Discipline and Industrial Capitalism. *Past and Present* 38: 56–97.

Thomson, J. E. (1996) *Mercenaries, Pirates, and Sovereigns*. Princeton, NJ: Princeton University Press.

Thumala, A., Goold, B. and Loader, I. (2011) A Tainted Trade? Moral Ambivalence and Legitimation Work in the Private Security Industry. *The British Journal of Sociology* 62 (2): 283–303.

Tilly, C. (1985) War Making and State Making as Organized Crime. In Evans, P., Rueschemeyer, D. and Skocpol, T. (eds) *Bringing the State Back In*. Cambridge: Cambridge University Press, pp. 169–91.

TM-Eye (2018) Conviction at St Albans Magistrates Court. Available at: https://tm-eye.co.uk/1772-bw-18-conviction-st-albans-magistrates-court/ (accessed 15 July 2019).

TM-Eye (2019) What We Offer. Available at: http://tm-eye.co.uk/what-we-offer/ (accessed 15 July 2019).

Topping, A. (2015) Security Contractor Not Adequately Vetted before Iraq Killings, Says Coroner. *The Guardian*, 11 May. Available at: www.theguardian.com/uk-news/2015/may/11/security-contractor-vetted-iraq-killings-coroner (accessed 9 August 2019).

Travis, A. (2013a) G4S Faces Fraud Investigation over Tagging Contracts. *The Guardian*, 12 July.

Travis, A. (2013b) Investigated Serco and G4S Can Bid for New Contracts, Says Chris Grayling. *The Guardian*, 15 September.

Travis, A. (2015) Probation Officers Face Redundancy in Plan to Replace Them With Machines. *The Guardian*, 30 March. Available at: www.theguardian.com/society/2015/mar/30/probation-officers-face-redundancy-in-plan-to-replace-them-with-machines (accessed 14 April 2019).

Travis, A. (2016) Seven G4S Staff Suspended over Abuse Claims at Youth Institution. *The Guardian*, 8 January. Available at: www.theguardian.com/business/2016/jan/08/g4s-staff-young-offenders-institution-suspended-medway-kent (accessed 31 July 2019).

Travis, A. (2017) Value of Asylum Housing Contracts Doubles after Criticism of Conditions. *The Guardian*, 23 November. Available at: www.theguardian.com/uk-news/2017/nov/23/value-of-asylum-housing-contracts-doubles-after-criticism-of-conditions (accessed 30 April 2019).

Travis, A. (2018) Private Probation Firms Face Huge Losses Despite £342m 'Bailout'. *The Guardian*, 17 January. Available at: www.theguardian.com/society/2018/jan/17/private-probation-companies-face-huge-losses-despite-342m-bailout (accessed 16 April 2019).

Travis, A. and Syal, R. (2014) 'Poison Pill' Privatisation Contracts Could Cost £300m–£400m to Cancel. *The Guardian*, 11 September. Available at: www.theguardian.com/politics/2014/sep/11/poison-pill-probation-contracts-moj-serco-g4s (accessed 14 April 2019).

Trevithick, J. (2017) US Military Reveals Contractors Flew to the Rescue in Niger, but Little Else. Available at: www.thedrive.com/the-war-zone/15121/us-military-reveals-contractors-flew-to-the-rescue-in-niger-but-little-else (accessed 22 June 2019).

UltimateSecurity (2018) Police and Justice. Available at: https://ultimatesecurity.co.uk/services/police-justice/.

UN (2017) UN Peacekeeping: 70 Years of Service & Sacrifice. Available at: https://peacekeeping.un.org/en/un-peacekeeping-70-years-of-service-sacrifice (accessed 28 May 2018).

UN (2018) Use of Mercenaries as a Means of Violating Human Rights and Impeding the Exercise of the Right of Peoples to Self-determination. UN General Assembly 73rd session A/73/303. Available at: www.securitycouncilreport.org/atf/cf/%7B65BFCF9B-6D27-4E9C-8CD3-CF6E4FF96FF9%7D/a_73_303.pdf.

van Brabant, K. (2010) *Managing Aid Agency Security in an Evolving World: The Larger Challenge*. London: European Interagency Security Forum.

van Creveld, M. (1991) *The Transformation of War*. New York: Free Press.

van Creveld, M. (1999) *The Rise and Decline of the State*. Cambridge: Cambridge University Press.

van der Pijl, K. (2006) *Global Rivalries From the Cold War to Iraq*. London and Ann Arbor, MI: Pluto Press.

van der Pijl, K. (2013) The Financial Crisis and the War for Global Governance. Available at: http://anticapitalists.org/2013/05/26/financial-crisis-and-war-for-global-governance (accessed 2 April 2015).

Vasagar, J. (2012) Public Spaces in Britain's Cities Fall Into Private Hands. *The Guardian*, 11 June. Available at: www.theguardian.com/uk/2012/jun/11/granary-square-privately-owned-public-space (accessed 27 November 2018).

Vaughan, B. (2000) Punishment and Conditional Citizenship. *Punishment & Society* 2 (1): 23–39.

VBID (2018) *Victoria Business Improvement District 2017/18 Annual Report*. London: Victoria Business Improvement District. Available at: www.victoriabid.co.uk/wp-content/themes/victoria/inc-download.php?PageDownloadID=10944.

Vitale, A. (2017) *The End of Policing*. London and New York: Verso.

Wacquant, L. (2004) *Deadly Symbiosis: Race and the Rise of Neoliberal Penalty*. Cambridge: Polity.

Wacquant, L. (2010) Crafting the Neoliberal State: Workfare, Prisonfare, and Social Insecurity. *Sociological Forum* 25 (2): 197–220.

Wakefield, A. (2005) The Public Surveillance Functions of Private Security. *Surveillance & Society* 2 (4): 529–45.

Walker, S., Annison, J. and Beckett, S. (2019) Transforming Rehabilitation: The Impact of Austerity and Privatisation on Day-to-Day Cultures and Working Practices in 'Probation'. *Probation Journal* 66 (1): 113–30.

Walkowitz, J. R. (1992) *City of Dreadful Delight: Narratives Of Sexual Danger In Late-Victorian London*. Chicago: University of Chicago Press.

War on Want (2016) *Mercenaries Unleashed: The Brave New World of Private Military and Security Companies*. London: War on Want.

Warrell, H. and Plimmer, G. (2012) Cuts Prompt Police to Use More Contractors. Available at: www.ft.com/content/7942437e-686e-11e1-a6cc-00144feabdco (accessed 15 January 2019).

Weaver, M. and Pidd, H. (2019) No Link between Knife Crime and Police Cuts, Says Theresa May. *The Guardian*, 4 March. Available at: www.theguardian.

com/uk-news/2019/mar/04/no-link-between-knife-and-police-cuts-says-theresa-may (accessed 15 August 2019).

Webb, S. and Webb, B. (1922) *English Prisons Under Local Government*. London: Longmans, Green.

Weber, M. (1946) Politics as a Vocation. In Gerth, H. and Mills, C. W. (eds) *From Max Weber: Essays in Sociology*. Oxford: Routledge, pp. 77–8.

Webster, R. (2017) What Does Prison Governor Autonomy Mean? Available at: www.russellwebster.com/prison-governor-autonomy/ (accessed 27 July 2019).

White, A. (2010) *The Politics of Private Security: Regulation, Reform and Re-Legitimation*. Basingstoke and New York: Palgrave Macmillan.

White, A. (2014a) Post-Crisis Policing and Public–Private Partnerships: The Case of Lincolnshire Police and G4S. *British Journal of Criminology* 54 (6): 1002–1022.

White, A. (2014b) The Politics of Police 'Privatization': A Multiple Streams Approach. *Criminology and Criminal Justice* 15(3): 283–99.

White, A. (2016) *Shadow State: Inside the Secret Companies That Run Britain*. London: Oneworld Publications.

White, A. (2018) Just Another Industry? (De)Regulation, Public Expectations and Private Security. In Hucklesby, A. and Lister, S. (eds) *The Private Sector and Criminal Justice*. London: Palgrave Macmillan, pp. 135–60.

Whitehead, P. (2010) *Exploring Modern Probation: Social Theory and Organisational Complexity*. Bristol: Policy Press.

Whitehead, P. and Crawshaw, P. (2013) Shaking the Foundations on the Moral Economy of Criminal Justice. *British Journal of Criminology* 53 (4): 588–604.

Whitehead, P. and Statham, R. (2005) *The History of Probation: Politics, Power and Cultural Change, 1876–2005*. Crayford: Shaw and Sons.

Whyte, D. (2015) Civilising the Corporate War. In Walklate, S. and McGarry, R. (eds) *Criminology and War: Transgressing the Borders*. London: Routledge.

Wiener, M. J. (1990) *Reconstructing the Criminal: Culture, Law, and Policy in England, 1830–1914*. Cambridge: Cambridge University Press.

Williams, C. (1998) *Police and Crime in Sheffield, 1818–1874*. University of Sheffield, History Department.

Williams, C. (2003) Britain's Police Forces: Forever Removed from Democratic Control? Available at: www.historyandpolicy.org/policy-papers/papers/britains-police-forces-forever-removed-from-democratic-control.

Williams, C. (2008) Constables for Hire: The History of Private 'Public' Policing in the UK. *Policing and Society* 18 (2): 190–205.

Williams, Z. (2019) In Clink Prison Restaurants, there is Fellowship in Food. *The Guardian*, 8 August.

Wilson, E. (2009) Deconstructing the Shadows. In Wilson, E. (ed.) *Government of the Shadows: Parapolitics and Criminal Sovereignty*. London: Pluto Press, pp. 13–55.

Worrall, A. (2008) Gender and Probation in the Second World War: Reflections on a Changing Occupational Culture. *Criminology and Criminal Justice* 8: 317–33.

Wrigley, C. (1999) *The Privatisation of Violence: New Mercenaries and the State*. London: Campaign Against Arms Trade. Available at: www.caat.org.uk/resources/publications/government/mercenaries-1999.

Wyld, G. and Noble, J. (2017) *Beyond Bars: Maximising the Voluntary Sector's Contribution in Criminal Justice*. London: New Philanthropy Capital.

Yeung, P. (2018) Loss of Senior Managers Led to UK's Prison Crisis. *The Observer*, 25 August. Available at: www.theguardian.com/society/2018/aug/25/staff-cuts-prison-leadership-crisis (accessed 15 August 2019).

Young, S. (2017) Prison Restaurant Beats Top Eateries to Number One Spot on TripAdvisor. *The Independent*, 27 November. Available at: www.independent.co.uk/life-style/the-clink-prison-restaurant-tripadvisor-number-one-reviews-cardiff-brixton-wilmslow-a8078056.html (accessed 27 July 2019).

Zedner, L. (2006) Policing Before and After the Police. *British Journal of Criminology* 46: 78.

Index